Christmas 2005

To Scott,
    This Book looks
like a good "read"
    I hope you will
enjoy it — Let me Know.

            with love
                Mom

"This book will be an 'impact player' from the boardroom to the locker room to the living room. With transparent honesty, Pat Williams shares it all. In doing so, he confesses, counsels, and challenges us to have a passion for distinction."

—Jay Strack, author and speaker

"Pat Williams' story is all about passion, both its positive and negative sides. This is a riveting personal story of the conflicts facing a sports executive superstar in his passion for Christianity, for his family, and for his work. My life is richer for reading it, and so will yours."

—Edwin Pope, *Miami Herald*

"Pat's autobiography is honestly refreshing and vastly informative. It brought back many memories we shared of early days in the NBA and tackles some of today's experiences."

—Jerry Sloan, head coach, Utah Jazz

"Pat Williams is a born storyteller with energy to burn and a dynamism that's always been impressive. It should come as no surprise that this book delivers in the usual Williams style: wit, passion, and a punch line."

—Chris Young, *Toronto Star*

"If players and coaches had as much energy and passion as Pat Williams, they'd all be undefeated. A catcher all his life, Pat masterfully pitches his philosophy. At the same time, he rekindles memories of the toughest times and most wonderful times."

—Phil Jasner, *Philadelphia Daily News*

"After reading this book, three thoughts came to mind: (1) Under the word *enthusiasm* in the dictionary, there should be a picture of Pat Williams; (2) the only sports people of the last 150 years Pat hasn't met are Cap Anson and Pele—and I'm not sure about Cap Anson; (3) you'll want to read this book in one long sitting."

—Bob Ryan, *Boston Globe*

"Pat Williams has become such a prolific author, I hear the trees are organizing a protest. However, even the forests will regard his latest, insightful tome as pulp well spent. Especially page-turning are the intimate accounts of divorce and remarriage under the pressures of a multifaceted career (NBA executive, author, speaker) that has always made me ashamed of being a devoted couch potato."

—Larry Guest, *Orlando Sentinel*

"Pat Williams' *Ahead of the Game* takes you with him through a life that has been one big adrenaline rush. It's like being on a roller coaster."

—Ron Green, *Charlotte Observer*

"I have always admired the skills and talent of Pat Williams. And I have been privileged over the past several years to become his friend and to get to know him from the inside out. His integrity, passion, and heart will inspire and encourage you."

—Dr. John C. Maxwell, author, speaker, and founder of INJOY

"Pat Williams has written a fascinating account of a remarkable life. His life is guaranteed to impact yours."

—Pat Summitt, head women's basketball coach,
University of Tennessee

"When Pat Williams writes, 'Have I got a story for you,' has he ever. It will astonish you, stun you, impress upon you that the good and the not-so-good can happen to anybody, even one with the gifts of God such as he. There's a textbook lesson about life here that can serve most any of us."

—Furman Bisher, *Atlanta Journal-Constitution*

"I love biographies! This is the best one I've read in years. What honesty and what a challenging and exciting life. Pat is a true credit to sports and to the Lord."

—Bill Glass, *Bill Glass Ministries*

"What a ride! Pat Williams is unbelievable."

—Jerry B. Jenkins, author

"We already knew that Pat Williams is an all-world general manager, wit, and dad. To that add world-class memoirist. *Ahead of the Game* is a pure pleasure."

—John Helyar, author of *Lords of the Realm*,
coauthor of *Barbarians at the Gate*

"Like Pat Williams himself, *Ahead of the Game* is inspirational and driven but also full of surprising laughs."

—Fran Blinebury, *Houston Chronicle*

"A true story of life from someone who truly understands the meaning of living. A wonderful read."

—Tom Enlund, *Milwaukee Journal Sentinel*

"Pat Williams writes about his wonderful life. It's an interesting one as well. Pat is candid about his successes and failures in his journey through faith and life."

—David Moore, *Dallas Morning News*

"As a sports historian, there is none better than Pat Williams. He has been there, and nobody has done it better."

—Sid Hartman, *Minneapolis Star Tribune*

"*Ahead of the Game* conveys a wonderful message of God's faithfulness. You will enjoy the exciting world of sports, but beyond that, from cover to cover you will see a man whose 'passion for distinction' drives him in a constant race to achieve, not only in business but also in good works. This autobiography reveals a man of distinct character whose passion for life has taken him on a journey over mountaintops as well as through valleys. His response to these challenges will bless and inspire you."

—Mrs. Paul Anderson, Vidalia, Georgia

Ahead of the Game

## Other Books by Pat Williams

*The Gingerbread Man*
*Go for the Magic*
*Jock Jokes*
*Just between Us*
*Keep the Fire Glowing*
*Kindling*
*Love Her, Like Him*
*The Magic of Team Work*
*Making Magic*
*Nothing but Winners*
*The Power within You*
*Rekindled*
*Twelve-Part Harmony*
*We Owed You One*

# Ahead of the Game

## The Pat Williams Story

**Pat Williams**

**with James D. Denney**

Fleming H. Revell
A Division of Baker Book House
Grand Rapids, Michigan 49516

Published by Fleming H. Revell
a division of Baker Book House Company
P.O. Box 6287, Grand Rapids, MI 49516-6287

Printed in the United States of America

**Library of Congress Cataloging-in-Publication Data**

Williams, Pat, 1940–
    Ahead of the game : the Pat Williams story / Pat Williams with James D. Denney.
        p.  cm.
    Includes bibliographical references.
    ISBN 0-8007-1763-5 (cloth)
    1. Williams, Pat, 1940–  . 2. Basketball coaches—United States—Biography. 3. Orlando Magic (Basketball team). 4. Baseball managers—United States—Biography. 5. Christian life. 6. Success. I. Denney, James D. II. Title.
GV884.W55A3  1999
796.323′092—dc21                              98-41194
[B]

For current information about all releases from Baker Book House, visit our web site:
http://www.bakerbooks.com

To Ruth,
a wonder, a gift from God,
a lifesaving miracle

You're a remarkable woman,
and I'm very proud of you
and eternally grateful.

# Contents

# Acknowledgments

My thanks to my editor, Bill Petersen, who believed in this book (for about ten years!), and to my collaborator, Jim Denney, who helped hammer it into existence. We make a great team! Special thanks for a marvelous editing job to John Phipps and Brian Phipps. My thanks to two good friends, Ken Hussar and Phil Jasner, who helped fine-tune the manuscript.

I also want to thank my colleagues at RDV Sports in Orlando for their support and encouragement. In particular, I'm grateful to our president, Bob Vander Weide, vice presidents Cari Coats and Alex Martins, my assistant, Marlin Bushur, and Adam Lippard.

# Prologue

## A Wonderful World

Wonderful!

That's my world, that's my life. Remarkable. Fun. Stimulating. Wonderful.

Wait! Not so fast—let's roll that word around a little: *Wonderful.*

As in wonder-full. Or full of wonder. Or even full of wonders, plural.

Any way you slice it, it fits. Not that there's anything so special about me. I'm just Pat Williams—an ordinary guy who gets to do extraordinary things and meet extraordinary people every day of the year. As the title of that great old Frank Capra movie says, it really is a wonderful life—and I'm *living* it! And if I can have a wonderful life, *anyone* can.

Have I had times of despair? Disappointment? Failure? You bet. I've had plenty of "learning experiences" in my time. I'm not afraid to talk about those, too. Because I know that failure is often an essential component of ultimate success. The pathway to the finish line is often littered with obstacles and hurdles.

As a former pro baseball player who can list a National Basketball Association championship on my sports management resume, I've had more incredible adrenaline-rush moments than I could ever count. I've spent thirty years on a white-knuckle emotional roller-coaster ride, working with such sports

11

legends as Julius Erving, Shaquille O'Neal, and Bill Veeck while building a career with such teams as the Chicago Bulls, Philadelphia 76ers, Atlanta Hawks, and Orlando Magic. And I've sat in a motorcade with some of the legendary names in basketball—Julius Erving, Moses Malone, Bobby Jones, Maurice Cheeks, and Billy Cunningham—riding down Broad Street while a million hysterical Philadelphia 76ers fans celebrated our NBA championship.

And what about the process of helping to bring a brand-new NBA franchise into existence—I mean, is there anything in the world more wonderful than *magic?* My association with the Orlando Magic has been, right from the start, one of the most wonder-filled experiences of my life!

And I've known the thrill of standing in airports to welcome fourteen adopted children into my arms and into our family— a thrill equaled only by being present at the delivery of each of my four birth-children.

But I failed at the most important goal in my life when my marriage collapsed in 1995. What good is it to have a successful career, a reputation as a motivational speaker, and a string of published books—including two on the art of sharing a life in marriage—if your most important relationships in life have broken down?

Yet out of that horrible, humbling sense of failure, God engineered a miracle. He proved he truly is the God of second chances. Even though I was forced against my will to bid goodbye to Jill, my wife of twenty-four years, my relationship with my children grew stronger and my relationship with God deepened. Then—wonder of wonders—God surprised me by giving me Ruth, who is my companion for the rest of my life.

The reason I'm opening up my life this way is simple: I'm hoping that my passion for distinction will challenge others to pursue a life of distinction. We are all capable of achieving far more than we can imagine. A passion for distinction means doing your best, trying your hardest, and never—ever—saying, "That's good enough."

One thing will be clear by the end of my story. I have never been content to live in the gray areas. As far back as I remember, I've always wanted everything I do to stand for something, to be significant, to make a difference.

How about you? Do you have a passion for distinction? Do you have a sense of wonder about your life? Is your life a *wonderful* life? If not, do you want it to be?

Turn the page, my friend. Walk with me a while. Let's talk it over.

Have I got a story for you.

# 1

# Williams vs. Williams

This was to be the fulfillment of the dream. This was the reason I had come to Orlando.

In just a few short years, we had taken the Orlando Magic from a struggling expansion franchise all the way to the 1995 National Basketball Association Finals. Best of all, we would begin the best-of-seven-games series with the home-court advantage against the defending champions, the Houston Rockets. As game one got under way, the Magic exploded to a fifteen-point lead in the first quarter—then extended that lead to twenty points by halftime.

As I watched our young team bruising and abusing the defending champs, I thought, *Boy-oh-boy, we've really got 'em on the ropes! I sure hope we don't embarrass Houston too badly. The NBA and NBC aren't going to be happy if we rout the Rockets in four straight—it's not good for the league or the ratings for the finals to be too one-sided!* Orlando was heavily favored to win. While the Rockets were seeded sixth in the Western Conference, having won only forty-seven regular-season games, the Magic had finished the season with a record of fifty-seven wins against twenty-five losses. We were confident that the Magic—

powered by the dynamic duo of Penny Hardaway and Shaquille O'Neal—would win the title.

But by the final quarter, the Rockets managed to battle their way back into the game. The truly heart-stopping moments occurred in the final moments of regulation play, as the Magic led 110-107. Nick Anderson was fouled and went to the line for two free throws, either of which would put the game away for sure—out of reach of even the luckiest desperation three-point basket by Houston.

Nick shot the first free throw—and missed. No problem, everyone misses now and then; even the sure hands of Nick Anderson are fallible. But he never misses two in a row.

This time, however, he did. As the ball rimmed out, Nick jumped and collected his own rebound—and was fouled again. So back to the line he went to shoot two more. I smiled and relaxed. He certainly couldn't miss four in a row! The game was in the bag.

Nick took his two shots. Missed both.

My jaw was on the floor. My heart was in my throat.

Houston took the ball back to its end of the court. With 1.6 seconds left in regulation, Houston's Kenny Smith launched a shot from beyond the three-point arc, sank it, and sent the game into overtime.

Where we lost it, 120-118.

Then we lost game two. And game three. And game four.

We had been swept, defeated, wounded. I felt emotionally bruised at the end of the NBA Finals.

But I didn't know what emotional pain was. The *real* pain was just around the corner. I was about to be wounded more deeply than I had ever been wounded before.

## The Letter

July 5, 1995 was the worst day of my life—the kind of day that marks you forever, the kind I pray my children never experience. If you have only one day like that in a lifetime, that's enough.

The previous day had been a glorious Fourth of July at the beach with my kids. The afterglow still warmed me as I strode into my office at the Orlando Arena. But even before I sat down at my desk, I saw the envelope—and my blood froze.

The letter had one of those official, ominous "return receipt requested" tags on the front. I instantly recognized the name on the return address: Mark Rabinowitz, Attorney at Law. Jill, my wife of twenty-two years, had hired him to represent her in her divorce action, which she had launched earlier that year.

For weeks, I had been racking my brain and soul, trying to think, talk, and pray my way out of this black hole our relationship had tumbled into. I was committed to the marriage, and I didn't want it to end. All along, I kept believing that the ultimate catastrophe could somehow be averted, that I could change Jill's mind. But the letter on my desk made it clear that something terrible was about to happen, and I couldn't stop it. I never felt so helpless in my life.

I sat down, took the letter in my hands, looked at it—then set it down unopened.

I tried to work up the courage to open it. I couldn't.

I slid the envelope over to the farthest corner of my desk and tried not to look at it, tried not to think about it. I didn't open it all day.

Months earlier, Jill had come to me and said, "I've hired a lawyer, Pat. I think it would be in your best interests to hire a lawyer, too."

"Jill," I said, "what can I do to change your mind?"

"Nothing, Pat," was her reply. "I'm not going to change my mind. This is the way it has to be."

Jill's decision came just as my professional career was reaching the top of the rainbow. The *Wall Street Journal* had just published a cover story on my life in Orlando, and the Magic was going into the NBA Finals against the Houston Rockets. Professionally, things couldn't have been better. But the marriage had hit rock-bottom. To be sure, it had not been a storybook marriage, and at times it had been downright turbulent. But *over?* I couldn't believe it.

Reluctantly, I contacted an attorney, Bill Barnett. He came highly recommended and had a reputation as a committed Christian. I wanted to be represented by someone who shared my values and would understand that I wanted to deal with this crisis as a Christian, not as Jill's adversary.

When I told him why I was in his office, his jaw dropped. He was familiar with my reputation and with our books, including two books I had written with Jill on marriage communication—*Rekindled* and *Keep the Fire Glowing*. My wife and I had literally "written the book" on how to keep a marriage healthy. Yet here I was, talking to an attorney about divorce. I felt humiliated and embarrassed.

"If this can happen in your marriage," Bill said, astonished, "it can happen to any of us."

"Bill," I said, "I don't want to give up on this marriage. I want you to do everything in your power to stall and block this process. I'm still hoping and praying that, somehow, Jill will change her mind and that we can save this marriage."

"I'll do what I can," Bill replied.

That was in June. Now it was a month later, and I was trying to ignore the letter that had arrived from Mark Rabinowitz.

The longer it sat there unopened, the more it was on my mind. Finally I thought, *This is stupid. It won't go away by ignoring it. I have to deal with this.* So I called Bill Barnett's office. His secretary told me he was on vacation in Colorado, but she would get a message to him.

Late that night, Bill called from Colorado. I told him about the letter.

"What does it say?" he asked.

"I don't know," I replied. "I haven't opened it yet."

"Well, open it!" he ordered. He didn't add, "you idiot," but that was the sense of it.

I slowly tore open the flap and unfolded the letter. The words were a blur. At the top of the page was a heading that made me feel ill. I read the heading to Bill. "It says 'Williams vs. Williams,'" I said. I flashed on the movie *Kramer vs. Kramer*—but instead of having one child, like the Kramers, Jill and I had eighteen.

I read further. Jill's attorney was a prominent divorce lawyer—the kind you want working with you, not against you. The letter began: "I have been retained by Ms. Jill Williams in her divorce proceedings against you. Please contact me or have your representative contact me as soon as possible. Ms. Williams wants these proceedings to be amicable, but we will take whatever steps are necessary."

It was a small point, but the abbreviation Ms. stuck out to me. I was used to Jill being Mrs. Williams, not Ms. Williams. It was a tiny but distinct sign of the huge gulf between us.

So began the darkest chapter of my life.

## A Line in the Sand

I had not been shocked when Jill told me she had retained a lawyer. It dropped on me with a sense of finality, but not as a surprise. This had been coming on for some years.

The problems in our marriage had first reached critical mass in December 1982, when I was general manager of the Philadelphia 76ers. As Jill and I chronicled in *Rekindled,* I sat down with her one Sunday afternoon to find out why she had been cool and silent toward me that morning. I assumed she was upset over some thoughtless remarks I had made before church. I figured I'd apologize for the remarks and that would be that. I was wrong. She delivered a stinging indictment of our marriage.

"I just don't care about this marriage anymore," she said, practically in a whisper—though I couldn't have been more shaken if she had shouted at the top of her lungs. "I hate this marriage. It's boring me to death. I don't even know if I love you anymore. I don't know if I ever loved you."

I had been oblivious. I was satisfied with my life, and I assumed Jill was, too. I certainly wasn't bored. Who could be, with a career like the fast-paced, high-intensity life of an NBA general manager? Who could be bored going to 76ers games, making multimillion-dollar deals with players, giving speeches and pep talks, writing books, and making media appearances?

Who could be bored with a house full of kids, and worshiping in an active, energetic church like ours?

I was happy in my world—but Jill was miserable in hers. And I didn't even know what she had been feeling.

The clues had been there all along, but I hadn't seen them. That Sunday, as Jill shattered my illusions about what I had assumed was our perfect storybook marriage, echoes came back to me of all the times she had tried to get my attention. For months, she had been telling me there was a major problem between us, but I just didn't get it.

She had said things like,

"You don't really care about this marriage."

"You don't notice me."

"You never share anything with me."

"Couldn't you come home early once in a while, just to be with me?"

"You never say nice things about me in front of other people."

"Why do I have to ask you to take care of the kids? Why don't you just see I need help and volunteer?"

I didn't agree with all of Jill's complaints, but I was never able to convince her to think otherwise.

Jill and I viewed our marriage differently—yet I didn't realize *how* differently. From my point of view, our marriage had problems, but was generally doing well. From Jill's point of view, our marriage was barely functioning. Was Jill too needy and demanding? Was I so optimistic that I couldn't see the real scope of our problems through my rose-tinted glasses? Or was the truth somewhere in-between? One thing was certain: The things Jill told me that day really rocked my world.

That conversation took place at the ten-year mark of our marriage—and I responded, making major changes in my behavior toward Jill. The last thing in the world I wanted to do was hurt her—or lose her. We experienced a time of great healing in our relationship after that.

But in the summer of 1986, we moved from Philadelphia to central Florida, where I became president and general manager of an expansion franchise, the Orlando Magic. Building a new NBA team from the ground up is an exciting but time-consuming challenge—and I plunged into it.

Meanwhile, our family continued to grow, so that by the end of 1993, we had eighteen children, fourteen of them adopted from four other countries. We had kids in elementary school, middle school, high school, and college at the same time. The logistics of running such a household—with all the school events, music lessons, dance recitals, swimming meets, soccer practices, and baseball games that entails—became very complicated, so we added a full-time nanny, chef, and handyman. I was spending a lot of my days and evenings on the road or at the arena, so the pressures and stresses of managing the home fell on Jill. It became so overwhelming she could no longer go on. All of her feelings toward me were dead.

She said to me regularly, "If it came to a choice between the Magic and me, you'd choose the Magic. If it came to a choice between the children and me, you'd choose the children. If it came to a choice between going somewhere to make a speech or being with me, you'd do the speech. If it was between working out and me, you would choose your workout." I'd heard that a lot over the past few years, and I know I'm not the first or last man to hear words to that effect. But I was stretched to the limit, and I felt powerless to do more than I was doing to support such a large family.

I believe my intentions were right. Jill was the only woman I had ever seriously dated or been with. I was convinced she was the one woman God had for me. I felt committed to making our marriage work.

But I've often thought that, with my job, with the many demands on my time, with my inner drive to excel, I'm probably tough to be married to. In my mind, I was not ignoring or neglecting her, but Jill didn't see it that way. She needed a lot of time and attention—more than I believed I could give her at that stage of my life.

"Jill," I often said, "I'm doing my best."

## "I'm Releasing You"

During those last few years of our marriage, Jill's mother was stricken with cancer. She spent the last weeks of her life in our little guest house and died on February 28, 1994. That time was wrenching for Jill. When her mother passed away, it was as if a piece of Jill died with her.

Jill began to pull away from me noticeably in the wake of her loss. One day I came home to find that Jill and many of her belongings were gone. Her closet was empty, her bedroom dresser was almost bare, inside and out. I was stunned. She hadn't given me any clue she was leaving.

I soon found that Jill had moved out of the main house and taken up residence in the guest house. I tried to talk to her to find out what could be done to heal the situation, but it was as if a curtain of finality had dropped between us. She had no interest in discussing anything with me. From that day forward, we never even had another meal together.

I could not engage Jill in any conversation about her decision. She was through talking about anything. Even polite conversation became impossible.

And what was there to talk about? Jill had not been happy in our relationship for some time. I knew her unhappiness was centered on the issue of my time and my attention—two commodities I had too little of to suit Jill. So after twenty-two years of marriage, she had drawn a line in the sand.

My first reaction was to suggest counseling. "I've been suggesting that for years," she replied, "but you never had time then." I said, "Let's spend more time together." She said, "You had your chance." I said, "Jill, let's take a trip and talk all this over." She replied, "I don't want to." "Jill, I'll do whatever it takes." "I've heard that before."

I thought back to our previous crisis in 1982 and of the things we had done to rekindle our love for each other. "Jill, we've done it once before," I said. "We can do it again." Her response was instantaneous. "Yeah, you were great for one year, Pat," she said, "but then you came to Florida and got consumed again."

Nothing I said or did penetrated. I had done everything I could, but nothing worked.

So we lived in a bleak state of separation. I didn't tell anyone what I was going through. I just prayed hard, tried to maintain an upbeat attitude and positive public front, tried to keep the family motivated, and tried to keep my professional life moving forward. I kept hoping something would change and we could resolve this crisis as we had before. I tried to keep in close contact with Jill—reaching out without groveling, always hoping she would change her mind. I did not want Jill to leave me. I loved her and was proud of her many talents.

Throughout the time Jill lived in that guest house, our lives were as separate as if she lived across town. We spoke from time to time, mostly about family business and situations involving the kids. When I tried to talk to her about restoring the marriage, she had nothing to say to me. There was no interest on her part.

I finally shared my dilemma with Jay Strack, a good friend in Orlando who is a nationally respected author and speaker. Jay listened sympathetically, then said, "Pat, you need to give it one more try. Here's what I suggest. Give her a big vase of flowers and a card with two plane tickets to any destination she wants. See what happens." So I did exactly what Jay suggested—and the next morning, I found the flowers and the card upside down in the trash can.

Eventually, Jill bought a house and completed the process of separating herself from me, leaving the children in my care. No one outside of our family knew of our separation. No one knew that our marriage had become an empty shell. It's very stressful living a fictional existence. It was hard on all of us.

It occurred to me that Jill must have felt like a prisoner in this twilight zone of a relationship—not married, but not divorced, either. I was sure she couldn't have been happier in that isolated state than when she was a part of the family. She must have felt trapped and terribly alone. Perhaps if she felt free, if she no longer felt imprisoned by our marriage, she would change. It was a certainty that nothing I had done up to that point had accomplished anything.

Some years earlier, I had read a book by Dr. James Dobson, *Love Must Be Tough,* and I remembered his advice for situations in which a mate is determined to leave. He said it was sometimes best to stop holding on, and to simply release your mate into the Lord's hands. So I went to her and said, "Jill, I've been hanging on, hoping things would change for close to a year and a half, but I want you to know right now that I'm releasing you." I put my clenched hand out in front of her and opened it. "I'm totally releasing you to the Lord. I'm not going to hold you here against your wishes. I can't fight anything you decide to do. From now on, this is in the Lord's hands, not mine."

I remember she cried a little bit, but she didn't say anything that I recall. I hoped that if she felt free, she would change— but I made up my mind that this was not going to be just a manipulation or a tactic. I was genuinely releasing my grasp and handing the situation over to God. Had it been a mere tactical move, I would have to chalk it up as a failure, because it was only a month later that her lawyer sent the letter that jolted my world.

But my talk with Jill was not part of some tactic to change her mind. It was something I genuinely had to do. I couldn't control Jill. I had to let go.

## A Matter of Public Record

Early 1995 was a tough time for me professionally, too. The Magic had worked hard through the season to get into the play-offs. But when we ended up losing four straight to the Rockets in the finals, it promised to be a long off-season.

Meanwhile, Jill's lawyers were moving forward aggressively and kept pressing for financial information and disclosure of personal assets. True to his word, Bill Barnett did everything he could within the law to delay. I asked him on several occasions to convey my request for counseling. Those requests were declined.

Finally, on the evening of December 21, 1995, we had our first face-to-face meeting since the start of the divorce action. Bill Barnett and I met with Jill and her lawyer in Bill's office. The meeting was structured as a meeting between opposing parties—which was a very weird feeling for me. This was the woman I had been with through the birth of four children. This was the woman I had gone to the airport with to meet fourteen adopted children. We had gone through tough times and high times together. Yet there she was, sitting across a table, an adversary according to the law—one half of "Williams vs. Williams."

As I had instructed him, Bill began by saying, "My client would like to open with a request for counseling with Mrs. Williams."

"Ms. Williams declines that invitation," Mark Rabinowitz answered with curt formality.

I said, "I would like to hear that from Mrs. Williams' lips."

"I have no interest," she said, softly but firmly.

The rest of the meeting was as unpleasant as any experience I've ever endured. Imagine a root canal without anesthetic—and you're not even close.

Jill and I had agreed that we wanted to resolve our situation quietly and amicably. One week later, the amicability ended. On the morning of December 29, Bill called me at home and said, "Well, we've been filed on." Jill's lawyers had filed divorce papers with the court of Seminole County. "Williams vs. Williams" had become a matter of public record.

That was a devastating day. I have a weekly interview show on a sports talk station in Orlando, and my guest that day was basketball star Bill Walton. As I drove him back to his hotel after the interview, I told him what had happened that morning.

"I've been through that myself," he said. "Let me tell you, it's going to be tough. When it's over, if you do everything right, you're going to walk away with three things: one, the love and respect of your children; two, your own self-respect and integrity; and three, your future. Your wife will walk away with one thing: your money."

At that point, my skies were so dark, I didn't quite grasp what he was telling me, but it was a word of hope—and hope was something I desperately needed.

Later that night, I went into the visiting team's locker room at the Orlando Arena. The Los Angeles Clippers were there for a game, and their coach, Bill Fitch, has been a good friend of mine for almost thirty years. I told him about my pending divorce, and he said, "I've been there, and let me tell you three things." That day, it seemed, advice was coming my way in threes. "Number one," said Bill, "before this is over, you'll end up hating your wife's lawyer. Number two, you'll wonder why she got such a smart lawyer and you got such a dumb one. And number three, you're going to go through some tough times. But if I was betting on anyone to make a comeback at age fifty-six, I'd bet on you."

Bill Fitch was mostly right. I did end up in a sense hating Mark Rabinowitz—not as a person, but certainly as a take-no-prisoners divorce attorney. And yes, I did go through some incredibly tough times. And yes, I did make my comeback. Bill was wrong about one thing, though: My own lawyer wasn't dumb. I couldn't have asked for a better, more caring, and more ethical representation than I got from Bill Barnett.

One of my biggest concerns was the media. I wondered what the newspapers would say about this, now that it was a matter of public record—and I dreaded it. I wanted to get a preemptive statement out to the press, so I worked all day on a statement. I wrote several drafts and showed it to various people for their input. By the end of the day I had structured a beautifully written press release.

The last person I shared it with was Rich DeVos, a good friend and advisor as well as the chairman of RDV Sports, the company that owns the Orlando Magic. He read it through, then said, "You don't need to say all that. All you need are these three sentences: 'My wife, Jill, has filed for divorce today. I regret this deeply. The children are with me and know they are loved and cared for.' That's all."

That was some of the best advice I ever received. I put out that single paragraph as a press release, and the story broke on the front page of the Orlando *Sentinel* the next day, a Saturday.

I didn't leave the house all day.

## My Past and My Future

The next year, 1996, was the toughest year of my life, a seemingly endless struggle to divide the assets of our marriage. It took twelve months to resolve—and I don't believe it would be resolved today if Jill and I had not agreed to go to a family counselor, Dr. Deborah Day, who sat us down with her partner, Guy Haines, and forced us to reach a resolution without our lawyers being involved.

The ordeal ended December 30, 1996, a year after the filing. The dissolution of our marriage left me with a whirl of mixed feelings—a sense of emptiness, sadness, and failure, but also of relief that a long nightmare was over. There was even a tinge of expectation, rooted in my attitude of optimism and curiosity, as I wondered what tomorrow might bring. The darkest, most tumultuous year of my life was finally in the past, and my future was about to begin again.

I'm not complaining, not one bit. My life has been an exciting, memorable journey—the most enjoyable any human could have. It's been my privilege to see, touch, taste, and experience things most people only dream about—and I'd like to share them with you. I've gotten to meet and know some of the most fascinating and dazzling personalities in the world—and I'd like to introduce them to you.

So come back with me to where the journey began—a little patch of grass in Wilmington, Delaware.

# 2

# The Wonder Years

If you go to the home where I grew up in Wilmington, you can still find two stones set into the front yard about sixty feet apart. One of those stones is about the size of home plate. The other is shaped like the rubber slab on a pitcher's mound. I spent most of my "wonder years" around those two stones, either throwing a ball, catching a ball, or swinging a bat.

My dad, Jim Williams, gave me my first baseball glove when I was three years old. He took my sister, Carol, and me to a major league game in 1947 when I was seven—my first big-league game ever. The Philadelphia Athletics, managed by Connie Mack, hosted the Cleveland Indians in a doubleheader at Shibe Park, and we sat through both games, up on the third base side, gobbling down hot dogs, slurping sodas, and cheering our heads off. It was one of the happiest days of my life, and I was hooked forever.

I vividly remember waking up the next morning, feeling I had truly had a vision of the rest of my life: I wanted to be a ballplayer. Playing major league baseball was my only goal. I never doubted that I would make it. Baseball was my food and drink. It was the air I breathed. It seems I always had a bat, a ball, and a baseball glove or two with me—one glove for me and one for anyone willing to play a game of catch.

If I couldn't go outside, I'd be in my room, a bat in my hands, swinging at imaginary pitches. There was a full-length mirror in my room, and I marked off the strike zone with tape and stood in front of the mirror for hours, practicing my swing.

I usually played catch with Dad—but my favorite childhood baseball story involves my mother, Ellen Williams. Mom has always been a baseball fan, and she and I spent a lot of time around those two rocks, throwing and catching and hitting balls. One day when I was seven, I was at the pitching rock and she was in her batting stance at the home plate rock. I gave her my best fastball, and Mom connected with a loud crack. She lined the pitch straight back at me, nailing me square in the eye. I hit the ground like I'd been shot. Everything went black. Mom ran to my side, calling out my name.

Now, it's funny. I kid Mom about it and tell her I should have gotten back on my feet and thrown her a brushback pitch—she was really crowding the plate! But it wasn't funny that day. She thought she had killed me, and I ended up with a black eye and a splitting headache.

Uncle Bill Parsons was Mom's only brother—a teacher, a coach, and a huge sports fan. He had an enormous influence on me, taking me to many major league games and my first college basketball games at the Palestra on the University of Pennsylvania campus. Uncle Bill was a Princeton man, and we went to many games at Palmer Stadium during the era of Dick Kazmaier, Princeton's Heisman Trophy–winning running back of the early '50s.

Uncle Bill taught me to keep a scorecard. On September 3, 1947, shortly after I had seen my first major league game, I was visiting at my grandparents' house in Ardmore, Pennsylvania. I was listening to a game on the radio—the Philadelphia A's and the Washington Senators. I was sitting on the front porch with my scorecard on my knees and having a hard time marking in the boxes—it was just a little too much for me at that age. But as the game progressed, I realized that Bill McCahan of the A's was pitching a no-hitter. In fact, if first baseman Ferris Fain hadn't made an error, McCahan would have had a perfect game.

Just as the game ended, my mother called. "Pat, your grandfather wants to see you!" So I ran into the house and dashed to my grandfather's room. He had been in poor health for a while, and he was sick in bed. As I came bounding into the room, I blurted out, "Grandpop! Grandpop! Bill McCahan pitched a no-hitter!" Those were probably the last words my grandfather heard. Within a couple of hours, he died.

I have been a Ted Williams fan almost as long as I can remember—an obsession I acquired from my Uncle Bill. Uncle Bill related everything—and I mean *everything*—to the great Red Sox star. If I didn't want to eat my brussels sprouts, he'd say, "You know, Ted would have eaten his brussels sprouts. You think maybe that's why he's such a great hitter?" Or he might just say, apropos of nothing, "I wonder what Ted is doing now." Or, "I wonder what Ted would think of this."

By 1954, when I was fourteen, my buddy, Gil Yule, and I would go to Philly for the games almost every weekend. I saw Ted Williams in person for the first time that summer, at an A's–Red Sox doubleheader. My team, the A's, lost both games. After the game, I waited outside the park where the Sox bus was parked. Ted sat in the front seat of the bus with the window open, while hordes of kids swarmed around him like mosquitoes in July, clamoring for autographs. I can still hear him roaring at those kids, "If you guys don't get in line, I'm not signing *any* autographs!" Well, those kids listened, and Ted signed autographs for every kid there, including an avid young fan named Pat Williams. I still have that signed photo.

Gil and I took the train back to Wilmington and I ran into the house that night, my Ted Williams memento in hand. Mom had heard the game on the radio, and she greeted me at the door, expecting me to be completely downcast. "Oh, boy," she said, "what a disappointing day! The A's lost twice."

"Disappointing?" I said. "It was a great day! I got Ted Williams's autograph!"

I liked all sports, but baseball was my passion. Practically every memory of my childhood is a baseball memory. The game ruled every waking moment of my early life. I papered my bedroom wall with photos of baseball players. I knew all the statistics of all the players, and I collected baseball cards and every other kind of baseball memorabilia—and I still have most of that stuff today. Back then, baseball cards came in packs of bubble gum, and I made my mother drive me all over Wilmington to find those nickel packs. You never knew what kind of treasure you'd find inside!

I learned how to read and do arithmetic from checking the box scores, keeping tabs on batting averages, and studying the won-lost columns in the newspaper. I also devoured the stats and player biographies printed on the backs of baseball cards. I read everything I could get my hands on that had to do with baseball players and tried to imitate the habits of the baseball greats. I read somewhere that Rogers Hornsby, the great National League hitter, never went to the movies because he believed that watching those flickering pictures in a darkened theater was bad for the eyesight. Hey, if it was good enough for Hornsby, it was good enough for Kid Williams! So I missed a lot of movies while growing up—but I can't really say I was a much better hitter after forgoing all those Hollywood thrills and buttered popcorn.

I also read that Don Mueller of the New York Giants used to sharpen himself for curveballs by hitting corncobs with a broomstick. So for weeks after I read that, I made my dad pitch corncobs to me in the backyard. I know he felt ridiculous—but he was a good sport about it.

My mother had a label for me: "monomaniac." I had never heard that word before, but she used it to describe my obsession with playing, talking, dreaming, and living sports.

## A Baseball Family

I came by this obsession honestly, being born into a sports-minded family in a Philadelphia hospital on May 3, 1940. My father wanted to cram as many Scottish-Irish names onto my birth certificate as would fit, so I was named Patrick Livingston Murphy Williams. My mother soon learned that it was not a good idea to call me by my entire name when she was angry with me. By the time she called out all four names, I'd be two blocks away!

My older sister, Carol, was born three years ahead of me, and two more sisters, Ruthie and Mary Ellen, followed me. I was a year and a half old when Pearl Harbor was bombed, and my dad left home to go to war soon after he gave me that baseball glove when I was three. A vision problem kept him out of combat, which is where he really wanted to be, so he ended up working with the American Red Cross in Australia and the Philippines and spending time in Japan during the postwar occupation. So I didn't really get to know my dad until he returned in 1945.

Dad was a thin, wiry, bespectacled man with an easygoing manner. I rarely saw him angry. Mom was much more emotional. In terms of personality, they were polar opposites—and perhaps that's why they had such a stable, effective relationship. I don't remember my parents being particularly demonstrative and affectionate in front of us kids, but that was an era when people were expected to be emotionally reserved. I would say theirs was a marriage of respect. They were both busy, driven, type-A people, and they were both involved in the community, volunteering time to civic projects. They were kindred spirits in that regard, and I don't remember many squabbles or fights between them.

My parents were firm but caring disciplinarians. I didn't give them too much trouble as a child, but I was a kid, and any kid, from time to time, needs to have "the board of education applied to the seat of knowledge." For that purpose, Dad kept a big paint paddle hanging in the kitchen—he called it his "Patrick Persuader."

I was seven years old when my youngest sister, Mary Ellen, was born, and I cried bitter tears when I learned that our new baby was a girl! I already had two sisters, and I really wanted a brother to play ball with. But there were deeper problems with Mary Ellen's birth that I didn't understand when I was seven. She was born with severe mental retardation, and she spent almost all of her life in an institution. She died in 1983 at age thirty-seven. The problems surrounding Mary Ellen's birth defect brought Mom and Dad closer together, and they both became involved in fund-raising and consciousness-raising on behalf of research and treatment of retardation.

One of the good things that came out of the difficult circumstances of Mary Ellen's disability was the Delaware High School Football All-Star Game, an annual event which helped raise funds to provide services to people with mental disabilities. The idea grew out of a behind-the-backstop discussion between Dad and Bob Carpenter, the owner of the Philadelphia Phillies, while they were watching their sons (Bob's son, Ruly, and me) play a summer league baseball game. The game has been held every year since then and continues to benefit work among the mentally retarded.

Even though Dad was the son of a Presbyterian minister and had once taught Sunday school, he never went to church while I was growing up. My mother took us to Westminster Presbyterian Church—I attended Sunday school or church every Sunday of my youth, right through high school. About all I remember of my many hours in church was that I was forced to memorize a lot of Bible verses. During the church service, I sat in the pew beside my mother and whiled away the sermon by daydreaming of hitting home runs for the Phillies or the A's.

For eighteen years, Dad taught and coached at Tower Hill School, a private all-grade school that catered to an elite clientele. Some of my earliest memories were of being around my father in the locker room or on the bench by the field. I would fetch the bats and baseball equipment for the Tower Hill teams, which, unfortunately, were never very good.

I remember going with my dad and another Tower Hill teacher, Bill Wild, to my first college football game. I was eight years old, and the game pitted Fordham University against Lafayette College in Easton, Pennsylvania. One memory I have is of a very animated, excited assistant coach who paced the Fordham sidelines. Perhaps you've heard of him—his name was Vince Lombardi.

Dad's job at Tower Hill didn't pay well, but the school did allow teachers' kids to attend free of charge. So I went to Tower Hill through the sixth grade—then Dad quit his teaching job in 1952 to go into the life insurance business. Even though we were able to continue on at Tower Hill, I cried and cried the day my father resigned, because I loved having everyone know that my father was the coach. But Dad knew best. He immediately began making good money selling life insurance, because he was a friendly, outgoing, likable guy.

Dad always stressed to me the importance of working hard. For six years, I had a paper route and Dad was always up with me at six A.M. to drive the car while I threw the papers on the porch. He also helped line up summer jobs for me in high school. I spent two summers working on a cattle farm and two summers on a construction job.

Jim Williams was an enthusiastic, proud father. He was always taking snapshots, shooting home movies, hollering at my games, and telling everybody, "That's my boy!" I should have been pleased that he was so proud of me, but it got to be embarrassing at times. Sometimes, I even gave him directions to the wrong ballpark to keep him from showing up and embarrassing me in front of the guys—but he always found me. I don't know if he ever realized I did that intentionally. I hope not, because I see now that there are lots of kids in this world who would kill for any scrap of attention from their parents. I was lucky to be so loved, and I wish I had appreciated it more at the time. Sometimes I wonder how I could have lived in the same house with the man for eighteen years without taking time to know and appreciate him better.

If there was a dark side to my father, it was that he didn't handle alcohol very well. He was not a regular drinker. He was more of a social drinker—but when he drank socially, it frequently got the better of him. Alcohol played a role in my extended family. My mother's father and uncle both had a problem with alcohol, and so did my father's brother, who was a broken alcoholic until he joined Alcoholics Anonymous and turned his life around.

Some of my most haunting memories are of New Year's mornings, after Dad had been to an all-night New Year's Eve party. I'd find him lying on the couch, fully dressed, either asleep or too toxed to function. I never saw him go into a rage or become abusive in any way, but it was disturbing enough to see my father unable to function because of alcohol.

My most devastating memory is of a time when I was fourteen or fifteen years old. We could always count on Dad getting up in the morning and waking the rest of us for school. But on this particular morning, I woke up to the distant sound of Dad's alarm clock ringing and ringing. I thought, *What's going on? Isn't Dad going to shut off that alarm?* I got up and went into his bedroom. He was lying across the bed with his clothes on, and the alarm was ringing and ringing—but he didn't move. I went closer and was shocked to see that there was blood on his face. That scared me.

I could see his chest rising and falling, so I knew he was alive—but something terrible had happened to him, and he couldn't respond to the alarm. I shut it off and backed out of the room, then went downstairs and saw Dad's Volkswagen in the garage—the whole front end was mangled. I later found out that he had driven his car under the rear end of a truck. That explained the blood on his face.

Mom was away at the time, and I remember thinking, *I've got to do something!* So I called Dr. Ward Briggs, our family physician, and he came over, got my dad to come around, and began treating him. I remember Dr. Briggs saying, "Jim, I wouldn't insure you for a nickel right now."

And that was the wakeup call for my father. He never took another drink the rest of his life. He lived another seven years.

The Volkswagen just disappeared—Dad didn't say what happened to it. A few months later, it reappeared, fully repaired and shined up. Dad gave it to me as a present on my sixteenth birthday, the day I got my driver's license.

That experience is probably one of the reasons I have never taken up drinking. But the bigger reason, I think, is that I simply understood from an early age that if I was going to be a big leaguer, I had to take good care of my body and stay away from things that would harm me or slow me down, such as alcohol or tobacco. (You never even heard of drugs in those days.) I remember reading *Pop Warner's Book for Boys,* in which the great college football coach wrote, "If you're going to be a great athlete, you don't drink, you don't smoke, you get your rest." I bought into that message as a young boy, and I only wish there were more influences like Pop Warner for kids today.

My Dad was a kind, caring man, and he was my biggest fan. He knew I was totally focused on being a big league ballplayer, and he was very supportive throughout my early years—except on one occasion when I was in high school. For some reason, out of a clear blue sky, he said, "You know, Pat, you're never going to play in the big leagues."

That stunned me. I think he meant to protect me against getting my hopes too high and feeling dashed when I didn't reach my goals. I think most parents want to make sure their children have something to fall back on. He probably wanted me to have a plan B in case baseball didn't work out. But when he told me, "You're never going to play in the big leagues," I was just wiped out.

He saw how hurt I was and tried to make it up to me. "I didn't mean to be hard on you, Pat," he said. "I really love you, and I believe in you. I know you're going to do great things someday."

But none of that cut any ice. All I wanted in life was a big league career. When he told me that my life's goal was out of reach, my reaction was to think, *Okay, I'll show you!* I never forgot that incident—and I've always tried, whenever I'm dealing with my own kids, to remember how I felt that day.

## A Well-Rounded Upbringing

My dad grew up in Greensboro, North Carolina, and came north after graduating from the University of North Carolina, where he majored in American history. Dad taught and coached at the Haverford School, a prep school near Philadelphia, and he also taught Sunday school at the Bryn Mawr Presbyterian

Church. He had a seventeen-year-old student in his Sunday school class named Ellen Parsons. Though he was eight years older than she, they began dating and continued after Ellen went on to college at Vassar in Poughkeepsie, New York. When she was in her junior year at Vassar, they decided to get married. After they were married, he took a position at the Tower Hill School in Wilmington.

Mom also had a big influence on me and my love for baseball. Even though Dad was a coach, Mom was really the more devoted baseball fan. While my father would occasionally take me to a ball game—especially that first game that made such an impression—most of my memories of watching major league baseball were of sitting next to Mom at an A's or Phillies game. We went practically every weekend and usually sat in the upper deck on the third base side.

Mom came from a family of baseball fans. Her father always talked about the legendary Detroit Tigers hitter Ty Cobb, and her brother just thought Walter "Big Train" Johnson of the old Washington Senators was the greatest pitcher who ever hurled a horsehide. My mother idolized Lefty Grove, the great pitcher of the Philadelphia Athletics during the 1920s and '30s—she often told me about the four World Series games he won. So the baseball tradition of the Parsons family was passed down through Mom; the Williams family was a baseball family, too.

I would give Mom an A+ as a mother. She was strict but very loving—and I always knew that our family rules were there for good reason, not because my parents were overbearing or capricious. From grade school through my senior year, I was never allowed out on a school night—those nights were for homework, and my mother was there every night to make sure I got it done. School work did not come easily for me. It was a daily struggle—but I had all the fun on weekends any kid could want.

Mom exposed me to many great influences, from sports to Cub Scouts to the arts. She was a fanatic about reading, and I vividly remember sitting with her while she read aloud to me when I was a little boy. No question, that's why I've been such a compulsive reader. My mother and sisters had a lot of musical ability, and music and the arts were a big part of our family life. We often went to New York and Philadelphia to visit museums, attend concerts, go to the zoo or the circus, and watch Broadway shows. I didn't have a lick of musical talent, but to this day I can enjoy and intelligently discuss Gilbert and Sullivan, *South Pacific,* and the whole Broadway scene. My friend Jerry Jenkins once called me a renaissance jock, and I think that's a good description of the well-rounded way I was raised. I owe it all to Mom.

Another really deep and positive impression my parents made on me was that they taught and modeled for me an abiding sense of fairness and acceptance of all people, regardless of superficial differences such as race or economic class. A good example of this occurred in 1956, following my sophomore year in high school. My father and Bob Carpenter, the Phillies owner, headed up the Delaware High School Football All-Star Game. It was North versus South, and it happened that two of the better football players in the North—Joe Peters and Alvin Hall— were African-American athletes from Wilmington's one largely black school, Howard High School.

For two weeks, all the players from high schools in the North trained at Sanford Prep outside of Wilmington. The only problem was that the headmaster at Sanford was nervous because there were students on campus from the Deep South, and the assumption was these students would be prejudiced against blacks. So he said that the school would only allow the practice facilities to be used if the two black players, Joe and Alvin, practiced during the day and stayed off-campus at night.

I remember my father remarking that it was a stupid and insulting condition to impose on those young athletes merely because of the color of their skin. "But if they have to stay off-campus," he said, "let them stay at our house." I had just gotten my driver's license at the time, so for two weeks, I got up early and drove Joe and Alvin out to the prep school every morning for practice. At the end of each day, I picked them up and brought them home, and they stayed in our guest room.

I was profoundly affected by this experience. I could see that here were a couple of guys who were just like everybody else in every way except the color of their skin, and I thought, *This is nuts! How could anyone think segregation is normal or moral?* Years later poet Maya Angelou expressed my feelings perfectly when she wrote, "Prejudice is a burden that confuses the past, threatens the future, and renders the present inaccessible."

## Guys and Girls

When I was in high school, my buddies Mike Castle (who later became governor of Delaware and a United States congressman) and Reeves Montague and I were so much into sports that we didn't have time for girls. Every weekend, we'd drive to Philadelphia to see college and pro basketball games and the Phillies and Eagles games. Personally, I just wasn't socially minded, and I didn't want to date girls. Outside of my circle of friends, I was painfully shy, and all I cared about was sports. Mike and Reeves and I always vowed that we would never have anything to do with girls.

I only broke that vow once in my early adolescence. That was when I was in the eighth grade and I invited Patsy Cox to go with me to a dance at Tower Hill School. She was the cutest girl at Wilmington Friends School—Tower Hill's fiercest rival. I didn't want Mike and Reeves and the guys to know I was calling her, because they'd accuse me of being a traitor—first for dating a girl and second for dating a girl from a rival school. But I couldn't help it—Patsy was really something.

It took me an hour to work up the courage to dial Patsy's number—but once I had her on the phone and managed to stammer out an invitation to the dance, she accepted. I think it was one of her first dates—and it was definitely a first for me. The night of the dance arrived—and before it was over, it would become one of the worst experiences of my young life.

Dad drove us to the dance—Patsy sat in the front seat of the family car between my dad and me. I bluffed my way through the dance, doing my best "suave and cool" impression. Small talk didn't come easily for me, but I managed to get through the dance without totally embarrassing myself.

Then Dad picked us up and we drove Patsy home. I walked Patsy to her door and stood there scuffing my shoes on the sidewalk for five minutes, telling her good-night. It was an agony of wondering: Should I kiss her good-night? Will she get mad at me if I do? Will she be hurt if I don't? Finally, my basic cowardice with girls prevailed. I shook her hand, and she went inside. I leaped back into the front seat with my dad, feeling relieved that the evening was finally over.

And then I heard the laughter. My big sister, Carol, was on the floor of the back seat, laughing her head off. Dad was laughing, too. We pulled away from the curb and I ranted and fumed all the way home. It was four years before I worked up the courage to ask another girl out on a date.

## In the Shadow of Shibe Park

I have always been goal-oriented. After that life-changing experience of seeing my first major league baseball game, I began to set goals. I intuitively bought into the American game plan of finding out what you enjoy in life, setting that as a goal, and pursuing it with everything you've got.

But even before I was seven, there were influences pointing me in the direction of a lifelong love affair with professional sports. I didn't realize it at the time, but one of the biggest breaks in my life took place when I was attending kindergarten at Tower Hill School, and one of my classmates was a kid named Ruly Carpenter. Little did I know the impact Ruly would have on my life.

In 1943, two years before I met Ruly, his grandfather had purchased the Philadelphia Phillies baseball team for four hundred thousand dollars and given it to Ruly's dad, Bob Carpenter, to run. By that time, both the Phillies and the A's played at Shibe Park. In socioeconomic terms, Ruly's family and mine had little in common. My dad was a school teacher making around four thousand dollars a year, while Ruly's parents were heirs to part of the du Pont fortune—his grandfather had married a du Pont. The only reason I got to know Ruly was that my dad could send his kids for free to a swank private school for the children of the well-to-do. So I got to be good friends with Ruly, and we came up through the school system together.

Tower Hill was a very demanding college preparatory school. I didn't enjoy school or studying, and everything came hard for me. What kept me going was athletics. Of course, I was probably helped by the fact that there were fewer distractions in those days—no pizza parlors or McDonald's or video arcades to hang out in, no CDs or MTV, and we didn't have a TV in our house. Life in the 1940s and '50s was pretty basic, compared with today.

But even sports activities were not as easy to come by then as they are today. This was in the days before youth sports got to be as important as they are now. There was no Little League baseball, no youth soccer, no basketball league, no Pop Warner football. The revolution in youth sports came in the '50s, and I was a decade too early. It was frustrating for me, and I had to be content with sandlot games in the neighborhood or intramural sports at Tower Hill.

I played in my first organized sporting event when I was a seventh grader, playing quarterback on the Midgets football team. Later, in the spring of my seventh-grade year, I played second base for the Midgets baseball team. I went 0 for 21 at the plate that year, and it was a humiliating experience because I was very competitive and very serious about the game and about winning. My only consolation was that Gil Hodges, the great Brooklyn Dodgers slugger, had gone 0 for 21 in the World Series the previous fall.

Throughout those years, Ruly Carpenter and I were the best of friends. I enjoyed going to his house for sleepovers. He lived in the most incredible house I had ever seen, and I was impressed that his family had a chauffeur named Alfred and a cook named Helen. Ruly and I did everything together: fishing, swimming, shooting baskets, shooting BB guns, skating, going to University of Delaware football games, and of course, playing lots of baseball.

Ruly even had his own baseball field. In 1957, Phillies first baseman Ed Bouchee worked out with us on Ruly's diamond. He had missed spring training, so he was getting in shape to rejoin the team—and Ruly and I got to work him out. I got to meet a lot of other major leaguers when Ruly and his dad would take me to see the Phillies play. After the games, they'd take me in the locker room, and there I was, a wide-eyed kid of ten, eleven, twelve years old, rubbing shoulders with all my heroes.

This was the heyday of the Phillies organization, too—the era of "The Whiz Kids," of Richie Ashburn, Del Ennis, and Robin Roberts of the legendary Phillies team that snatched the National League pennant from the heavily favored Brooklyn Dodgers in 1950. I still have all the clippings and programs and magazines I collected while I was growing up with Ruly, in the shadow of Shibe Park, in the shadow of my heroes.

You would never have guessed that Ruly was from an upper-crust family. He was as plain as an old shoe and always getting into some kind of minor mischief. I'm not sure my parents ever quite trusted Ruly or fully approved of our friendship—they viewed Ruly Carpenter with the same wariness that Ward and June Cleaver reserved for Eddie Haskell on *Leave It to Beaver*.

But Ruly was a great guy, and the good times I had with him were worth all the occasional scares he gave me. How many kids can say they have maintained even one friendship from kindergarten all the way through high school and beyond? And what kid wouldn't give his comic book collection, his pet hamster, and his Captain Midnight decoder ring to be best friends with the son of a major league owner? I look back and realize I had a wonderful childhood—the best. I wouldn't have traded those years for a squillion bucks.

## A Taste of the Big Leagues

Ruly would get a bunch of us guys together—Mike Castle, Reeves Montague, me, and a couple of other guys—and we'd go to the train station at the start of spring vacation, ride the night train to Clearwater, Florida, and watch the Phillies at spring training. The Carpenter family had a home in Clearwater, and we'd either stay there or at a hotel and have access to the ballpark. Whenever the Phillies weren't using the field, Ruly and the rest of us would go out and have our own little spring training.

By 1958, my senior year in high school, the Phillies had really hit the skids. Their losing record, combined with the fact that Ruly and I were approaching graduation and getting full of the cockiness of youth, had taken a lot of the shine off these guys who had been our heroes. We'd sit in the stands and watch the Phillies play, and we'd say stuff like, "Can you believe these guys get paid to play like that? Can you believe that strikeout? Man, my little sister coulda hit that one!"

Well, one day in the spring of that year, the bunch of us were sitting in the stands at Al Lopez Field in Tampa, watching an exhibition game between the Phillies and the Cincinnati Reds. The last three hitters in the lineup were shortstop Roy Smalley Sr., catcher Joe Lonnett, and third baseman Woody Smith. They were hitting sixth, seventh, and eighth for the Phillies. Together, those three guys went 0 for 12 in that game, and let me tell you, the Phillies got waffled by the Reds that day.

All through dinner that night, Ruly needled his dad about how bad his team was. "You take those guys at the bottom of the order—Smalley, Lonnett, and Smith," he said. "Even I could strike those bums out!"

Well, Bob Carpenter had heard just about enough bluster from his son. He said, "You think you're better than the big leaguers on the Phillies? Let's just see you prove it." And he bet Ruly twenty bucks that he couldn't pitch three innings against Smalley, Lonnett, and Smith without giving up four runs. Ruly could pick his defense.

The next day, Bob Carpenter went to his manager, Mayo Smith, and set up the game. Ruly was on the mound, and I was catching. All the other defensive positions were manned by Phillies players—real major leaguers. It was the most incredible thing I had ever experienced. The entire Phillies organization gathered around to watch, and there were reporters and photographers. We even had major league umpires.

I was in my T-shirt and khakis, and Joe Lonnett lent me his catcher's mask and pads. I hunkered down behind the plate, Ruly went out to the mound, and the game began. Ruly just had to pitch three innings with a little break between innings—our side didn't have to bat. So Ruly started pitching, and right away he gave up two runs. Then he got some help from the infield and outfield to close the inning. In the second inning, Joe Lonnett clobbered a homer over the right centerfield fence. It was beginning to look like Ruly's dad was going to win that bet.

But then Ruly settled down and even struck out Roy Smalley. Roy Smalley! Even though Smalley was in his thirties and in the twilight of his career, he had enjoyed a long run as a pretty good hitter for the Chicago Cubs. So it was really humiliating for him to be struck out by the owner's kid, who was still playing high school ball. As Smalley walked away from the plate, I heard him mutter, "What a way to leave the big leagues!"

By the end of three innings, Ruly had given up three runs— and he had won the bet with his dad. The "game" was widely reported. In fact, syndicated political writer Sandy Grady, who was then a sports writer for the *Philadelphia Daily News,* wrote an entire column on that contest. Being a part of it was the highlight of my high school years.

Ruly was an outstanding athlete. From the ninth grade through graduation, he won a dozen varsity letters. He went on to be a star football and baseball player at Yale. Ruly and I played on the same varsity teams, both football and baseball. On the baseball team, Ruly was the pitcher and I was the catcher, so he was throwing to me. On the football team, I played quarterback and he was an end, so I threw to Ruly. I threw him ten touchdown passes in our senior year. Our coach was Bob De Groat, the kind of coach and mentor you remember the rest of your life. I can still hear his voice, and the lessons I learned from him resonate in my life today.

Our football team was undefeated during our last two years in high school. In four years, we lost only two games. Our baseball team was also outstanding during those years. Our senior year, Ruly threw three no-hitters and I batted .523, after hitting .428 as a junior.

As the baseball season drew toward its conclusion, I had two big worries—the game against our traditional rivals, Wilmington Friends School, and my senior term paper. At breakfast the morning of the game, Dad teased me. "Go four-for-four today," he said, "and I'll type your term paper for you."

"Are you kidding?" I asked incredulously.

"I'm dead serious, son!" And he was.

That day, in my four times at bat, I hit three singles and a double. I can still see my dad laboring over the typewriter, banging out my senior masterpiece, "Islam as a Force in Africa."

Did my dad know how to motivate me or what?

I played baseball every summer after the high school season ended. I had some excellent coaches—Buddy Clark in sandlot ball, Leroy Hill in American Legion baseball, and Peanuts Riley in a semipro league. Peanuts was a fiery little guy who had been a minor league infielder in the Phillies system. He knew baseball inside out and really took a personal interest in Ruly Carpenter and me. After I went away to college, Peanuts stayed in touch with me. I got a letter from him once that I kept in my wallet for years. Two statements really left an impression on me:

> Glad to hear you have someone pushing you for the catching job. That helps you and the ball club. Hustle a little more every day.

> Don't ever lose your confidence. Remember, the other fellows put their uniforms on the same way you do. Never stop swinging, and you'll be rough on all of them.

## Wake Forest Days

My football career ended in the summer of '58 when I played in the third annual Delaware High School Football All-Star Game. I played for the North squad, and we won. It was a great game, and a gratifying experience to be part of this event that had been such an important part of my dad's life.

I briefly considered playing college football. Then I thought about how it would feel to wind up at the bottom of a pile of 250-pound, college-level defensive linemen—and I decided to stick with my original passion, baseball.

All my friends went north to college, most to the Ivy League schools. I wanted a small college with a good baseball program, warm weather, a physical education department, and some scholarship help. I figured I would have a glorious career in baseball, then move into the front office when my athletic career wound down. Thanks to my friendship with Ruly Carpenter, I had a real good idea of how the pro sports world operated—from the locker room to the front office, from spring training to the World Series—so I had my career path all mapped out. I figured the best school to prepare me was Wake Forest in Winston-Salem, North Carolina.

Baseball practice started in the fall, right after we arrived on campus. I scrimmaged against the varsity players and handled myself well defensively and at bat, getting a couple of base hits in the exhibition games. I felt good knowing I could really compete at that level.

Our coach, Gene Hooks, was one of the early advocates of weight training for athletes. Up to that time, ballplayers were told not to work out with weights lest they become muscle-bound. But Hooks said, "Nonsense! A stronger athlete is a better athlete!" He wrote a book called *The Application of Weight Training to Athletics* which was way ahead of its time. Today, the whole world knows Hooks was right all along, but I'm glad I was introduced to weight training at an early age. I work out with weights to this day—and no one's ever accused me of being muscle-bound!

The classroom regimen at Wake Forest was tough, and I had to work at it. I was fortunate to have attended Tower Hill, or I don't think I could have hacked it at Wake Forest. I didn't want to be pushed, and learning still didn't come easily. I have to confess that I got through some of the required reading in the classics by buying Classics Illustrated comic books of *Ivanhoe* and the Cliff Notes summaries of *Wuthering Heights* and *The Scarlet Letter*. After all, this was the 1950s—I couldn't run out and rent the video like kids do today.

Dad continued to be my cheerleader and number one fan, driving all the way from Delaware to North Carolina—a nine-hour haul one way, sometimes straight through the night—to watch me play a freshman game. He'd even go to the varsity games, even though I wasn't in them. He just wanted to be involved with my school.

One weekend the varsity was playing at the University of Maryland. Sure enough, Dad drove down to Maryland to see the game—and I wasn't even in it! He even bought popsicles from a Good Humor man and passed them out to the players in the Wake Forest dugout. I really heard about it from the varsity players when they got back to campus. I was known as Popsicle for a long time after that.

I made a lot of good friends at Wake Forest—future TV analyst Billy Packer; future NBA players Len Chappell and Dave Budd; Ernie Accorsi, who went on to become the general manager of the Baltimore Colts, the Cleveland Browns, and the New York Giants; my baseball coaches, Gene Hooks and Jack Stallings; Norm Snead, who later quarterbacked for several National Football League clubs; John Mackovic, who coached the Kansas City Chiefs and several college teams; Brian Piccolo, who played for the Chicago Bears, and whose untimely death due to cancer inspired the movie *Brian's Song;* pitcher Jerry Galehouse, whose dad, Denny, had pitched for fifteen years in the American League, from 1934–49; and future pro golfer Jay Sigel.

The summer after my freshman year, I went to Canada and played semipro ball in Dartmouth, Nova Scotia. The players were good, my skills were challenged and sharpened, and I even hit a couple of home runs—one off a big right-hander named Rollie Sheldon, who went on to a good career as a pitcher for the Yankees.

At the start of my sophomore year, I began to get over my shyness with women. I let a friend set me up with a blind date, and that's how I was introduced to a stunning freshman named Ann Herring. It was your usual college date—a hamburger and a movie—and that night I came reeling back to my dorm room. I thought she was fantastic. I was so smitten that I managed to work up the courage to ask her out again—but she said she had other plans. Well, that was as much courage as I could muster—I couldn't stand the thought of another turndown, so I never asked her again. That summer, I was watching the Miss America pageant on television when who should I see but Ann Herring—Miss North Carolina. She finished as the second runner-up in the 1960 pageant.

After my sophomore year, I played a summer in the Tobacco State League in Smithfield, North Carolina, which enabled me to get another forty games or so under my belt—all good experience. My most "fragrant" recollection of playing in Smithfield was living at the White Swan Motel on the edge of town, where they put up the team for the season. The White Swan was right across from a big slaughterhouse for hogs. All day and all night, you could hear the sound of squealing pigs, and an odor wafted over from that place that remains strong in my memory to this day.

In the summer of 1961, I played Basin League semipro ball in Huron, South Dakota. It was a wonderful experience, even though my performance was not distinguished. I did hit a home run in the opening game, though, off a pitcher named Eddie Watt, who went on to have a long career with the Baltimore Orioles and the Phillies.

I really came out of my shell in the fall of my junior year—and to this day, I'm not sure why. But I had always listened with admiration to radio sports announcers, and I long held a secret wish to broadcast games. One day, I just thought, *Well, why not?* And I walked over to the campus radio station and asked Dr. Julian Burroughs, the station manager, if I could give it a whirl.

I was given the job of broadcasting freshman basketball games and doing a sports interview show (amazingly like the sports interview show I do today on Radio 540 in Orlando). I put myself in a position where I was *forced* to communicate with thousands of people from behind a microphone. (Okay, it might have been dozens—but I *believed* it was thousands.) I just didn't have time to be shy.

The show was called *The Pat Williams Show,* and the people who ran the radio station gave me a free hand to develop it. Sometimes I'd interview people in the studio, and sometimes I'd hear that someone was in the area, so I'd grab a tape recorder and do the interview on location. Once I heard that my baseball idol, Ted Williams, was in Greensboro, so I looked him up and got the interview of a lifetime. I interviewed golfing great (and Wake Forest grad) Arnold Palmer, and Bill Sharman of the Boston Celtics. I got interviews with big leaguers Roger Maris, Jim Gentile, and Harmon Killebrew, who were in Winston-Salem for a home run-hitting contest. Maris had set a record of sixty-one home runs during the 1961 season, so it was a fascinating interview. Talking to these legendary players made me feel like I was practically in the majors myself. I wanted it so badly, I could taste it.

One of my favorite interviews was with a man who was not a sports figure at all: Dr. Billy Graham. He came to Wake Forest to speak at chapel, so I lined up a sports interview with the famous evangelist. He talked about his baseball background and all the sports he loved to play, plus the athletes he knew. He was knowledgeable about sports and gave me one of my best interviews ever.

That show also taught me that whenever you try to build something, there will be people—including some who consider themselves your friends—who will try to tear it down. I had put the entire show together—designed the format, arranged the guests, selected the theme music, everything. After my first broadcast, I came back to my room and found a note my roommate had placed on my bed. It was written as if to put words in my mouth: "I'm not a broadcaster, but I tried."

Maybe he meant it as friendly advice: "Don't delude yourself, Pat. Don't embarrass yourself. You're terrible, so just give up." Or maybe he was a little jealous that I was asserting myself, that I had this passion for distinction that propelled me into the public arena. Whatever his motivation, the note left a wound.

But it served as a motivator in my life: *So he thinks I'm not a broadcaster? Fine. I'll prove him wrong!* There's a lesson for anyone who would try to distinguish himself or herself in any field: People will always try to stop you and diminish your accomplishments; just ignore them and keep moving toward your goal.

I loved broadcasting, and my radio show made me something of a campus celebrity. It also did a lot for my confidence as a speaker. I studied speech in my junior and senior years, and the techniques and skills I learned from speech professor James Walton still serve me well. Learning to communicate before a group was a major turning point in my life.

I've heard it said that the number one fear among people in this country is not the fear of death, but the fear of having to give a speech. From my early classroom experiences with public speaking, I can testify that it's the truth. Over the years, I've given thousands of speeches, and I've often thought back in amazement to my experience in Miss Barbara Bullard's ninth-grade English class. She allowed us only one index card for notes—and I had my first speech written out word for word in such tiny lettering I couldn't even read it when I stood in front of the class. I froze like a deer in the headlights. It's a wonder I ever got up to give a speech again! But I did—and public speaking has been a major part of my life ever since.

Another turning point came in November 1960. Jerry Steele, president of the Monogram Club for varsity letter winners, needed someone to head up the freshmen-versus-varsity basketball game. "Pat," he said, "I'm volunteering you." Since Jerry was 6'8", 235 pounds, and he had me in a headlock at the time, how could I say no? So I agreed to be volunteered.

I enlisted the help of other club members and worked harder than I had ever worked in my life. I had the tickets printed and sold and directed the publicity campaign and made arrangements for the halftime show and the band and the presentation of the homecoming queen and everything. I was merchandising, packaging, and selling basketball as fun and entertainment—in short, everything I would later get paid to do by the Philadelphia 76ers, Chicago Bulls, Atlanta Hawks, and Orlando Magic.

The event came off without a hitch. I was ecstatic. I went to bed feeling so excited and pleased I could hardly sleep. I knew then that someday I would like to get involved with the promotional end of pro sports—after a full, rich career as a major league baseball player, of course.

The spring of my junior year was terrific—I hit over .300 as the varsity catcher and, in a game at Georgia Southern, I collected four hits in five at-bats, including a home run. I figured after just one more year at Wake Forest, it was on to the big leagues and the fulfillment of my lifelong dream! Another team we played that year was Yale—so I got a chance to play against my old buddy Ruly Carpenter. I didn't get a chance to bat against him though. He played left field and got one hit—but we won the game.

During my junior and senior years, a scout from the Philadelphia Phillies organization, Wes Livengood, was watching my progress and sending regular reports back to the front office. We talked a lot about baseball, and I hoped he was telling the people in Philly what a great baseball player I was. He had seen the job I did on the homecoming promotion, and he had heard my radio show. Though I didn't realize it at the time, I later learned that his reports often dealt more with my front-office potential than my baseball ability.

## The End of Summer

As I entered my senior year, I was having enough success as a baseball player to be encouraged—but I knew I was not competing against the top college players in the country. In the summer leagues, I was facing players who had stepped up to the next level—and I knew there was at least a level beyond that— maybe more—on the way to the majors. It was a definite reality check. My mindset had gone from, "It's just a matter of time till I'm in the major leagues," to, "Man, I sure hope I get a chance." All I wanted was an opportunity to play pro ball.

During the spring of 1962, we had an excellent ballclub, although I was not hitting as well as in previous years. We tied for the Atlantic Coast Conference championship, then beat out cochampion, Virginia, in a playoff game and won the right to represent the ACC in the NCAA regional tournament in Gastonia, North Carolina. Going to the tournament in June meant missing graduation ceremonies back in Winston-Salem—but if we moved on from Gastonia to the College World Series in Omaha, Nebraska, it would be worth the sacrifice. We just had to win.

Three other schools were in Gastonia for the double elimination tournament—Florida, West Virginia, and Florida State. The winner would go to Omaha. We opened by beating West Virginia rather handily. The next day, we decked Florida. In double elimination play, you have to lose twice to be knocked out of contention—and we hadn't even lost once. With a double-header left to play against Florida State, which had one loss, we were just one victory away from going to the World Series.

So the pressure was on Florida State to win both games to advance to the World Series, while we could split the twinbill and still come out on top.

My family drove down from Delaware for the final game—my mother and sisters in one car, my father in a separate car.

The first game was a real slugfest—a lot of runs, a lot of action—but we lost it, 11-8. As we prepared to go into the second game, we knew our pitching staff was depleted. We went with Don Roth on the mound—Don had been my roommate and close friend on campus. By then it was dark and drizzling and the lights were on. It was a totally different game from the first one—a wrestling match instead of a slugging contest. Don pitched a beautiful game and he never let up. The teams struggled and struggled with each other, going inning after inning with nothing to show for it but a 1-1 tie.

In the top of the eighth inning, I came up to bat. Because I had not been hitting well that season, I was not exactly brimming with confidence. I let a couple of pitches slide past—and then the pitcher gave me a pitch I really liked. I hit that one out. It sailed over the left field fence, and I practically somersaulted around the bases, I was so ecstatic. We had taken the lead by one run—*my* home run!—and if we could hold Florida State for two more innings, we were on our way to Omaha.

We went to the bottom of the eighth, and there was a close play at the plate. The throw was coming home, so I ripped off my catcher's mask and positioned myself to make the play. But the throw bounced in the dirt, hit me in the face, and kept going. I chased it down, but it was too late—the runner scored. The ball in the face didn't hurt me, but it banged me up and made me angry.

By the end of the ninth inning, the score was still tied at two, and we went into extra innings. At that point, we had no bullpen, and poor Don Roth had already pitched his heart out. But he hung in there on what had become a miserable rainy night. We struggled into the tenth inning, then the eleventh inning. I kept signaling for Don's wicked curveball, and he kept putting hitters away—six in a row.

Came the bottom of the twelfth inning, we were still knotted at two. The first Florida State hitter got a double. Don struck out the next hitter—and the hitter after that. We were still in great shape. Just one more out and we'd be up at bat again in the thirteenth.

Don threw a strike. And another strike. I put down a signal for a curveball. Don nodded, went into his windup, released, the ball hooked in, the batter swung—and the ball sailed into left field for a single. The runner who was at second was already rounding third, and the left fielder, Mike Budd, scooped up the ball and threw it home. That ball just seemed to float in slow motion while the runner kept coming like a freight train with afterburners. I could see the mud flying from his cleats as he sprinted for home. I straddled the plate, reached for the throw, and waited forever, it seemed. The ball hit my mitt.

But the runner had already crossed the plate. It was over. Florida State won, and we could only go home.

As the Florida State side began celebrating, I felt a lump in my throat. In that instant, it hit me. This was our last game. When that runner crossed the plate, our college days ended, my class graduated. It was really over.

I didn't want to see or talk to anyone. I was filled with a deep, aching, empty feeling.

And as I absorbed the feelings of that loss while taking off my chest protector and shin guards, I looked up and there was Dad. Didn't he know I didn't want to talk? Didn't he understand what I was going through?

"Tough break, son," he said.

"Yeah, tough."

"You almost had 'em. It was so close."

"Yeah."

I saw my mother and Carol and Ruthie standing a little ways away. They waved to me, and I waved back, but I didn't want to talk. I was too devastated.

"Well, I guess we'll be going, son," said Dad. "I'll be dropping Carol off in Washington, D.C., then I'll go on home to Wilmington. Your mother and Ruthie are taking the other car straight home."

"Yeah, okay. Listen, Dad, could you check with Mr. Carpenter and see what my chances are with the Phillies organization?"

"Bob Carpenter knows you. When you get home, you can talk to him yourself."

"Yeah, I guess so. Well, good-bye, Dad. See you back home."

I trudged off to the team bus for the last ride back to Winston-Salem. It began to rain hard as we boarded the bus. That was fine with me. It fit my mood.

For my teammates and me, it was a quiet, somber hour and a half ride. We all knew that our team was splitting up, and we didn't want it to end. Some of us had been together all four years. We were a unit—and we were never going to be together again.

Four friends who lived north of Wilmington traveled with me the next morning. We had slept late, then taken our time loading the car before heading north. We didn't talk much. I wanted to shake off the past and think about breaking into pro ball, but the pain of that loss kept intruding on my thoughts. I've suffered plenty of losses since then, but few hurt as much as that one.

We didn't push it on the interstate. We were in no hurry to leave four years behind. We noticed the lights of a minor league ballpark in Richmond, Virginia, so we stopped and watched a Triple A game between Memphis and Richmond. Tim McCarver played for Memphis that night. We stayed overnight in Richmond and got a late start in the morning.

I invited the guys to spend the night at our house, and they readily accepted. We arrived in Wilmington around five o'clock that evening. I was surprised to see a lot of cars in front of our house and people in the yard. That was strange.

As we pulled up in the driveway, several people approached looking somber. One was my mother.

"Oh, Pat," she said, "I have terrible news. Your dad had an accident after he left Carol off in Washington."

"An accident? How bad?"

"Pat, your dad was killed."

# 3

# Old Dreams and New

If my buddies and I had been listening to the radio, we'd have heard about the accident. Dad was prominent in Delaware, so the story of his death was carried on all the stations. My mother's biggest fear was that I would get the news about Dad from a radio bulletin. She wanted me to hear it from her. She didn't have any way to contact me on the road—she didn't even know where I was—so she prayed I wouldn't listen to the radio, and her prayer was answered.

When she broke the news to me there in our driveway, she gave it to me very directly, no beating around the bush. She handled it just right—Mom's very wise and very direct in matters like these. She'd had a couple of days to get used to the fact that Dad wasn't coming home, and she was thinking of her kids.

My father and Carol had driven all night to Washington, where Carol got out at her home. Dad was driving alone on the Washington-Baltimore Expressway in the wee hours of the morning. He probably fell asleep at the wheel. His car went off the highway into a bridge abutment. No other cars were involved in the accident.

As my mother was giving me the news, my friends got out of the car. They were almost as stunned as I was, and didn't know what to do or say. They all knew my dad because he had been to all the games and knew each of them by name. They all told me how sorry they were, then they left, not wanting to intrude on our family's grief.

I didn't cry when Mom told me the news, or for several days afterward. I kept thinking, *I've got to be strong. Dad would want me to be strong. Real men don't cry.* That's wrong, of course, but that's what I thought. That was the jock mentality in those days. After a couple of days, Mom became concerned that I was not handling my grief in a healthy way, and called in Don Wilson, our pastor, to visit with me. We talked for a while, and I just kept telling him I was fine, just fine, don't worry about me.

The closest I came to breaking down was at the funeral. There were tears in my eyes several times during the service—but I was careful not to let anybody see. All of Dad's friends were there. Even Jack Stallings, my baseball coach from Wake Forest, came up for the funeral, and I was really touched by that. Bob Carpenter was there, of course. I made a point of going around and personally thanking everyone for being there. I must have shaken several hundred hands that day.

The hardest part for me was the viewing. To see my dad's face composed in death that way was difficult, and the image haunted me for a long time after that. Even though I had gone to church as a boy, I really had not integrated a Christian faith into my life, so I had no faith to hold on to at that time. Seeing him in that casket and remembering that I had just seen him a short time earlier in Gastonia and that I had scarcely said good-bye to him—that was hard, very hard.

After the funeral, Uncle Worth—Dad's older brother—pulled me aside and said, "Your dad didn't leave you much money, but he did leave you a heritage of hundreds of lives he impacted for the better—and that's quite a legacy, when you think about it." Well, Uncle Worth was right about that—but he was mistaken about the money. Dad left me forty thousand dollars in life insurance, which allowed me to get started in life.

My Grandmother Williams, who was in her eighties and not in the best of health when Dad died, lived in Greensboro. I vividly recall a letter she wrote to Mother in which she copied down a number of Bible verses that had helped her in times of trouble. Though I didn't have a living faith at the time, I was profoundly impressed that, having just lost her son in a tragic accident, she was sending encouragement by writing out these verses of faith and comfort. I was especially struck by one verse she wrote down, Job 1:21—"The LORD gave, and the LORD has taken away; Blessed be the name of the LORD."[1]

## In Pursuit of the Dream

I dealt with the loss by trying to move forward with my baseball career. I had a letter of acceptance to graduate school at Indiana University, and I was planning to go there after the summer was over—but that was just it: What was I going to do with my summer? The only thing I wanted to do was play baseball. I wasn't even thinking of the big leagues. I just wanted a chance to play pro baseball anywhere and at any level. In the back of my mind was a vague notion that if I was behind the plate, with my mind on the game, I could somehow get over losing my dad.

One of the last things I had said to Dad was, "Could you check with Mr. Carpenter and see what my chances are with the Phillies organization?" And he had said, "When you get home, you can talk to him yourself." The day after we buried my father, I pondered that conversation. I remember thinking, *Dad was right. I can talk to him myself.* It's not easy for young people to approach adults, especially for a favor. Even though I had known Mr. Carpenter since I was five years old, even though his son had been my best friend for years, it wasn't easy for me to approach him. But that's what Dad had wanted me to do, so I picked up the phone and dialed up Mr. Carpenter's office.

He came on the line. "Pat! Good to hear your voice. It was a fine service yesterday. Your dad was a wonderful man. I'm really going to miss him."

"Yes, sir. Our family really appreciated you being at the funeral service."

"What can I do for you?"

"Well, sir—I hate to impose on you . . ."

"Just name it, Pat. How can I help you?"

"Well, I would really like to continue playing baseball. I know your scout, Mr. Livengood, has been reporting on me. I was just wondering what your thinking might be—do you think there might be a place for me? Maybe one of the farm clubs? I just want to play."

"Pat, I'll see what I can do. Let me get back to you."

"Thank you, sir. Thank you very much."

I put the phone down and thought, *I've gone all the way to the top, to the owner of the Philadelphia Phillies. Now all I can do is wait.*

I didn't have to wait long. The phone rang later that day, and it was Bob Carpenter. "Pat," he said, "we have an opening with our farm club in Miami. It pays four hundred a month."

*Yes,* I thought. *I'm going to play ball!* I knew all the Phillies farm teams, and I was familiar with the Miami Marlins. It was a Class D club in the Florida State League, a long way from the big leagues—but it was baseball. At that point, that's all I cared about.

"How are your finances, son?" said Mr. Carpenter. "I bet you could use some cash to start out with."

"Yes, sir," I said, "I sure could."

"Well, we'll give you a five-hundred-dollar bonus. That'll get you down to Miami. Come on up to the office tomorrow."

Sometimes when I tell that story, I joke that when Mr. Carpenter advised me to keep the terms of that contract confidential, I replied, "Don't worry—I'm just as ashamed of this contract as you are." But the truth is that I thought it was a lot of money back then, and I was so relieved that I was going to get into professional baseball, I didn't care how much they paid me. In fact, I'd have paid them.

So I drove to Philly—a route I'd taken a thousand times. At the Phillies office all the papers were ready for me to sign. I talked to Gene Martin, the Phillies farm director, and received the five-hundred-dollar bonus right on the spot. I had never seen so much money in my life.

The next afternoon, the Wilmington newspaper carried a story that read, "Pat Williams, former Tower Hill ballplayer, signs with the Phillies." Later that day, the phone rang. It was Al Cartwright, sports editor of the *Wilmington News-Journal*. "Pat," he said, "I'd like you to do a weekly column for the paper about your experiences in the minors. We'll call it 'The Class D Rookie.' Just write down everything that happens, everything you think and feel and go through, then mail it to me. I'll edit it and run the column once a week. Can you handle it?"

"Sure, Mr. Cartwright. I'll do it."

I wrote the column every week and loved it. That column sparked a lifelong interest in writing, collecting and telling stories, and expressing myself publicly.

As I got ready to take off for my new career, my mother was very supportive. She could have said, "Pat, please don't go. Your father hasn't been gone a week yet, and I need you here." But she didn't do that. She knew I needed to pursue my dream, and she wanted me to go after it. Despite her loss, she was strong enough and independent enough to send me off with her blessing. In fact, she was probably as thrilled as I was that I had the opportunity to play pro ball.

## Miami Days

A week to the day after my last Wake Forest game, I was on my way to Miami. That week had completely changed my life. I had left college, lost my dad, and found my career within the space of a few days. My head was spinning.

The only thing I knew about Miami was that it was the home of the ultraswank Fontainebleau Hotel. I pulled in at the Fontainebleau on Miami Beach at a little after midnight. I felt like a big shot baseball player, and I wanted to spend one night in the best place in town—only there were no vacancies. I went to the coffee shop, ordered a piece of apple pie, downed it, and found another place to spend the night.

The next day, I reported to the manager, Andy Seminick—the Phillies catcher in the late '40s, early '50s. When I was a boy, Andy had been my idol, and I had gotten to know him while I was a teenager hanging around Shibe Park. Andy was one of the Whiz Kids, the National League pennant-winning Phillies of 1950. So it was a thrill to have Andy as my first manager in the pros.

Right after I arrived, we had a road trip, and our first stop was in Tampa to play the Cincinnati Reds farm club at Al Lopez Field. Yep, that's the same field where we watched the Reds-Phillies exhibition game in 1958 as high school seniors. So there I was, four years later, making my pro debut—but not as a player. I got my start as an umpire, of all things! The ump who worked the bases didn't show up, so the managers decided to name one player from each team to act as umpires. Andy Seminick pointed at me and said, "Williams! You umpire first base!"

At the end of that road trip, we returned to Miami Stadium for our home debut. Playing my first game at home against the Fort Lauderdale Yankees, I struck out my first two times at bat on six consecutive pitches. Ouch! My third time at bat, I quickly fell two strikes behind, putting me one strike away from fanning three times straight. I began to sweat artillery shells.

The next pitch was an outside pitch, and I took my cut—and connected for a line drive up the alley in right center. The ball bounced off the wall, and I legged out a standup double.

Talk about a sense of relief! I was standing out at second base thinking how proud my dad was at that moment. Even though I had no real faith or spiritual foundation, I felt Dad's presence and believed he had seen it all and was proud of me. I'd have even taken one of his popsicles that night!

I got to third on an infield out. Coaching third was Max Patkin, the Clown Prince of Baseball. This legendary performer traveled to all the major and minor league ballparks, entertaining the crowds with his antics. As I rounded third, Max grabbed me by the neck, dragged me back to the bag, gave me a big kiss right on the mouth, then continued on with his show. The inning ended with me stranded at third.

Later that summer, we returned to Al Lopez Field, where I had my best game ever as a pro player. I started in left field and got four hits in five times at bat. That was the pinnacle of my pro career—it never happened again.

We had quite a team that year in Miami. One of our players was an incredible young hurler, Ferguson Jenkins, who would become the first pitcher in the majors to achieve three thousand strikeouts with fewer than one thousand walks. Fergie went on to have six consecutive twenty-game winning seasons with the Chicago Cubs. He won the Cy Young award in '71, and was the first Canadian inducted into the Baseball Hall of Fame. In Miami, I caught five of his seven victories in the 1962 season. I often say that Fergie was once asked who was the toughest player he ever pitched to, and his answer was, "My catcher—Pat Williams." He didn't *really* say that—but the line always gets a laugh on the banquet circuit.

I vividly remember one Sunday night in July 1962, we were playing the Kansas City A's farm club from Daytona Beach at Miami Stadium. Daytona had just signed a seventeen-year-old high school infielder from Tampa. I was catching and Fergie was pitching, and the runner on second was this young Daytona infielder. There was a base hit to the outfield, the runner rounded third and put his shoulder down to plow into me. I went feet over teakettle, hung on to the ball, and came up with it in my hand. The umpire called him out. The next day, in the *Miami News*, a five-frame sequence, like movie film, detailed that showdown at the plate with that seventeen-year-old infielder, whose name was Tony LaRussa. He went on to become one of the top managers in baseball for the last twenty years with the White Sox, Athletics, and Cardinals.

Alex Johnson was just a kid outfielder for the Miami Marlins in '62, but it was clear even then that he was a natural hitter. He liked to razz me all the time. One day while I was taking batting practice, he stood outside the cage and baited me. "Williams," he called, "I hit 'em when I want to. You hit 'em when you can." He led the Florida State League in hitting that year, and he went on to play for a number of teams in the National and American Leagues. One year, he led the AL in hitting while playing for the Angels.

And then there was Pat Williams. I didn't know then what was in those scouting reports Wes Livengood sent back to Philly when I was at Wake Forest, but I later found out he wrote, "Good receiver, adequate arm, poor speed, weak bat. His future is in the front office." I doubt that anyone who read the report expected me to hit .295 my first season in Miami—but I did. I went 18 for 61 with two doubles and a triple.

I battled extra hard for one of those hits. In Daytona Beach I hit a ground ball to deep short. The shortstop knocked the ball down and recovered to throw to first, but too late to get me. The scorer ruled it an error. My teammates were incredulous and told me I had been robbed of a hit. The next morning, I found the scorer, pleaded my case, and in the official report, he gave me credit for a hit.

That Miami experience in 1962 and '63 laid the groundwork for everything that has happened to me in sports. It gave me the experience of riding the buses on road trips, feeling the insecurities and fears of a pro athlete, the highs and the lows of competition, the successes and the failures. It gave me a valuable perspective for all the years ahead as an administrator in sports. I didn't fully appreciate it then, but I realize now that it gave me a wonderful advantage. Many times I've been the one to sit down with a player and tell him that he's being waived or traded. I've had to dash a lot of dreams—and that's the hardest part of this business. Knowing how an athlete feels and how badly he wants to make it, and having had the same thing happen to me, I'm better equipped to deal with pro athletes.

I always remembered one piece of advice Bob Carpenter gave me before I left for Miami: "Keep your eyes and ears open—on the field and off." I wanted to absorb everything I could about every aspect of the game. I spent a lot of time with the Miami general manager, Bill Durney. Normally, players don't get all that chummy with front-office personnel, but I found Durney to be an interesting guy with an interesting history. He had been

Bill Veeck's traveling secretary when Veeck ran the St. Louis Browns in the early 1950s. I had always been fascinated by the promotional genius of Veeck, and I continually pumped Durney for stories and information.

I also kept my eyes open to the racial situation in the South. This was in the days just before Dr. Martin Luther King came into prominence, when segregation was a fact of life across the South. It was before such terms as black or African-American were used, when a black man was called a Negro. The black ballplayers on our club could not stay at many of the motels with us or eat at the same restaurants. We often brought food out to the black players who had to wait for us on the bus. I found it disgusting that people should be treated that way for no reason and that it was simply considered normal. I couldn't understand it then, and I can't understand it today.

One of our veteran black players, Fred Mason, was from Wilmington, so I offered him a ride home at the end of the season. We finished the season by going to the playoffs, where we lost to Fort Lauderdale. After the last game, Fred and I drove from Fort Lauderdale to Jacksonville, where I thought we'd tank up the car and find a place to spend the night.

I told the attendant to fill it up, then I went into the station to get a soda. While I was at the vending machine, I heard a vicious ugly yell: "Get outta here, you nigger, or I'll kill you!" I looked and saw that Fred had gotten out of the car to go to the rest room—but the attendant had blocked his path, waving a huge monkey wrench while screaming at Fred at the top of his lungs. Fred backed away from the man and got back into the car. The service station attendant continued to swear at Fred. It was the most insane behavior I had ever seen.

My hands shook as I paid for the gas. I got into the car and we drove straight on to Wilmington, taking turns sleeping and driving for the next five hundred miles. For the first few hours, neither of us said anything. Finally, Fred spoke quietly. "Some of my friends would've torn that place apart," he said. "I'm just not that way." If he had, I wouldn't have blamed him a bit.

## Veeck—as in Wreck

Reflecting on the season, I wished Dad could have seen some of my games. How he would have enjoyed watching me play as a pro, however minor the league. I know he gladly would have driven all the way to Miami. I thought about all the times I had given him wrong directions to my high school games and all the times I was embarrassed by his cheering and his fatherly pride—and I wished I had appreciated his loud enthusiasm. I never would have imagined that I could miss his shouting, his carrying on, his passing out ice cream bars to the guys in the dugout—but I did. I really did.

So there was a bittersweet feeling to the close of the summer. I had gotten a real taste of professional baseball, and I had played in a lot of minor league ballparks against a lot of good, future major league players. If only I could have shared it all with my dad.

Bill Durney told me I should look up Bill Veeck sometime. Veeck was living in retirement at his Easton, Maryland, estate, about two hours from Wilmington. I had been a fan of Bill Veeck almost as long as I had been a baseball fan. We have Bill Veeck to thank for so many innovations in baseball. He was responsible for putting names on the back of players' uniforms and for setting off fireworks after a home team triumph. Never a skybox sort of owner, Veeck preferred to sit in the bleachers with the rest of the fans. His dad presided over the Chicago Cubs for years, so Veeck grew up around Wrigley Field. The game of baseball was Bill Veeck's life.

Veeck knew what winning was about. His Cleveland Indians had won the World Series in '48 and his White Sox had taken the American League pennant in '59. But what Veeck is most remembered for by the fans is that he made baseball fun—win or lose. He was a master showman. I was endlessly fascinated and profoundly influenced by his colorful promotions and stunts. His most famous gimmick was sending in vertically challenged (3'7") Eddie Gaedel to pinch-hit for the St. Louis Browns in 1951.

But Veeck was more than just a stunt promoter. He was dead serious about fairness, freedom, and simple human decency. He broke the color barrier in the American League, signing Larry Doby to play for the Cleveland Indians in '47. He received a certain amount of hate mail for that decision, and he personally answered each letter. Typically, he would congratulate the bigoted letter-writers for their wisdom in having selected parents belonging to the majority race. But since not everyone was able to choose parentage and skin color, he continued, he was going to select his players on the basis of personal merit— whether a given player "happened to be black, or blue with pink polka dots."

Bill Veeck actually had planned to integrate baseball before Branch Rickey brought Jackie Robinson up to break the color barrier with the Brooklyn Dodgers in 1947. Five years earlier, Veeck attempted to buy the Philadelphia Phillies from then-owner Gerry Nugent—and he had planned to stack the roster with powerhouse players from the Negro Leagues, including Roy Campanella, Satchel Paige, and Monte Irvin. But before the deal could be finalized, Nugent—who was on the brink of bankruptcy—turned the team over to the control of National League president Ford Frick, who sold it to a lumber merchant named William Cox for a quarter of a million dollars (Veeck had been willing to pay twice that amount). In late 1943, Cox was banned from baseball because of his involvement with gamblers, and the team was sold to my father's friend, Bob Carpenter.

By the summer of 1962, when Bill Durney urged me to give Veeck a call, his autobiography, *Veeck as in Wreck,* had been out a few months and was an instant best-seller. I had already read it (I still make a point of reading it once a year), and I was eager to talk to this man who had left such an imprint on sports promotion. I was planning to leave for graduate school in Indiana soon, but I wanted to meet Bill Veeck before I left, so I called Bill Durney and asked him to open the door for me.

While I had not given up on the idea of getting to the majors, I was slowly coming to realize that the dream was becoming ever more distant. I was beginning to face facts: It would take more than a .295 batting average in the low minors to land a position on a major league team. So the front-office career of sports promotion began to beckon—and who better to teach that end of the business than the great Bill Veeck?

It was a beautiful, sunny day in early September as I drove up the tree-lined drive that wound around to Veeck's beautiful home overlooking Chesapeake Bay. And there he was, right on the front steps: Bill Veeck himself. He was burr-headed, bare-chested, and clad in a pair of tan shorts. He had lost one leg during World War II, and he wasn't wearing his artificial leg at the time. In his hands was a book of Civil War poetry.

I expected Veeck to be a loud, brash Leo Durocher type. I was surprised to find instead this warm, gentle, soft-spoken man. Yes, he sported a rough exterior, but inside that seamed and grizzled head was a mind that moved at the speed of light. He was a great listener, he seemed interested in everything I had to say, and his responses were thoughtful and laced with a rich vocabulary, the result of extensive reading.

After an hour or so, I thought, *I shouldn't take up too much more of his time*—and I began to plan a graceful exit. But then Veeck said, "If Bill Durney finds out you were here and I didn't invite you for lunch, he'll really be mad at me." So I stayed through lunch, and we chatted on into the afternoon. Later, he strapped on his artificial leg and we played a game of badminton—I could hardly believe it!

He gave me four pieces of advice I've never forgotten. "First," he said, "know somebody. It's almost impossible to get inside this game if you don't know somebody." I told him of my relationship with Bob and Ruly Carpenter, and he said, "That's good, that's good. Now, three more things: Learn to type. Learn all you can about advertising and marketing. And get some kind of business background." I left feeling I had been to the mountain and received a revelation.

In the weeks that followed, I took those four points to heart. The following week, as I was traveling to graduate school in Bloomington, Indiana, I memorized the typewriter keyboard, and for the next eight years I did most of my own typing. I also picked up advertising and business training through books and on-the-job training. In the years since that meeting with Bill

Veeck, I saw over and over again how wise his advice was. It was the beginning of a friendship with him that continued until his death in 1986.

## Letting Go of the Dream

I chose Indiana University for my grad work for two reasons: the school of health, physical education, and recreation, and the campus radio station. I had fallen in love with sports broadcasting at Wake Forest and wanted to stay involved with radio. I couldn't have asked for a better situation. I no sooner arrived on campus when I met John Gutowsky (who is now well-known as John Gordon, announcer for the Minnesota Twins). John announced football and basketball on the campus radio station, WFIU. We became fast friends and spent hours working together.

The director of the school's radio and television department, Dick Yoakam, informed John and me that we would be the broadcast team for the IU network. "Now, we're counting on you two young fellas," he told us, "and, by the way, you've got very big shoes to fill. The announcer who was working the games the last couple of years is a graduate student who has been very well-received throughout the state of Indiana. And I hope you can live up to his work. His name is Dick Enberg." The name meant nothing to me then, but looking back at it now—wow! We succeeded Dick Enberg, who has become one of America's most successful sportscasters.

I stayed at Indiana for two semesters to get as many of my master's requirements out of the way as possible. Meanwhile, the Phillies organization sent me a new contract to play in Miami for fifty dollars a month more. By the spring of 1963, I had pretty well leveled with myself about my baseball future. I skipped spring training to complete courses at Indiana—something I never would have done if I was still banking on making the majors. By the time I joined the team in Miami, the regular season was under way and I was way behind the other players.

They threw me into the lineup right away and I quickly developed a sore arm. My first night back, I played in a doubleheader against Daytona Beach. In the first game, I got a single to drive in the winning run. In the second game, my squeeze bunt in the last inning brought in another winning run. But it was all downhill from there.

It was a disappointing summer. I didn't feel good, I didn't play well, and I just wasn't doing my job. There's no shortcut to getting in shape, physically or mentally. I wasn't physically ready to play, and I wasn't mentally sharp. When Clay Dennis, the Phillies' minor league director, visited Miami in July, I went to him and said, "I know I'm not contributing on the field, but I still want to be useful to the organization. If you'd have me, I'd be interested in spending the last month of the season helping out in the front office. I'll be content to help Bill Durney any way I can."

Dennis okayed the arrangement, so for the last few weeks of the '63 season, I did everything from typing news releases and selling tickets to sorting paper clips and rubber bands. I still caught batting practice and warmed up pitchers, but I didn't go on road trips or suit up for games. I was close enough to the team to feel a part of things, so the fact that I was finally giving up a lifelong ambition didn't seem as painful as if I had just walked away from the team.

Bill Durney took me under his wing in an encouraging, mentoring, fatherly way. He was a big man in every dimension—tall, rotund, with a large heart, a large love of the game, and a large knowledge of the business of baseball. I enjoyed working with him and learned something from him every day.

One of the duties in the front office was assisting in the team's publicity effort. We promoted the team any way we could, and we used radio extensively. A young radio talk-show host who broadcast his local late-night show from a houseboat off Miami Beach had a big following, and it was always great exposure to get on his show. I would make the arrangements, then accompany our manager (Andy Seminick in '63, succeeded by Bobby Morgan in '64) out to the houseboat. It was called *Surfside 6* and was the very boat used in the TV series by that name. We'd get aboard, our guy would do his hour-long interview, and I would sit and watch. That talk-show host has come a long way since the early 1960s. His name is Larry King, and over the years, he's been very friendly to me. He's endorsed several of my books, and we've been guests on each other's shows.

When I left Miami at the end of the season, I headed for Indiana and one more semester of graduate work to complete requirements for a master's degree in physical education.

It was a pivotal time for me. I was confronted with the fact that something was missing from my life: a clear sense of direction. From the time I was seven years old, I had known exactly what I wanted, where I was going, and how I was going to get there. But that summer, I finally faced facts and let go of that dream. Only I didn't know where my next steps would take me. Should I teach? Coach? Broadcast? Administer? I didn't know. It was a strange feeling. A little scary—but exciting, too. Even while I was mourning the loss of my original dream, I had the feeling there was another adventure on my horizon.

## "Wouldn't Wanna Buy One, Would Ya?"

In November 1963, I got a call from Clay Dennis, who wanted to set up a meeting. We got together at Chicago's O'Hare Inn, where he told me that Bill Durney wanted me back in Miami. "Bill really liked the job you did and the attitude you displayed at the end of the season," he told me. "He wants you to spend the '64 season as assistant general manager of the Miami club. The pay will be the same as last year, and at the end of the season we'll decide where to go from there. If we like it and you like it—who knows?"

I was speechless. It was a chance to stay connected to the world of baseball—and they were even going to pay me! Maybe this was the new dream of the future I was looking for.

When the Indiana University basketball broadcasting schedule ended in early March, I packed my new master's degree in a suitcase, jumped in the car, and sped off for Miami. Bill Durney put me to work right away. He was a fun-loving, hard-working, hard-driving man who gobbled up life and never slowed down. He seldom slept, but made up for it by eating constantly. The first assignment he gave me was to sell advertising in the Marlins' season program. The team would arrive soon for spring training, so we had to get rolling.

The thought of selling advertising terrified me. I had never sold anything in my life. It should have been easy, but my approach was all wrong. I went around saying, "We've got these programs, see, and you can buy an ad in it. You wouldn't wanna buy one, would ya?" For two and a half days, I was a complete flop. The ad space was cheap, and we had good attendance at the games, which meant good ad exposure—but I hadn't sold even an eighth of a page. I was sick about it.

At around noon of the third day, I returned to Durney's office feeling dejected. "I'm a failure, Bill," I said. "I just can't do this. I haven't sold one ad." I was seriously considering going back to the safety of old familiar haunts in Wilmington.

"I think I know what your problem is, Pat," Bill said gently. "You think you're going out there asking merchants for money. That's not what you're doing at all. You're out there doing those merchants a favor. For just a few dollars, he can put his business in front of the sports-loving public at every ball game. You see that program?"

I looked down at the Marlin program I had rolled up in my hand.

"That program," he continued, "is a great advertising medium. When merchants advertise in that program, it doesn't cost—it pays."

"I never thought of it that way," I said.

"Here's another piece of advice: Always give your client a choice—'Do you want your ad next to the Marlins lineup or next to the visitors lineup?' Don't ask him if he wants to buy an ad. Ask him where he wants his ad to appear. Now, do you think you can go out and sell ads in that program?"

I grinned. "Sure, I can!"

"Good. Selling is the key to success in any business, Pat—especially the baseball business. Whether it's your outfield walls, or tickets to the game, or ads in the program, selling is the name of the game. If you can sell, you'll always have a job in sports."

That was one of many times I took note of what Bill Durney told me—sometimes I took mental notes, but I also filled a notebook with ideas, principles, and sage advice he gave me. I left my meeting with Durney believing I could sell iceboxes to Eskimos. First stop: Mugge's Restaurant. Could I sell ad space to Mr. Mugge? Not a problem—I was doing him a favor! I was giving him a bargain. For a pittance, I was going to bring a lot of new traffic into his establishment. When I believed it, the merchants believed it. Mr. Mugge bought a seventy-five-dollar ad, and I went on to sell the rest of the space in just a few days. I celebrated by ordering a piece of his superb key lime pie.

Once the program was sold out, I went back to Bill and said, "What's my next assignment?" I was ready for anything.

Durney gave me lots of freedom. We bounced promotional ideas off each other every day. He was never at a loss for a gimmick, and he never shied away from new or crazy ideas. It could be a contest, a musical event, a celebrity appearance, or a giveaway, but whatever it was, it was creative and fun. Watching this human whirlwind at work had a profound effect on my career.

I was constantly trying to express myself through new ideas for marketing baseball. I pushed to have music played on the public address system between innings—upbeat recorded music, Top Forty stuff. Durney didn't like the idea, but he finally let me do it. I knew I had really arrived when John Quinn, the general manager of the Phillies, came to the park and sat in the press box. Quinn was the arch conservative of baseball—hardly the sort you would call innovative or receptive to new ideas. But when my music came on (most likely a pop song by the Four Tops or the Four Seasons or the Fab Four), there was John Quinn, tapping his fingers to the beat of the music. In fact, he was even *smiling*.

I met Bill Durney in '62, and he died of a heart attack in '68, so I didn't know him for many years. But in that short span, he made a deep impression on me, personally and professionally. Many times after he was gone, I wondered, *What would Bill*

*Durney do in a situation like this?* One of my favorite pictures is one Bill signed in 1963. He wrote, "To Pat Williams—a guy with a great present but a much greater future."

## Spartanburg and Mr. R. E.

In the summer of 1964, the Philadelphia Phillies were in the thick of the National League pennant race. They had been leading the league all year, and the City of Brotherly Love was going wild over the possibility of a pennant—and maybe even the World Series! Because the minor league season ends earlier than the majors', the Phillies' front office asked me to help with promotion and ticket sales in the event Philadelphia played in the series. By that time I was so psyched up about a career in baseball administration, I would have done anything to help them out—anything, that is, except spending time in an Army brig.

The problem was that I had joined the Army Reserves, which up to that time had no more impact on my life than requiring me to attend a few meetings. But the same week the Phillies contacted me, I got a piece of mail that said, "You are hereby ordered to report for active duty." I had a five-month Army obligation to serve, beginning in September, and couldn't get away short of going AWOL. As it turned out, the Phillies blew the '64 pennant drive, rendering the whole question moot.

Brief though it was, I hated my Army stint. After being on my own for several years and getting a taste of the world, I found it humiliating to spend twenty weeks being treated like a number. For the first few weeks of basic training at Fort Jackson, near Columbia, South Carolina, I was treated like a nonperson. No phone calls, no leave, no mail, no nothing. But when I got to feeling really low, I considered the alternative: Vietnam. Compared to "the 'Nam," Fort Jackson was a day at Coney Island.

When I got back to Winston-Salem, WSJS radio offered me a job as sports director. It was tempting, but in the end, I opted for a career in baseball administration, while keeping open to doing radio on the side. As it turned out, I was able to do exactly that. During my years to come as a front-office man in Spartanburg, I also broadcast Wake Forest football and basketball, Clemson and Georgia Tech football, and Duke basketball. Only after I left Spartanburg did I go full-time as a sports executive.

While home for Christmas, I made a side trip to Philly for an important chat with Clay Dennis, the Phillies' farm director. "Pat," he said, "we have two general manager jobs open in our farm system. One is in Bakersfield, California. The other is with the Spartanburg Phillies down in South Carolina. We've been watching you and preparing you in Miami. We also have another young man we've been preparing, an ex-pitcher named Dick Smith."

"Oh, yes," I said. "I know Dick. He's the assistant GM in Little Rock."

"That's right. We want to put you in charge of one team and Dick in charge of the other. Both jobs are open and you can take your pick. The pay is five hundred a month. Are you interested?"

Well, I sure was. I talked to Dick Smith and asked him which position he wanted, and he said, "It doesn't matter to me."

"Well," I said, "I spent four years at Wake Forest, and my family is from the South—so if it's okay with you, I'll take Spartanburg."

"Fine," Dick replied, "I've got Bakersfield."

Talk about a break! I wasn't twenty-five years old, and I was going to operate my own ballclub. Here was my first real chance to run the show. I flew to Miami for a couple of days of heavy briefing with Bill Durney, then returned home for a few days with my family in Wilmington. Then I loaded everything I owned into my car and drove to Spartanburg. For all my familiarity with South Carolina, I had never been to Spartanburg, and I didn't know a soul. The first person I was to look up in town was Mr. R. E. Littlejohn, one of the two owners of the Spartanburg Phillies. It was cold and rainy when I arrived that first Sunday in February 1965. Though the day was miserable, I could feel the excitement right down to my toes.

R. E. Littlejohn was a successful petroleum carrier executive, and he lived in a fabulously beautiful home. Mrs. Littlejohn answered my knock. She was a warm and friendly woman in her fifties. "We were expecting you," she said in a euphonious southern manner. "Mister R. E. was called out of town unexpectedly to attend a funeral, but please come in."

I was a little surprised that Mrs. Littlejohn called her husband "Mister R. E.," but I was soon to learn that everyone in Spartanburg called him that. That's what I called him at first—but I later nicknamed him "Coach."

And what to call Mrs. Littlejohn? She insisted I call her Sam. Her real name was Marion, and she had been nicknamed Sam when her two daughters, Caroline and Dixie, were young. In the years to come, Coach and Sam would become my closest friends in Spartanburg—and they would have a profound influence on my life.

Sam was a gracious hostess, offering refreshments and engaging me in conversation. "You'll never meet another man like Mister R. E.," she said. "You'll never again work for anyone like him, no matter how long you're around. He's the greatest man in the world."

I had never heard anything like that in my life. I didn't take it seriously then, but I would soon find that Mrs. Littlejohn's description of her husband was not empty hyperbole. She was exactly right.

Two days later, after I had found a place of my own and was settled in, I met Mister R. E. at his office. I was instantly and profoundly impressed by this gray-haired Southern gentleman. He was courteous and soft-spoken, with a gift for putting people at ease. No one was ever intimidated in his presence. He took a genuine and personal interest in everyone. I never observed him to be annoyed, impatient, or sarcastic with anyone. He truly was unlike anyone I had ever met—just as Sam had described him. I couldn't put my finger on just what struck me so about the man, but I was intrigued.

After our first meeting, I got down to business. The season would open in just two months, and we had a lot of work to do.

## The Fixer-Upper

Duncan Park was set low in a hilly, tree-filled area—a beautiful location. But the stadium was rundown, dirty, and unpainted. The office was tiny and cold, and the rest rooms were filthy beyond belief. When I so blithely chose the job in Spartanburg, it never occurred to me that I would be getting such a fixer-upper of a ballyard.

At first, I wondered how the owners, Mister R. E. and Leo Hughes, could have allowed the place to become so dilapidated. Then I realized that they were businessmen with their own enterprises to run. They had no time to run the Spartanburg Phillies—that's what I was hired to do. I looked around and shook my head slowly. All my promotional ideas would have to wait until the ballpark was fit to attend. No wonder crowds had been so sparse in recent years.

I decided to take on the renovation of that ballpark as a challenge. I was going to sell baseball to that town and I was going to get the people to come out, see a great show, and have a good time. From that moment, I never looked back.

The fear of failure drove me through eighteen-hour days, seven days a week. Everything took a back seat to the ballpark. For me, there was no dating, no socializing, no church. We labored over that field from dawn to dusk, cutting the grass, building a new press box, overhauling the locker rooms, painting the outfield walls, and refurbishing the rest rooms.

Ah, let me tell you about the rest rooms! We slapped some paint around in the men's room—that was good enough for us guys. But the ladies room—now, *that* was the masterpiece. We hired carpenters and really went to town on it. We air-conditioned it, painted it, wallpapered it, put in curtains and red carpeting and full-length mirrors, piped in music, hired an attendant, and arranged for fresh flowers for every game. The ladies room at Duncan Park was a work of art. Whenever we showed anyone our ballpark—even the visiting commissioner of major league baseball—the first stop on the tour was the ladies room.

I had plenty of other chores that could not be ignored—meeting with the city fathers to plead for moral and financial support from City Hall, getting programs and tickets printed, getting uniforms altered and mended, and selling advertising space. We also needed to come up with some really eye-popping, pulse-pounding promotional ideas to draw the crowds.

I called my old sportscasting buddy from Indiana—John Gutowsky—and invited him to become the voice of the Spartanburg Phillies (by this time, he had changed his name to John Gordon). He agreed and became my roommate for the next four years.

I began to realize that I couldn't get the job done without some help, so I put out the word that the club needed a secretary. I didn't even get a nibble until two days before the season started. At an open house for the ballplayers, a woman named Claire Johns took me by the arm and said, "I heard through the grapevine that you need a secretary. Is the job still open?"

I said, "That depends. How fast do you type?"

"I don't know. I've never used a typewriter before."

"Ever do any filing?"

"Not really."

"What kind of office experience do you have? Ever worked as a receptionist?"

"'Fraid not. I've never worked in an office before."

"Can you show up for work at eight in the morning?"

"Sure, I can!"

"Congratulations. You've got the job."

As it turned out, I never could have run the club without her. She took care of the details so I was free to promote. I nicknamed her "Mama Johns," and she worked with me for four years. She was terrific!

## Executive of the Year

As the ballpark took shape and opening day neared, Mister R. E. kept in constant contact with me. He often said he believed in me and thought I was the greatest. Those pep talks really meant a lot to me and kept my motivation high. He seemed to notice everything I did right and somehow knew that I would learn from my mistakes without having them pointed out to me. He wanted me to learn and succeed. I grew to love him like a father.

I had found my new dream: operating a baseball team. But not just any little bush-league team in the sticks! I had decided I was going to play my cards very carefully, do some self-promotion, publicity gathering, and noise-making—and soon I'd be operating in the big leagues. It might take a few years—but then again, maybe I could make the leap to the big leagues in just a year or so!

Day and night, I thought of nothing else. I was headed for the big leagues! People would know Pat Williams, yessir! Sure, I'd push the ballclub. Sure, I'd make it fun and exciting in the tradition of Bill Veeck. But all that stuff was just icing on the cake—my real goal was to grab the glory, status, and ego-inflation that come with success in the sports world.

As opening day approached, my rapidly swelling head began to fill with ideas and gimmicks. Our first opponent was the Greenville Mets. We borrowed a goat and named him Greenburg—a combination of Greenville and Spartanburg. We made a deal with the general manager of the Mets: Whoever lost the opener had to keep the goat as a mascot for the rest of the season.

I kept another idea top secret until game day. We hired a skydiver to drop in on the field just before the start of the game. It was a night game, and our plan was to surprise the audience by turning out the lights—which would also keep the skydiver from hitting a live wire on the way down. Then we'd turn the lights back on as he landed on the pitcher's mound.

The idea might have looked a bit brighter if I had at least warned the other team that the lights were going off. Dick Selma, who later pitched for the Mets, Cubs, and Phillies in the majors, was warming up on the sidelines when the lights went off. He released a fastball—and the stadium suddenly went as black as the inside of a sack. A collective gasp went up from the stands. Meanwhile, a sizzling fastball was hurtling unseen through the blackness—straight for the warm-up catcher. He hit the ground, covering his face with his mitt, as the ball whizzed past his ear. He could have easily gotten beaned, maybe even killed—and how would *that* have looked on my resume?

At the arranged moment, I flicked the lights back on so Dick Montgomery, the skydiver, could see the field. But when the lights came on, I looked—and couldn't find our skydiver. He was supposed to land on the pitcher's mound—or at least somewhere inside the diamond. Where was he? Then I saw him. He was floating down into the trees beyond the outfield. My blood froze. I had just missed killing the Mets' catcher, but I still had a chance to kill a skydiver.

I turned to the PA man and had him announce, "Mr. Montgomery, your tickets are waiting at the will-call window if you want to get into the ballpark tonight." When Dick Montgomery came walking into the park, unhurt, I could have hugged him. I managed to get through opening night without killing anybody—and that was quite an accomplishment.

We received a lot of great publicity that season, and the fans clearly enjoyed themselves. Even though we wound up having to buy three Greenburgs that season (one goat died and another ran off), most of the later promotions were successful. Our team played poorly, but we drew 114,000 fans in sixty home dates.

On the Fourth of July, we had planned to treat the fans to a fireworks display after the night game. I hadn't figured on the game going into extra innings. By the time we fired off the show, it was well after midnight. The police department and the mayor's office received so many calls from irate Spartanburgers that a city ordinance was passed the next day: No fireworks after 10 P.M.

Later that month we brought in Satchel Paige to pitch a few exhibition innings. Ol' Satch, the ageless wonder, whizzed through our batting order, striking out several players and allowing just one hit and no runs. The crowd loved it, and so did Satchel. He signed a photo for me, "Best wishes to Pat Williams from Satchel Paige, who would love to pitch in Spartanburg." He enjoyed himself so much he didn't want to leave.

I'll never forget the day we scheduled a big-league exhibition game at Duncan Park—the Philadelphia Phillies and the Pittsburgh Pirates. I hadn't realized how many towels big leaguers use, but after batting practice, word came from both batboys that the teams needed more towels. Well, where was I going to get more towels on a Saturday night with the stores closed? Mama Johns sent the batboys to her house to round up some towels—and every one of her good, colored hand and bath towels wound up in those grimy, grubby locker rooms!

As the stadium filled up, it appeared we might have to rope off the outfield and let some of the fans sit inside the fence. I was so harried with all the other details that when Claire asked how much rope we needed, I replied rather curtly, "I don't care what you do, Claire. Get a thousand yards of rope, if that's what it takes."

An hour later, as the game was about to start, Claire came to me. "Pat," she said, "the man is at the gate with the thousand yards of rope. Do you want to pay him for it?" She had taken me literally. As it turned out, we didn't need any rope at all—and if we had needed it, a hundred yards would have done the job. I traded the poor guy some tickets to cool him off—and I never let Claire forget the day she bought enough rope to hang both teams.

## The Whiz Kid

In 1965, a new manager joined the Cardinals farm club in Rock Hill, South Carolina. Since we were both in the Western Carolinas League, we became acquainted. I had no way of knowing then that George "Sparky" Anderson would one day become the third winningest manager in major league baseball history, behind Connie Mack and John McGraw, and a future Hall of Famer.

The parent organization in Philadelphia was pleased with our season, and I was named Executive of the Year in the Western Carolinas League—and, of course, I knew I deserved it. By this time, I had made a name in town. Everyone was pleased with the spiffed-up ballpark. People in town and in the organization felt sorry for me because the team didn't play as well as the front office promoted. Word on the street was that this Williams fella was a child prodigy, a whiz kid, a real sophisticate. And I was beginning to believe it.

I was twenty-five years old and honestly thought my next step was to be president of the Yankees or some similar team. No offers were coming in, but I knew that, once the word got around, the big leagues would be calling any day. Spartanburg had been fun, but hey—when a ballplayer has a good year, he moves up, right? I figured the same goes for execs.

The night the season ended, I sat and talked with Mister R. E. in his car. "It's been a great season, Coach," I said, "and I really want to thank you for all the help and encouragement you've given me."

Mister R. E. could read the subtext: I was thinking of moving up. He knew I wasn't ready, wasn't mature enough—but how was he going to break the news to me? "Patience is the key word, Pat," he began. "You've had a very good year, a successful year, and I'm proud of you. The club has come a long way and this town is finally getting interested in baseball again. I'd like to see us get a better team in here, so our win-loss record will be as good as our promotions."

"Well, sure," I said. "I've paved the way for the next guy who comes in here as GM, so it shouldn't be that hard for him to put together a winning organization."

"Patience, Pat, patience," Mister R. E. continued, realizing that he was going to have to be blunt to penetrate my cockiness. "The fact is, you're not ready to move on yet. You have one year under your belt. It's been a good year—but it could have been a lot better. Anyone can be a one-shot, one-year salesman. The measure of real success is how well you can build. You need to stay and prove yourself. Show the league and the Phillies organization what you're *really* capable of."

We talked for a couple of hours, and I inwardly rebelled against every word of advice Littlejohn gave me. He really didn't understand that I was ready to take on the Yankees! He didn't believe that the big leagues would be ringing my phone any day now! That really hurt.

But a couple of days passed. The phone didn't ring. Mister R. E.'s words began to sink in. I realized he was right. I wasn't going anywhere—not yet, anyway.

That fall and winter, I commuted to Winston-Salem and worked as a broadcaster for the Wake Forest football and basketball games with Woody Durham, who has become a legendary announcer in North Carolina. With each lonely mile I drove across the Carolinas, I vowed to make the '66 Spartanburg Phillies the most successful franchise in the history of minor league baseball. I'd show 'em. I'd show Littlejohn and everybody else that I was good enough to be in the big leagues. I had a mission, and I would not be stopped. I wanted nothing short of having *The Sporting News* choose me as Minor League Executive of the Year. Getting the Western Carolinas League award was nice, but it was too local. I wanted national recognition.

I called Bill Veeck to tell him about the season. "It was a bit disappointing," I told him. "The club didn't win many games."

"How many fans did you draw?" he asked.

"A hundred fourteen thousand."

"How many more followed the team on radio?"

"I dunno. Thousands more, I'd say."

"Let me ask you this: How else could you entertain so many people? You gave a lot of people a lot of happiness and fun. You brightened a lot of summer nights for the folks in Spartanburg. You're in the entertainment business, and don't ever apologize for it. Compete hard for that entertainment dollar."

We talked for quite a while that night, and Bill left me with a piece of advice I've never forgotten: "Be accessible. Don't screen your calls. Don't screen your mail. Let the people see you and talk to you, let them grab you by the lapels and tell you what they think. Stand at the exits after the game and thank them for coming. Show them you're not just out for their money, but that you care for them and want them to have a good time. Do all that—and you'll make fans out of spectators. Don't sell the games on the won and lost column—that's too risky. Instead, guarantee your fans a good time every time they come to the park. Promise them a pleasant experience and lots of fun." I never forgot those words.

The Wake Forest football season ended in November, which gave me an extra couple of months to prepare for the season ahead. With a head start, we could make 1966 better than '65. I threw myself into the running of the club, and narrowed my vision until all I could see was success for Pat Williams.

We got a great bunch of new ballplayers from the Phillies organization, including two rookie infielders, Denny Doyle and Larry Bowa, who went on to long major league careers. I couldn't take credit for the new talent on our team—though I would have if I could have. I had big plans for the season—wild, outrageous, crazy promotions for every game. We had a Miss Spartanburg Phillies pageant, a watermelon-eating contest, some find-the-lucky-number-under-your-seat giveaways, a drawing for a vacation, Texas barbecues and Hawaiian luaus, cow-milking contests, limbo dancers, egg-tossing contests, musical chairs, tug-of-war, donkey baseball games, and even a barnyard scramble, in which our team chased farm animals all over the field.

We opened the 1966 season at home against our arch-rivals, the Greenville Mets. They had two great pitchers who went on to stellar major league careers, Nolan Ryan and Jerry Koosman. In that game, the starting pitcher was Ryan, the right-hander out of Alvin, Texas. Our lead-off hitter was nineteen-year-old shortstop Larry Bowa, the future Phillies star. Bowa struck out four consecutive times that night, and after the game he called his father in Sacramento. "Dad," he lamented, "if all the pitchers in pro ball are like this guy I faced tonight, I'll be back home real soon." Well, fortunately for Bowa, there's only one Nolan Ryan.

We had a great team that year, and we even beat the Greenville Mets for the pennant. We had a twenty-five game winning streak—and the town just about came unglued!

We had "Pack 'Em in Tight for the Commissioner Night" to honor William Eckert, commissioner of baseball. When Bill Veeck visited our park, we had "Impress Bill Veeck Night."

Veeck later wrote an article about his visit that was published in papers around the country. One paragraph really thrilled me: "Pat is a fellow who dares. He'll try anything once. And if it doesn't work? Well, then he'll try something else."

On one occasion, we had a little guy named Henri LaMothe perform for the crowd—he climbed a forty-foot ladder and dove into sixteen inches of water. Boy, did he make a splash with the fans! We had to delay the start of the game fifteen minutes until we could dry out the infield near first base.

One of our best promotions that year involved Ron Allen, younger brother of Dick Allen, who was playing with the Phillies. Ron was our first baseman and was named the outstanding player for the month of June in the Western Carolinas League. We had a Ron Allen Night for him and we tried to fly his mother in from Wampum, Pennsylvania—but an airline strike put the kibosh on that idea. The morning of the game we got a call from Mrs. Allen. "Where are you?" I asked.

"The Spartanburg bus station." She had ridden a bus all night to get to Spartanburg in time for Ron Allen Night. We arranged for a hotel room for her and told her to stay there all day and not tell anyone she was in town. At game time we sent a police car to pick her up. While we were making presentations to Ron, the squad car pulled onto the field and out jumped his mother. People in the stands actually wept as mother and son embraced.

"Wouldn't you know it?" Ron said. "You're only in this town one day and the police have already got you!"

## Bush-League Big Shot

I reveled in my success as a manager and promoter. All I cared about was me. I drove an Oldsmobile Toronado and wore sharp clothes. I was a legend in my own mind. I covered up my self-centeredness by playing the part of a generous, gregarious sports exec. I was good at making people believe I cared about them—and on one level, I did. But deep down, all I really cared about was my own success. I had worked hard, sacrificed, and paid the price to reach this level of notoriety. And it paid off. The Spartanburg Jaycees named me their Outstanding Young Man of the Year.

However selfish my motives, the Spartanburg Phillies finished with one of the best seasons ever enjoyed by a minor league club. We had packed the fans in every night, and we had won the championship. I had achieved my goals—and once again, I was named Executive of the Year by the league.

The people in the front office in Philly knew what I had accomplished during my two seasons in Spartanburg. In September 1966, I got a call from Bob Carpenter. He said the Phillies were planning to start a new team in a Double-A league in Reading, Pennsylvania. He wanted me to come to Philadelphia to discuss taking over the operation of the club.

It was a step to a higher level of the minors—but Mr. Littlejohn didn't think I needed to move to the majors by a step in this town, another step in another town. "You can develop recognition right where you are," he said. "And you can learn just as much here to prepare you for the big leagues as you can learn anywhere else." I called Bill Veeck and asked him what he thought. Veeck agreed with Littlejohn.

That's all I wanted to hear. I didn't want to go to Reading. Who knew how I would be received or what I'd have to go through in starting a new team from scratch? Spartanburg was a sure thing. Reading meant starting all over again. I could fall flat on my face! I should have felt flattered by the offer, but my swelled head got in the way.

The organization flew me up for a meeting at the Philadelphia office. I decided I was a pretty important guy, being flown all the way to Philly just so I could turn down their offer. I strode into the executive offices, and everybody was there: Dad's old friend, owner Bob Carpenter; general manager John Quinn; farm director Paul Owens; and my old pal, Ruly Carpenter. Having graduated from Yale, Ruly was well on his way up the executive ladder.

Bob Carpenter did the talking. He told me the organization was pleased with my progress, and the team wanted to offer me the Reading position as a vote of confidence. I cringe when

I remember my bush-league response. I told this elite group of executives that I didn't need their Reading Double-A team. "I'm not about to jeopardize my career by getting myself mixed up in that town," I said. "Who knows how the city will respond? How do I know it's really a baseball town? Why risk everything I've built in Spartanburg for a set of unknowns in Reading?"

What an idiot I was! I easily could have given them a warm, gracious thanks-but-no-thanks. I could have told them I had made a commitment in Spartanburg for the '67 season and wanted to stand by it. I could have taken time to consider the offer. I could have shown some gratitude for their faith in me. But, no. I had to play the big shot.

Even while my big fat mouth was still in gear, I knew that I had riled Bob Carpenter. I could see from the way the glances darted around the room that *everybody* knew I had blown it. In my youthful arrogance, I still wasn't fully aware of just how ridiculous I had been. A few months later, I would get a complete earful of it—but at that moment, I was just standing there with smoke curling from the bullet hole in my wing-tip shoe, a hot-barreled pistol in my hand, and a smug grin on my face confirming I had no clue that I'd just shot myself in the foot—big-time.

I went back to Spartanburg and waited for *The Sporting News* to announce in November that Pat Williams had won the award as the Outstanding Sports Executive of the Year. When November came, Mr. Littlejohn called me over to his house and sat me down on the couch. "Pat," he said, "I just got word that the award went to someone else." I couldn't believe it. I had earned that award! How could they give it to someone else?

"We just have to learn to accept these things and not let them affect us," Mister R. E. continued. "You just have to work a little harder, that's all." He was being kind, but I was bitter. Here I had worked my head off to draw 173,000 fans in a town of 46,000—and what did I get? But I never considered the possibility that *The Sporting News* might consult with the parent club in Philadelphia when making its selection. Looking back, I'd be willing to bet it was my obnoxious behavior in the meeting in Philly that cost me the award.

Our club did get a consolation prize that year—the Larry MacPhail Promotional Trophy, presented by the National Association of Minor League Clubs. I decided to regroup and redouble my efforts to earn the award from *The Sporting News* the following year.

In December, I was back in Wilmington visiting Mom, when Bob Carpenter called and asked me to visit him at his home. It was three months after my shameful performance in his office. Though he didn't tell me what he wanted to talk about, I felt the tension between us as we talked on the phone. My stomach was knotted as I drove to his house. I had known the man since I was seven years old, I had been best friends with his son, I had stayed in his house and eaten at his table many times, and had been virtually a junior member of his family. Bob Carpenter had given me my start in baseball and all my subsequent breaks.

But now something was wrong—and I knew what it was. My arrogant display had driven a wedge between us. As we sat down, he got right down to business. "Pat," he said, "I'm going to give it to you straight. You're not the same young man I sent to Spartanburg two years ago. What in the world have they been feeding you down there? What happened to you in the past two years that changed you?"

I tried to think of a response. Nothing came. What could I say? The man was right. I'm sure that conversation was as frustrating for Mr. Carpenter as it was frightening for me.

In Spartanburg after Christmas, I told Mister R. E. what had happened. He took much of the blame for counseling me not to take the job in Reading—but it wasn't Mister R. E.'s fault, not one bit. I could have turned down that job gracefully instead of tossing it back in his face. I sat down and wrote a letter of apology to Mr. Carpenter, and I heard later that he appreciated receiving it.

But being forgiven doesn't mean there are no consequences. I had torpedoed my chances for upward mobility in the Phillies organization. If I spent the rest of my career in Spartanburg, it was only what I had earned.

The following season was another big summer in Spartanburg. I focused on big-name personal appearances, spending about ten thousand dollars for promotions. A Who's Who of sports celebrities paraded through beautiful Duncan Park: Bart Starr, Paul Hornung, Johnny Unitas, Bob Feller, Furman Bisher, Oscar Robertson, Robin Roberts, Larry MacPhail, Paul Hahn, Frank Lane, Satchel Paige, and more. Looking back, I realize that I was making a major mistake—I wasn't trying to draw fans to a baseball game, I was trying to buy spectators. Fact is, if you have to pay a celebrity that much money to get him to your stadium, it's unlikely he'll draw enough extra fans to make it worth the money. Mister R. E. knew that—but he allowed me to learn at his expense.

By the end of the season, I received what I had been angling for ever since I arrived in Spartanburg: I was named The Outstanding Class A Minor League Baseball Executive of 1967 by *The Sporting News*. We drew over 145,000 people and won both halves of the season. We had received all sorts of national publicity, including two interviews with broadcasting legends Bill Stern and Walter Winchell. Sandy Grady, my old friend from the *Philadelphia Daily News*, came to town to write a feature on us. The Spartanburg Phillies and I looked like a resounding success story. But if you looked closely at the bottom line, you'd see that the Phillies organization had very little profit to show at the end of the year. Where had all the money gone? I had spent it buying myself that award.

# 4

# God and the Gingerbread Man

My target in life had always been distinction—and I felt I had hit the bull's-eye. I had gained as much success in my field as a person my age could ask for. I knew all along what would come with success: a deep sense of joy and satisfaction. I'd be on top of the hill. I'd be happy, content, fulfilled, and at peace with myself.

So it was baffling that I still wasn't happy. I didn't feel satisfied. I felt restless, unfulfilled, and empty.

How could that be?

For most of my life, I had assumed that the key to happiness was to have goals to strive for—and to achieve them. Knock down one goal, notch up the excitement, and keep moving toward bigger achievements. If that doesn't make you happy, what will?

But with each new triumph, I discovered to my disappointment that the satisfaction faded long before the newspaper clippings turned yellow. Instead of being on an endless high, I found myself on a roller-coaster existence of up days and down days.

Though continually in pursuit of happiness and satisfaction, I never seemed to catch up to it.

Remember the children's story *The Gingerbread Man*? The little Gingerbread Man was baked by a farmer's wife, with a frosting face and raisin eyes. He came to life, escaped from the kitchen, and dashed across the countryside, having a series of adventures and close calls—always getting away just in time to avoid being a snack for some dog, cow, or other animal. As the story ended, he wound up being outsmarted—and gobbled up— by a wily fox. Remember the Gingerbread Man's theme song? It goes like this:

> Run, run, run
> As fast as you can!
> You can't catch me—
> I'm the Gingerbread Man!

That's how I felt: I was always on the run, always uncatchable—but I constantly had a hunch that a hungry fox was waiting for me just around the corner. I was living a superficial and selfish life—but I didn't know where to find depth and meaning.

By 1967, I was named president of the Spartanburg Phillies, and the city of Spartanburg had selected me to head the March of Dimes drive. I'd spent three years as a broadcaster for Wake Forest, Clemson, Duke, Davidson, and Georgia Tech football and basketball games, and in my year with Georgia Tech, my partner was Al Ciraldo, a Tech legend. I enjoyed the popularity, but I hardly considered myself a public-spirited philanthropist. If anyone was an honest-to-goodness do-gooder in that town, it was Mr. Littlejohn. I was forming a higher opinion of him every day.

The only time I even thought about God or the Christian faith was when I was talking with Mister R. E. He had such an impressive, unforgettable personality, yet he was a completely humble man. I never saw him behave in an out-of-control or vengeful way and only saw him angry once—and then it was righteous anger.

After the 1965 season, John Gordon was fired by the radio station that broadcast our games, and in a meeting after the firing, Mister R. E. launched at station owner Bob Brown for what he saw as unfair treatment of a good announcer. He was angry, and everyone knew it. I learned right then that Mister R. E. wouldn't display anger to defend himself, but he could be as fierce as a grizzly bear when others needed defending or there was injustice to be stamped out. At the conclusion of that meeting, Mister R. E. picked up everything and moved to another radio station—and John Gordon was back in action, broadcasting our games on the new station.

To me, Mister R. E. personified Christianity—yet I couldn't put my finger on what it was about him that seemed so Christ-like. All I knew was that I wanted to be like Mister R. E. the way a monotone yearns to be an opera singer—but I figured I was just not that kind of guy. Whatever it was that made Mr. Littlejohn special seemed to be something he was born with.

One day I said, "You know, Coach, it seems to me that Jesus Christ must have been a lot like you."

I meant it as a compliment—but to his ears, it must have verged on sacrilege. Mister R. E. was clearly embarrassed. "No man can compare with the Lord Jesus," he replied.

Looking at my own life, I figured I was doing okay. I was honest and hardworking. I didn't have any bad habits. My motto was, "I don't drink or smoke or chew, and I don't go out with the girls who do." I was kind to my mother, and I didn't kick stray dogs. In my mind, I was in at least the ninety-fifth percentile of humanity.

Oh, sure, I knew I wasn't perfect. For example, I had a temper. There was that time a man was late delivering some ponies for a pregame kids promotion. I got so mad, I smashed the glass on my desktop with a baseball bat. So I had my flaws, but I figured God was grading humanity on a curve. I was bound to come out as good as the next guy—maybe better. As long as my good deeds outweighed my bad deeds, God would say, "Williams, you're okay in my book."

In the spring of 1967, something happened that made me realize my life could have far more excitement, meaning, and satisfaction than I had ever imagined.

## An Outstanding Human Being

In April of '67, the Phillies organization sent Bobby Malkmus, the former big-league utility infielder, to Spartanburg. His job was to help coach some of the ballplayers for a few weeks (including a future major league infielder named Manny Trillo). I was glad to have Bobby come to town, because his reputation might draw a few more fans to the games. Only one thing bothered me about Bobby Malkmus: it was well-known in baseball circles that the guy was very *religious*. I was concerned that a Bible-thumping religious fanatic might scare off some of our customers.

I had nothing against religion—in its proper place, of course. And the proper place was in church on Sunday mornings. A little religion was good for business, so I made it a point to visit various churches on behalf of the ballclub. I seldom went to the same church twice in a row—I spread my presence around to all the churches in town. I wanted all to see that Pat Williams was a good guy, so they'd know that the team was worthy of their support. In addition to family attendance at the ballpark, I wanted the Christian businessmen in town to advertise in our program. I had no particular interest in the songs or the sermon or the prayers—church was simply a good place to be seen for social and business reasons.

But these Bible-thumpers like Bobby Malkmus—well, I just wasn't sure what to expect. Was he going to preach to me? Was I going to have to endure a lot of talk about my soul roasting slowly on the barbecue spit of Hades?

When Bobby showed up, he wasn't at all what I expected. He didn't shout, "Hallelujah! Praise the Lord!" He didn't call me "brother" and ask me if I knew my soul was "bound for glory."

He didn't ask me if I had been "washed in the cleansing blood." He was—well, he was a normal guy.

No, he was better than normal. He was a *terrific* guy. In fact, he reminded me a lot of Mister R. E.

He was different from a lot of the big leaguers I'd met, because he didn't go around with a chaw of tobacco in his cheek and he didn't drink beer or cuss. But he was friendly and open and as likable as anyone I'd ever met. And he was savvy about the game of baseball. This guy really knew his stuff.

I was struck by the way he had just the right word to say in any situation. For example, I got an early Saturday morning call from the Spartanburg police department, telling me that three of our ballplayers had torn up a tavern and put one of the bar patrons in the hospital. The players involved had left with the team for a road trip that morning, so I spent much of the day talking with the minor league brass in Philadelphia and leaving messages for our manager, Dick Teed, in Lexington, North Carolina.

The Phillies took a hard line with players who stepped out of line—as they should. The Philadelphia office ordered Teed to send the players back to Spartanburg. Once they arrived, I was to give two of the players outright releases, and I was to fine and suspend the other player. Just before the players were to arrive on Sunday, I had dinner with Bobby Malkmus and filled him in on what had happened.

"Are you feeling a little queasy about meeting those guys?" asked Bobby.

"Well—yeah. Sorta." Actually, I was scared out of my socks. They had already beaten up some guy in a bar. If I had to tell these fellas their baseball career was over, what would they do to me? What would they have to lose by working me over? Nothing. I knew these guys, and they were tough.

Bobby could see I was more worried than I let on. "Tell you what," he said. "I usually go to the evening service at church, but I can skip it tonight. Let's you and me go out to the ballpark together. If there are two of us there when they arrive, there shouldn't be any trouble."

What a relief! I could've hugged the guy.

We went to the ballpark. A few minutes later, a taxi pulled up and the three players stepped out, pale and shaken. They didn't look so tough anymore. Fact is, they looked defeated. I had thought I would need Bobby there for protection. I was wrong. What I needed at that moment was the right words to say—and I didn't have any. But Bobby did. As the three young men walked toward us, Bobby stepped forward to meet them. He put his arms around the two guys who had been cut from the team and said, "I'm so sorry, fellas. I feel terrible for you. Please let me know if there's anything I can do for you—anything at all."

Of course, there was nothing anybody could do—but Bobby had said just the right words under the circumstances. He didn't suggest to them that they were being punished too harshly—but he didn't rub their noses in it, either. He was simply a friend.

I was amazed that evening by what I saw, and I was drawn to the quiet, steady wisdom Bobby displayed in that situation and many others. Bobby never preached to me, but I soon began to wish he would. I was so struck by the power of his personality and by the confident, upright way he lived that I wanted to be like him. Maybe if he preached to me, he would reveal the secret of being such an outstanding human being.

## "This Is Your Life"

If you're from my generation, you no doubt remember the old TV show *This Is Your Life*. The guest of honor is given a surprise party, and people significant to him give testimonials and tell stories of events from his lifetime. In May of '67, Claire Johns surprised me with a "This Is Your Life" birthday party. She brought in my mother and sisters, cousins, aunts, uncles, and several old friends, including Bill Durney from my Miami days and my college coach, Jack Stallings. I was flabbergasted—and humbled. It was one of the finest things anyone ever did for me, and I am eternally grateful to Mama Johns for the memories of that day.

That same month, I met another man who would have a powerful impact on my life. His name was Paul Anderson, and he ran a home for troubled boys in Vidalia, Georgia, with his wife Glenda. I had once seen him put on an amazing show of strength, so I asked him to appear at one of our ball games. He had never been a side act, so he wrote back to say he would only do it for five hundred dollars plus expenses. I learned later that he had not expected to hear from me again. But we wanted him, so we paid, and he came.

The first thing he did in his show was to drive a big nail through two one-inch-thick planks of wood. Now, a lot of guys could do that with a hammer, no problem. But Paul Anderson drove the nails with his bare hand. That was unbelievable enough—but it got even more incredible. Using only his little fingers, he lifted eighty-five pound dumbbells in each hand, holding them straight out from his sides. This guy had biceps on his pinkie fingers!

Next, he pressed a 250 pound barbell over his head eight times. But that was just the warm-up for the really big test. We had rigged a special wooden platform according to his specifications. He called out our eight heaviest ballplayers and sat them on the platform, four on each side. Each weighed more than two hundred pounds, and the platform must have made the total weight more than a ton. Paul got beneath the platform, found where the weight was balanced evenly on his shoulders, then hoisted the whole thing off the ground. The crowd went nuts.

Paul Anderson was an immense man—5'9", 375 pounds. He ignored the field mike we set up and addressed the crowd of 2,200 in his own unamplified voice. "I've lifted more weight than anyone in the history of mankind!" he boomed. "I once lifted over 6,000 pounds in a back lift. I've been declared a wonder of nature from the United States to Russia. I've been written up in Ripley's *Believe It or Not*. I've stood on the center platform at the Olympic Games. They call me the strongest man in the world.

"But I want you to know," he continued, "that all of those accomplishments are secondary in my life. I, Paul Anderson, the strongest man who ever walked the face of the earth, can't get through a minute of the day without Jesus Christ!"

Well, that statement really got my attention.

"The greatest thing in my life is being a Christian," he added. "If I can't make it without Christ, how about the rest of you?"

The crowd hadn't expected to hear a sermon at a baseball game—but this was a Bible Belt town, and the fans gave Paul one of the biggest ovations I had ever heard in beautiful Duncan Park. His message didn't really reach me at that moment, but I was impressed that this guy had the guts to talk about Jesus to a baseball crowd. He could have done his feats of strength, soaked up the applause, and gone home with his paycheck. Instead, he bared his soul to the crowd. I thought, *Man, I could never do that—get up and talk about religion to a bunch of sports fans!*

Then it hit me. Paul Anderson hadn't said a word about *religion.* He had talked about *Jesus Christ*—not about going to church or doing religious rituals. In fact, when he talked about Jesus Christ, it was as if he was talking about a friend, about a person he knew and talked to every day. That was a new one on me.

I had a picture of Paul and me together, taken some months earlier when I had first met him, so I asked him if he'd drop by the office and sign it on his way home. The photo shows me trying to lift him from behind. He came by the office and signed it, "To Pat, your friend in Christ, Paul Anderson." After he left, I framed it and showed it to Claire Johns. "Look at that, Mama," I said with a chuckle, "Paul Anderson is my friend *in Christ.*"

Claire detected the mocking tone of my voice. "Watch what you say, young man," she said. There aren't many women who would talk that way to the boss—but Claire Johns wouldn't hesitate to set me straight. And she was right.

## My Neck in a Noose

Over the next few weeks, my mind kept returning to what Paul Anderson had told the crowd that night in May. I had to admit it—he had a point. If the strongest man in the world couldn't make it through the day without Jesus Christ, what about me? I started reading books about other Christian athletes. I had always been an avid reader of sports books, and whenever I read a book about or by a Christian athlete, I usually just flipped past the "religious stuff." But after hearing Anderson's talk, I began to pay attention to Christian athletes, and I noticed that there was a common thread tying all the Christian sports books together.

The story that intrigued me the most was the biography of Bobby Richardson, former second baseman of the New York Yankees. Baseball stories were my favorite, of course, and here was Bobby Richardson, a South Carolinan and one of the biggest baseball names in the country. I wondered if I could get him to come to Spartanburg for a promotion in '68—but I knew that would be expensive. Then I had an idea. In view of Richardson's outspoken Christian testimony, maybe the Spartanburg churches would want to share expenses with the Phillies, and we could bring him down for a baseball appearance and a talk to Spartanburg young people about Christ.

But there was a snag: I couldn't convince area pastors that it was a good idea. Finally, Joe Brooks, pastor of the Westminster Presbyterian Church, stepped up to the plate. One of his parishioners, Charlie Sanders, saw a personal appearance by Bobby Richardson as an opportunity to go one step further on behalf of local youth. "Let's start a Fellowship of Christian Athletes chapter here in Spartanburg," he said. "Bobby's active in FCA, and we could bring him to town under the auspices of the group."

I knew next to nothing about the FCA, but I figured if that would help me get Bobby Richardson to our ballpark (cheap), I was all for it. To me, FCA was no different from the Heart Fund or the United Way—just another good cause. We set up a series of meetings from December 1967 through February 1968, talking about setting up the FCA chapter. My goal was to get the details settled so that we could get Richardson to town by April. I pushed and pushed, and couldn't understand what was so difficult about getting the group off the ground.

Finally, at one meeting in mid-February, I was sitting with the group of pastors along with our announcer, John Gordon. There was a new man there, Rev. Alastair C. Walker, who had just come up from Griffin, Georgia, to serve as pastor of Mister R. E.'s congregation, First Baptist Church in Spartanburg. When it came time to nominate a chapter chairman, Reverend Walker stood and in a thick Scottish brogue nominated—

Me!

*Oh, no!* I thought. Everyone in the room cheered, and I was elected by acclamation, without even a vote. I knew that these pastors wanted an FCA chapter to minister to the spiritual needs of young people, but all I wanted was to get Bobby Richardson to my ballpark. Now I was stuck with the job of putting together a Christian ministry. I accepted—but I felt as if I had just stuck my neck into a noose.

## Four Laws

A week after that meeting, on Thursday, February 22, 1968, I went to the Spartanburg gym-auditorium building to watch a couple of games of the state girls' basketball tournament. Someone handed me a flier about a singing group, the New Folk, that was giving a concert in the same building that evening. I watched the first game along with Art Fowler, the former major league pitcher (he was also Billy Martin's pitching coach wherever Martin was managing; Art lived in Spartanburg during the off-season). After the first game, I said, "Art, I'm going upstairs to listen to the concert."

"Aw, c'mon, Pat," Art drawled, "stay and watch the second game."

Normally, I would have stayed. Art's a great guy, and I always had fun talking baseball with him, but this time, something inside me just said, *Go on upstairs.* It was as if I was being led to the concert by a will higher than my own. "No," I said, "I'm going to check out the concert."

Art shrugged, and I took off. I got up to the auditorium just as the concert was starting. The New Folk were eight young men and women doing the kind of guitar-accompanied folk music (in the Peter, Paul, and Mary and New Christy Minstrels style) that was popular in the '60s. They were *great*.

I loved it—but I wanted to see the next game, so at intermission I got up to leave. But the leader of the New Folk said, "Please don't leave, folks, because in the second half we'd like to tell you what the Lord has been doing in our lives." Whoa! I hadn't heard anyone talk like that to a crowd since Paul Anderson. Almost against my will, I found myself settling back into my seat.

In the second half of the show, the tempo of the songs changed. The New Folk began singing about God. They took turns talking about their "faith in Christ" and "receiving Christ." The terms made no sense to me. At the end of the concert, the leader said, "We want to meet you, so stick around."

Well, there was a petite blonde in the group whom I was really interested in meeting. During the introductions, she had said her name was Sandy Johnson and she was attending nursing school at Northwestern University in Illinois. I went up and introduced myself. "You know, I went to grad school in Indiana." I tried to steer the conversation in such a way that I could casually mention that I was a big-shot exec in minor league baseball, but every time I said something to her, she turned it around to the subject of what the Lord was doing in her life.

"You guys really sound terrific," I said.

"Well," she replied, "we've dedicated ourselves and our talent to Jesus Christ, and it's our privilege to share his message with people."

We just weren't connecting. I wasn't finding any way to get the conversation around to my status—and how much I'd like to take her out after the concert.

Finally, she handed me a little booklet. "Here, let me leave this with you," she said. "If you read it, I think it will help you a lot." I stuck the booklet in my pocket, feeling very let down and disappointed. I had made my best play for this girl, and she had deflected it with ease. What's worse, I could see that she had something I really wanted—a radiance, a confidence, a joy. It was the same elusive quality I had seen in Mister R. E., in Bobby Malkmus, and in Paul Anderson—a quality I couldn't put my finger on, but which I really craved.

I went back to my apartment, flopped onto the bed, and noticed something jabbing me from my pocket. I pulled it out and saw it was the little booklet Sandy had given me. The title of the booklet was *Have You Heard of the Four Spiritual Laws?* I flipped it open and began to read. It only took a couple of minutes to get through the booklet. At the end of it, I said to myself, "Is *that* what makes those people different? Is *that* the 'something' I see in Sandy and Bobby Malkmus and Paul Anderson and Mister R. E.? Is *that* why I have all this success, yet they are the ones who are happy?"

I had to know more. I needed to talk to Sandy again—but how? I didn't know where she was staying. On a hunch, I called the motel across the street from the auditorium where the concert had been. The desk clerk confirmed the New Folk were staying there, and a few moments later, I heard Sandy's voice. "Hello?"

"Hello, Sandy Johnson? This is Pat Williams. We talked at the concert tonight. I'd really like to talk to you again—say, for breakfast tomorrow morning?"

"Well, we're leaving town at 11 A.M.—"

"Great," I said, using the sales techniques I had learned from Bill Durney. "I'll see you at nine-thirty."

I know she thought I was just trying to get a date with her—but that wasn't it at all. I really *was* interested in her message.

I didn't sleep well that night.

The next morning, I woke up early. When my roommate, John Gordon, began to stir, I said, "Hey, John, I want you to hear something."

"Huh? Whuzzat?"

"Just tell me what you make of this: 'Law One: God loves you and has a wonderful plan for your life. Law Two: Man is sinful and separated from God. Therefore, he cannot know and experience God's love and plan for his life. Law Three: Jesus Christ is God's only provision for man's sin. Through him you can know and experience God's love and plan for your life. Law Four: We must individually receive Jesus Christ as Savior and Lord, then we can know and experience God's love and plan for our lives.'"[2]

"What have you got there?" asked John, his eyes beginning to focus as he sat up in bed.

"It's a booklet I got from one of the New Folk singers at the concert last night."

"Concert? I thought you went to a basketball game."

"I did. But then I went to a concert. And I met this young lady—Sandy Johnson—and she gave me this booklet. Here, listen to this verse: 'Behold, I stand at the door and knock. If anyone hears my voice and opens the door, I will come in to him, and dine with him, and he with me.' This is something I really need to think about."

John nodded thoughtfully—but said nothing in response. I had no idea (and John didn't tell me) that he was also wrestling with the same issues that were troubling me. He had been going to church a bit, and he had heard Paul Anderson the year before and was a part of the effort to start the Fellowship of Christian Athletes chapter in Spartanburg. He already had an appointment that day to meet with Reverend Walker of First Baptist Church to find out more about the Christian faith. While I got ready to meet Sandy Johnson for breakfast, he was getting ready to meet with the pastor.

I found Sandy waiting at a little pancake house next to her motel. She was polite but guarded—and I could hardly blame her for being suspicious of my motives after the way I had come on the previous night. I bought her breakfast and asked her to go over the booklet and explain the four spiritual laws to me again. We talked for quite a while, and when the time came for her to leave, I still had many things to ask her.

At eleven o'clock she boarded the van with the other singers of the New Folk. She smiled and waved from the window. I waved back, a fake smile frozen on my face, hiding a confused and frustrated heart. As the van took off down the road and dwindled in the distance, I still had the booklet she had given me—and a lot of unanswered questions.

## "I'm In Now!"

I was miserable. I had a head full of questions and no one to ask. The New Folk had something I wanted, even though I wasn't sure what it was—but they were on their way to Columbia, South Carolina. They were normal-looking, happy people—but they talked about "the Lord" in a bold, uninhibited way. The only people I'd ever met who were that openly religious were sign-carrying kooks and weirdos. But the New Folk were happy. I wasn't. I needed to figure out what this thing was all about.

I tried to throw myself back into work. On the way to the ballpark, I made some sales calls, but my heart wasn't in it. I couldn't concentrate. I felt lonely and frustrated. I wanted that van to turn around, and I wanted those young people to come back and explain the four spiritual laws to me until I understood what it was I was missing. I had a gnawing, unsettled feeling inside, and I wanted to settle it.

After lunch, I puttered around in the office, tormented and without any peace of mind. All I could think of was the look of joy on the faces of the New Folk. If I'd known where my roommate was at that moment, I *really* would have been blown away: John Gordon was sitting in our messy apartment, talking with Rev. Alastair C. Walker. "I want to know more about being a Christian," John was saying.

"In that case," Reverend Walker replied in his thick Scottish brogue, "I would like to share with you a passage from God's Word. In Revelation 3:20, Jesus says, 'Behold, I stand at the door and knock. If anyone hears my voice and opens the door—'"

Before Reverend Walker could finish quoting the verse, John leaped excitedly to his feet. "I know where I heard those words! Just this morning, Pat Williams read that verse to me from some booklet he has. You know what? That's the only verse in the whole Bible anyone ever read just for me—and now I've heard it twice in one day! God is really trying to get through to me!" Reverend Walker—the same man who nominated me to head up the drive to start a new FCA chapter—probably thought that

I had been trying to share my faith with John. Little did he know that I was no more a Christian than John was.

By two o'clock, I finally decided I wasn't going to get anything done. I had to talk with someone. *Maybe Mr. Littlejohn can help me,* I thought. *He's a churchgoing man.* I decided to tell him exactly what had happened during the last eighteen hours and see what he had to say.

I got in my car and drove to Mister R. E.'s office—and was surprised to see John Gordon and Reverend Walker arriving in John's car. The three of us went into Mr. Littlejohn's office and sat in silence for a few moments—no one knew where to start. Reverend Walker and John were smiling at Mister R. E. and he was smiling at them. In fact, everyone in that room was positively beaming—except me.

Finally, Reverend Walker leaned forward in his chair. "Mister R. E.," he said, "I've got some wonderful news. This young man here, John Gordon, committed his life to Jesus Christ this afternoon."

Well, that was a shocker. I had been agonizing over the same decision all last night, all morning, and all afternoon—and my roommate was the one who actually made the big decision. I thought, *Wait just a darn minute! That's what I want! Somebody explain this thing to me, because I want to do it, too!* But I still didn't know how to put my feelings into words, so I just sat there.

I saw Mr. Littlejohn's eyes glisten with joy. "Oh, that's wonderful," he said softly, "just wonderful!" I had never seen him so happy. And then I grasped what I had always seen in R. E. Littlejohn but never understood: The source of the joy in his life—that indefinable extra something I had seen in him—was due to his relationship with Jesus Christ. That's what was so different about him. I had known him for three years, and I had completely missed the secret of his amazing personality.

The three of them sat and talked about John's decision for about fifteen minutes or so—and I just sat there dumbfounded. No—I felt worse than dumbfounded. I was *jealous.* John had the same look those singers in the New Folk had. John was one of *them* now—and I was an outsider.

After a while, John and Reverend Walker stood to leave, and I stood, too. "Pat," said Mister R. E. after they left and we were alone, "I want you to know that Reverend Walker and I have been praying for you. Fact is, my wife and I have been praying for you ever since you came to Spartanburg. You could have such an impact in sharing Christ, using the platform of your success in the sports field. When you talk, people listen. You know, Pat, you could make the same decision for Christ that Johnny made."

In that instant, everything seemed to pop into focus. I suddenly understood why all my successes and accomplishments had left me feeling empty. I understood what the four spiritual laws were trying to tell me—that God loved me, that he wanted to use my life and make it meaningful and rich and full, that I was a sinner but that Jesus had taken all the punishment for my sin on himself. Most of all, I finally saw what I needed to do—the decision I had to make. All my life, I had set my own agenda and plans for success. I had been the captain of my own soul. Now it was time to let go, to die to myself and my ambitions, to let Jesus Christ take the reins and set the direction of my life.

Even at that moment, while I teetered on the brink of finally obtaining the elusive thing I had sought for so long—that *something* I saw within R. E. Littlejohn, within Bobby Malkmus, within Paul Anderson, within Sandy Johnson and the New Folk—even then, I felt a tug of self-will. Something faintly whispered to me, *Don't surrender control!* It was the refrain of the Gingerbread Man:

> Run, run, run
> As fast as you can!
> You can't catch me—
> I'm the Gingerbread Man!

My life had been a race—run, run, run, don't get caught, don't surrender, stay in control. You can't catch me, God! I'm in control. I'm Pat Williams, I'm successful, I'm running the show, I'm doing it all. I'm the Gingerbread Man!

But in that instant, I knew my running days were over. I had been caught—not by the hungry fox, as I had always feared. I had been caught by the one the Bible called the Lamb of God, Jesus Christ. My long struggle was finally over. Jesus had won.

My soul flooded with emotion, and I began to cry. Mister R. E. put his arms around me without a word. Now I understood why he had reminded me so much of Jesus Christ—Jesus was his lord and example, and everything Mister R. E. did, he did in imitation of the Lord he loved. Now I could live that way, too!

I lifted my head, no longer crying, and my heart was racing with excitement. I was a new man, and I knew it. For the first time in my life, I had been freed from the need to be somebody other than myself. Success was no longer my god. I felt I had been scrubbed clean from the inside out with a strong detergent. I was no longer on the outside looking in, wondering what was different about Christians. Now I knew. The Gingerbread Man had come home.

"I'm *in* now!" I said, sitting down.

Mister R. E. chuckled. "Yes, Pat," he said. "You're in."

## From Religion to Relationship

Mister R. E. suggested I make an appointment with Reverend Walker. I had a lot to learn about my new faith—and I was ready to begin the process.

I left Mr. Littlejohn's office and thought, *I want to tell someone what just happened to me! But who?* I decided to go by the office at the ballpark and see if Claire Johns was there. I remembered the time I had mocked Paul Anderson's inscription on the photo: "Look at that, Mama," I had laughed, "Paul Anderson is my friend *in Christ.*" I knew she would understand what had just happened to me—and she would be as happy as Mr. Littlejohn.

I burst into the office, and sure enough, there she was. "Mama Johns," I shouted, "I've become a Christian!" She was elated, and she gave me a big hug.

Now R. E. Littlejohn and Claire Johns knew—but that wasn't enough. I wanted to tell *everybody!* I needed to tell John Gordon, and I needed to tell Reverend Walker and—

And Sandy Johnson. Sure! I needed to tell her! She was the one who had given me that booklet. She was a part of this change in my life, too. Where did she say they were going next? Columbia, South Carolina. It was five o'clock. If I was going to get to Columbia and find out where the New Folk were performing, I'd have to hustle. I raced home to shower and change, and there I ran into John. The moment he saw me, he read it in my face. He knew that we were brothers—brothers in Christ, as Paul Anderson had put it. John and I carried on like little kids. We shared something special: We had been reborn on the same day.

Later, we would both look back on that day as the best day in our lives. Not only was it the day we gave our lives to Jesus Christ, but that evening John had his first date with a young lady, Nancy, who would later become his wife. It was also the first time John Gordon ever let me get in the shower first. As I was getting dressed, Johnny jumped into the shower and yelped, "Hey! It's cold! What kind of Christian are you? You used up all the hot water."

We laughed. Hot water or cold, life was suddenly unbelievably good!

I straightened my tie, jumped in my car, and sped off for Columbia. Ninety minutes later, I was cruising into town without a clue where the New Folk might be performing. The only landmark I knew in that town was the University of South Carolina Auditorium. I drove straight there—and the place was lit up, the parking lot was filled with cars, and music was coming from the building. I had come right to the place where the New Folk were performing.

I went inside and moved up as close to the front as possible. The New Folk were doing the same songs they had played the night before in Spartanburg—but the music seemed brand-new to me. I understood those songs now. It was as if every word had been written and sung just for me. As they strummed the guitars and banged the tambourine and praised the Lord—*my*

Lord!—I sat there with my face lit up like the evening sky on Independence Day.

After the program, I sought out Sandy Johnson. She saw me coming, and she had a surprised look on her face. It may have even been a look of dismay—as in, *Oh, no, this guy never gives up.* I didn't want her to get the wrong impression. I just wanted her to know what had happened. "Sandy," I said, "everything you told me last night—everything in the booklet you gave me— it all makes sense to me now. This afternoon I received Jesus Christ into my life."

Sandy's eyes widened, and a look of joy spread across her face. "Oh, Pat, that's—that's—" Her eyes glistened. "Oh, praise the Lord!"

I didn't want to keep her—other people wanted to talk to her, possibly others who needed the same change I had just experienced. So I said good-night and walked back to my car. All the way home, I had a lump of joy in my throat, and I had to keep brushing tears from my eyes. I had never had such feelings in my life before—never.

People often ask, "Then what happened? Did you end up marrying this girl?" Actually, I did look her up in 1969, when I was with the Chicago Bulls. She was living in Lisle, Illinois, at the time, and I went out with her a couple of times, but we never became romantically involved.

The next day, I called Mom in Wilmington and told her what had happened to me—but I don't think I explained it too well. I told her I had become a Christian, and she said that she had raised me to be a Christian. After all, she had taken me to Westminster Presbyterian Church and to Sunday school; I had grown up to be a fine, successful young man who didn't drink or smoke or chew tobacco. So I was already a Christian. "Are you sure this isn't some sort of—well, some kind of emotional experience?" she asked.

Well, it surely had been emotional. I had gone through more emotions in the past twenty-four hours than in all my preceding years on the planet. But it wasn't just an emotional experience—it was real, and I told her so. This wasn't just some new religious kick I was on. None of the Christians I had talked to and been around even mentioned religion. This was not about religion or emotion—this was about a relationship with a person.

In the years that followed, Mom admitted that the "experience" (as she called it) was good for me, and she couldn't deny that I stuck with it; it was not just a phase or a religious kick I was on. But the truth is not that I stuck with it, but that God stuck with me. He showed me that I could stop running in search of happiness and satisfaction. I didn't have to earn the praise of people or the favor of God. Now I had Jesus.

Years later, I was talking with my Uncle R. Murphy Williams about my conversion experience. A Presbyterian minister for many years throughout the South, Uncle Murph co-officiated with Dr. Warren Wiersbe at my first wedding in Chicago. As I talked with him about my encounter with Jesus Christ, I asked him, "Why didn't somebody tell me this before, Uncle Murph?"

"Oh, you've heard it," he replied. "You just didn't listen." And, of course, he was right.

The day after I told Mom what had happened, I had an Army Reserve meeting. Before, I had always dreaded those meetings. But as a brand-new Christian, I even found myself enjoying the Army.

The following weekend, I attended a Christian conference in Athens, Georgia, that the New Folk had told me about. The speaker was a fellow named Hal Lindsey—the same Hal Lindsey who would later become world-famous as the author of *The Late Great Planet Earth*. I was hungry for fellowship with other Christians, and I knew I had so much to learn. I walked into a large Methodist church where dozens of college kids milled about. I didn't know a soul. I stopped and asked a dark-haired lady, "Do you know if Hal Lindsey is here yet?"

"He's here somewhere," the woman replied. "I'm his wife, Jan. Can I help you?"

"Well, I'm Pat Williams from Spartanburg and I've been a Christian for about a week. Fact is, I'm not even sure why I'm here, but I want to be around other Christians, and I know I have a lot to learn."

Jan Lindsey kept track of me from then on, making sure I knew where to go, introducing me to people, and generally watching out for me. She introduced me to Hal, and when they found out I didn't have a place to stay in Athens, they invited me to stay with them.

That weekend was the greatest thing that could have happened to me as a new Christian. It helped cement my understanding of the faith and confirmed that Christians are not fanatical oddballs but genuine, happy, loving people who care about others and about their Lord. I was immediately drawn into their fellowship, and they made me feel I really belonged. We studied and discussed the Bible, we applied it to real-life situations and problems, and we prayed together. It was the first time I heard people pray as if they were just talking to a friend—or to a caring father.

One thing I learned at that retreat was that I had to be totally willing to do anything God might ask of me. That was hard. I had to be willing to give up even my life in pro sports, if that's what God wanted, and go wherever he might lead me. I even had to be willing to become a missionary. At first, I resisted that thought, but as I talked and prayed with my newfound friends, I began to realize the point was not that God was going to send me off to some distant desert or jungle, but that I should be *willing* to love and serve him to that extent.

Coming to that place of willingness and obedience was a big step for me. For years, I had maneuvered myself to be seen at the right places to advance my career and enlarge my ego. Now I was letting God handle all my plans. If he wanted me to go, I'd go. If he wanted me to stay put and tell the Spartanburgers about Jesus the rest of my life—well, that was cool with me, too. He's the Lord, not me.

I left that retreat eager to talk about my faith with everyone I met. I'm sure I scared off as many people as I attracted to the gospel—but there was no stopping me. I wanted everyone to know Christ, just as I did. The first place I talked publicly about my faith was in an adult Sunday school class at First Baptist Church in Gaffney, South Carolina. There I discovered that promoting Christ was even more fun than promoting baseball!

When the Phillies farm director, Paul Owens, canceled out on a speaking engagement at the Spartanburg Lions Club, I filled in. I told the hundred or so most influential men in town about my new relationship with Jesus Christ. That little speech hit the meeting like a blockbuster, and the news spread through town like a firestorm. Within a couple of days, the whole town was buzzing.

Reverend Walker asked me to tell my story from his pulpit at a televised Youth Sunday event. People all across the state saw that broadcast, and soon my speaking schedule was packed. I was asked to speak at churches I had never even heard of. Being a new Christian, I was able to communicate my experience without a lot of Christian jargon—and that seemed to connect with a lot of people.

Reverend Walker and R. E. Littlejohn stressed the importance of a daily walk with God—that is, a daily experience of Bible study and prayer, and regular fellowship with other Christians. They warned me that the emotional high I was feeling would wear off, and I would probably wonder about the validity of my relationship with Christ—and they were right. They warned me that my new faith would not insulate me against problems and would actually present me with a new set of problems and temptations—and they were right. They warned me that I undoubtedly would have times of slipping back into old habits and old selfish attitudes—and they were right.

But they also told me that if I persevered in studying the Word, talking to God, worshiping with Christians, confessing sin and returning to God, I would continue growing in Christ. So I did what they said. The Christian faith, once just a rigamarole of rituals, had become a living relationship. I could really talk to God—and he really listened. I wasn't embarrassed to use everyday language and ignore the thee's and thou's I had always associated with prayer. There's nothing wrong with praying in King James English, if you believe it lends an air of reverence to your attitude in prayer—but that just wasn't me. And God, I realized, was happy to let me be me, and to accept my conversational prayers. Daily prayer and Bible study kept me going and believing long after the emotional high wore off.

## A Whole New Ballgame

Bobby Malkmus was ecstatic when John Gordon and I told him of the change in our lives. He was selected to be the Spartanburg Phillies manager for 1968, and it was great to see him again in the spring.

Around that same time, I got a call from Pam Smith, an airline flight attendant I had dated a few times. She wondered why I hadn't called in a while. "Well," I said, "I've really been busy as a new Christian—"

"What?"

"The thing is, I've received Jesus Christ into my life and I'm a new person." I told Pam the whole story—and she wanted to come to Spartanburg and find out more. She had more questions than I could answer, so I introduced her to Bobby Malkmus and Reverend Walker—and she accepted Christ into her life. That was a profound experience, seeing this young woman make the same big decision I had made. Nothing compares with seeing someone come to Christ. To this day, I get a chill down my spine and tears in my eyes when I hear that someone has received Christ as Lord and Savior.

There was a special bond among the ballpark personnel that year. The owner, general manager, manager, radio sportscaster, and office secretary were all Christians—and we had some wonderful times. More than once, Johnny and I said that we wished we had found Christ years earlier. For all the success and fun we'd had before, nothing compared to this. Never again would I wonder, *Is that all there is?*

The team started strong and finished in first place for the first half of the season. It was the fifth straight half-season championship for Spartanburg, and we had good crowds again.

By April we had started a thriving FCA chapter—and succeeded in bringing Bobby Richardson to Duncan Park. The stands were packed with young people when Bobby got up and said, "When you receive Christ by faith, God will pardon all your sins past and present. He'll give you real peace with yourself and your neighbor. He'll give you a true purpose for living.

And he'll give you the power to live up on top of your daily circumstances. Jesus will never leave you nor forsake you, and you'll never have to feel empty or afraid again." Bobby signed hundreds of autographs that day.

Mr. Littlejohn told me that now, more than ever, I had every reason to be the best promotional man I could be. I continued to seek publicity and the spotlight—not for myself, but for the ballclub and for Christ. I shared my faith in him every chance I got to speak.

I was happier and calmer than I had ever been. Problems and foul-ups which used to set me off became opportunities to rely on Christ and allow his character to be exhibited in me. I could see change and growth in my character, and that was exciting. I consumed Christian books like popcorn—anything and everything that might help me to better understand and live out my new relationship with Christ: *The Hiding Place, Make Love Your Aim, The Cross and the Switchblade, God's Smuggler,* and more.

On July 8, 1968, I walked into the ballpark office and found a phone message on my desk from a Jack Ramsay in Inglewood, California. The only Jack Ramsay I had ever heard of was the one who had coached basketball so successfully at St. Joseph's College in Philadelphia before becoming general manager of the NBA's Philadelphia 76ers. But I knew it couldn't be *that* Jack Ramsay—he didn't even know me. I returned the call and was astonished to find out it *was* that Jack Ramsay.

"Have you been following what's been happening with our team?" he asked.

I certainly had. There was speculation all over the sports world that one of the biggest trade deals in history was about to be struck between the 76ers and the Los Angeles Lakers.

"Well, I'm out here in California to work out the final details of our trade with Los Angeles," he continued. "We're getting Darrall Imhoff, Archie Clark, and Jerry Chambers in exchange for Wilt Chamberlain. The trade will be announced later this afternoon. You know our coach, Alex Hannum, resigned, and we haven't been able to get anyone to replace him yet, so I'm going to coach the team this season. That won't leave me much time to manage the team, so we're going to need a business manager. Would you like the job?"

I managed to stammer out an affirmative. I couldn't have been more surprised if he had asked me to replace Chamberlain as the starting center. "Fine," he said. "Let's talk in Philadelphia in a few days."

For years, my whole focus had been baseball. Now, out of the blue came a chance to work in NBA basketball. It was the major leagues all right, but this was a whole new ball game. This break was so clearly from the Lord, I couldn't pass it up. I realized that once I finally resigned myself to whatever the Lord wanted—whether it meant staying in Spartanburg or putting on a missionary pith helmet and going to the far side of the world—he had big plans for me. He had just been waiting until I was completely sold out to him.

The Gingerbread Man was dead. An entirely new man—Pat Williams, follower of Christ—was being rebuilt and put into service. I didn't realize it then, but my life had just turned a corner and was heading in an entirely new and exciting direction.

# 5

# Brotherly Love
# and Big Shoulders

I flew to Philadelphia and Jack Ramsay offered me a three-year contract at twenty thousand dollars a year—a lot of money for a guy in his twenties in 1968. It took a lot of faith for Ramsay to turn over the business end of the Philadelphia 76ers to a twenty-eight-year-old kid whose only experience was in minor league baseball. I later asked Jack how he knew about me, and all he would ever say is, "A lot more is known about you here in Philadelphia than you realize."

The main thing was that I had the job. This was the big league, and I would be entrusted with promotion, publicity, ticket sales—everything but personnel. I liked the idea.

I took a cab to the Phillies' offices to talk to Paul Owens, the farm director. I told him what was brewing, and he asked me to wait until he had a chance to talk to my old pal Ruly Carpenter, who was by then a top executive in the organization. I returned home to Spartanburg, and the next day I got a call from Ruly. "Wait a few more days," he said. "I want to check out the 76ers' front office and their owner, Irv Kosloff, to make sure everything is solid." I appreciated that, and he soon called back to say that everything seemed to check out.

I called Ramsay and said, "I'm with you, sir. I'll finish out the baseball season here and I can join you by Labor Day."

A few days went by, and then I got an unexpected call from Jack Ramsay. "We've got a small snag," he said. *Uh-oh,* I thought. *What now?* "Mr. Kosloff would like to talk to you before we make this official," Ramsay continued. "Do me a favor and give him a call, and I'm sure everything will work out."

I called Kosloff, who was also the owner of a major paper company. "I want you to do two things for me," he said. "First, I want you to have three people who know you call me collect so I can talk to them about you. Second, I want you to come to Philadelphia next Monday and go to the following address by ten o'clock in the morning." He read off the address and hung up. *What's this?* I wondered. *Some kind of test to see if I can follow directions?*

I asked three people to call Mr. Kosloff with their recommendations: Bill Veeck; Vic Bubas, the basketball coach at Duke; and Andy Musser, the 76ers' radio announcer. Then I flew in for the mysterious ten o'clock appointment the following Monday. It turned out to be the office of Dr. Norman Gekoski of Management Psychologists Inc. I was greeted by the receptionist and told that I had five hours of testing in front of me. Kosloff hadn't told me about it, and I resented having this testing sprung on me as a surprise. I was so angry, I was on the verge of walking out—but I did want that job.

Then I met Dr. Gekoski. He called me into his office for an hour of interviewing—chatting, actually. He was a delightful man, and quite a basketball fan. He would become a close friend during my time with the 76ers. It was a good thing I got to talk to him or I might have taken that initial bad attitude all the way through the testing.

Later that afternoon I met with Kosloff's banker, who was another of Kosloff's trusted advisors. By the time I met with Irv Kosloff himself, he had gotten reports from his banker and Gekoski.

The first question Kosloff asked was, "What qualifies you for this job?" I hadn't prepared any answers to this or any other question. But somehow I stammered out a response, and I guess I didn't embarrass myself too badly, because he nodded and went on to the next question: "What are your strengths?" Then: "What are your weaknesses?" I sure didn't want to answer that one! Then: "What difference will your presence here make in my franchise?" It was a direct, intense interview, and I gave honest, direct answers.

On the way to the airport for the flight back to South Carolina, Kosloff told me the job was mine. It had been a long, tough, exasperating day, but I had learned a valuable lesson in patience.

## City of Brotherly Love

R. E. Littlejohn wanted me to stay in Spartanburg. He offered an incredible inducement to stay: complete ownership of the Spartanburg Phillies. But he knew I had my sights set on the big leagues, and he encouraged me to do what was best for my career. The most important thing to him was that I had my feet on the ground and that I knew who I was, why I was here, and where I was going. Well, I knew.

I was going to a pro basketball team which had just traded away the biggest draw ever. Wilt Chamberlain was headed for L.A., and the sports pundits and prophets of doom predicted that the 76ers would never again draw the crowds that once came to see Wilt the Stilt. The challenge I faced was to prove the pundits and prophets wrong. I looked forward to that challenge. Conventional wisdom said that the kind of outrageous fun-and-games promotions I had tried so successfully in the minors would never work in the big-city atmosphere of the major leagues. I disagreed, and I wanted to disprove that notion. To me, people are people and fun is fun anywhere you go. I had no doubt that Philadelphians could enjoy a good laugh and some uninhibited fun as much as the Spartanburgers had.

119

On the way up to Philly, I stopped in Wilmington to visit Mother. I no sooner had walked in the door when the phone rang. It was Jim Fanning, general manager of the Montreal Expos expansion team, which would begin its first National League season in 1969. I had known Jim for years. "Pat," he said, "we'd like you to join our front office here in Montreal." My heart sank. This was what I really wanted—a job in major league baseball. All the time I had been in Spartanburg, I had been waiting for this call, but it had never come. Ironically, Fanning's call came just days after I had accepted the NBA job in Philadelphia. With a lump in my throat, I had to say "thanks, but no thanks" to the Expos and major league baseball.

I arrived in the City of Brotherly Love the day after Labor Day 1968. Jack Ramsay said our club was going to do just fine without Wilt Chamberlain. "We've still got Billy Cunningham, Hal Greer, Chet Walker, Luke Jackson, and Wally Jones," he said. "We'll be playing a more varied and interesting game." He was right; they did—and that helped. In fact, Philadelphia would end up in the playoffs again before losing to Boston in the first round.

I received five days of intense training and instruction from Jack—then I was on my own. The only time I saw him after that was when the team was in town. Talk about on-the-job training! I hit the ground running and soon found that promoting basketball is not so different from promoting baseball. Any differences are mostly superficial. For example, in basketball you schedule the shows for halftime instead of before the game. In both games, you want to keep the people entertained as they wait for the game to commence, while still giving them a chance to hit the rest rooms and the concession stands. You don't want anyone going home feeling there was nothing to see or do.

The difference between trying to fill a five-thousand-seat minor league baseball stadium and the Spectrum, a fifteen-thousand-seat basketball arena (which was then less than two-thirds full on an average night) seemed daunting at first—until I remembered that if I was in major league baseball, I'd be worrying about filling fifty thousand seats for eighty-one home dates. Basketball has only forty-one home games.

One thing I really liked about pro basketball was the noise. Basketball arenas are enclosed by lots of reflective surfaces, such as concrete walls, low ceilings, and hardwood floors. The noise echoes and re-echoes, and a really great crowd can be like having a rock band in one ear and a jumbo jet in the other. There's nothing like an overtime game with a house full of screaming fans rocking the roof off the house.

## Big Victor and Little Arlene

I went to work coming up with outrageous, goofy promotions for each home game. Jack Ramsay let me do anything that came to mind. I had always thought that sports events and popular music made a good combination, and I got a great idea when I heard of a couple of big concerts coming to Philly in the fall of '68—one by Motown stars Martha and the Vandellas, the other by that smooth crooner Andy Williams. I used my 76ers connections to slip backstage with some typewritten copy and a portable tape recorder, introduced myself to the stars, and asked them to read some promotional blurbs into the tape recorder.

At a local radio station, an engineer mixed in some background music—"Dancing in the Street" for the Martha Reeves promo and "Moon River" for the Andy Williams promo. The voice-over went something like this: "Hi, this is Andy Williams, and you know, the 76ers are coming on strong this season, and you don't want to miss a single exciting game. So make sure you get your tickets by calling this number. . . ." Everyone was amazed that I had gotten endorsements from such big stars. You'd never get a celebrity to do you a favor like that now, but in some ways, the '60s were a kinder, gentler time.

Back when doubleheaders were still played in the NBA, we played the New York Knicks early in the season. That double dose of basketball would have been enough to bring out most fans, but I decided it would be a great time to pile on the hoopla along with the hoops. So during halftime of the first game, we brought out Victor the Wrestling Bear. Any fan who dared grapple with that 700-pound grizzly would get a couple of free tickets to the next ball game. And anyone who pinned Victor to the floor would win some cash.

I don't remember how much we offered, because it never occurred to us that we would ever have to pay off. Though declawed, defanged, and muzzled, Victor had such power in his arms that no one stood a chance. That bear even pinned a 275-pound NFL football special teams player in a matter of seconds. The few daring (foolhardy, foolish, out of their cotton-picking minds) fans who took on Victor were instantly pancaked. It was hilarious.

The New York sportswriters came to Philly to cover the Knicks—but they ended up writing a lot of column inches about Victor. A photo and story made the front page of the *New York Daily News*.

For the halftime show in the second game, I brought in Dick Allen (who was then the superstar third baseman for the Philadelphia Phillies) to perform with his rock group, the Ebonistics. Dick had been a controversial figure in Philly. Because of his tempestuous relationship with the fans, he was often the subject of taunts and boos. He had cut a record called *Echoes of November* on—I kid you not—the Groovy Grooves label. Even though the fans had booed Allen all summer at the ballpark, he got a standing ovation when he performed that song in our arena. Soon, everyone was talking about 76ers games and how much fun they were, and the team quickly became known for more than just good basketball.

The idea for another really insane promotion came from one of our players, Craig Raymond. He had heard of a young lady named Arlene whose thing was eating. He said she helped promote the opening of a hamburger stand by eating hamburgers there all evening. I had visions of some porky slob who would get laughed out of the stadium—but as a promoter, I considered nothing beyond the pale, so I called her.

She sounded sweet and dainty over the phone. Sure, she said, she'd be happy to help us with a show. All we had to pay was her expenses—how could we lose? For weeks, we billed the coming attraction as "Little Arlene." She claimed she could out-eat any five men put together, so we challenged the five biggest eaters in town to come to the ballgame and try to outconsume Little Arlene.

Shortly before Little Arlene arrived, I got a call from a guy who had been to one of our recent games. He was vacationing in Florida and had found four other big guys who agreed to challenge Arlene. They called themselves "the Philadelphia Fillups, featuring the Galloping Glutton." I couldn't imagine a girl outeating five healthy college guys, but we started advertising in earnest.

When the big night came, the Spectrum was packed. The eating binge was to tip off at seven o'clock and continue right through the ball game until we had a winner. Arlene said she had no preference as to the food, so we agreed upon hot dogs without the buns, medium pizzas, and Cokes. The food was brought out by stadium personnel dressed as chefs. Little Arlene—who was quite petite—began eating slowly and daintily. By contrast, the guys started horsing down hot dogs, pizzas, and Coke as if it was all going out of style.

By eight o'clock, the guys had slowed way down. Each had eaten a couple of medium pizzas and about fifteen hot dogs with several Cokes. But it wasn't a speed contest. This was for quantity. Arlene was still munching away, showing not the least sign of fatigue. The crowd began to take notice.

A few minutes after eight, the guys were through. They were sitting, standing, lying, groaning, and turning green. Arlene was still eating. If I hadn't seen it, I never would have believed it. In slightly less than three hours, delicate Little Arlene personally chewed up and swallowed seventy-six hot dogs and twenty-one medium pizzas. She drank twenty-five Cokes. She won the great American pig-out, hands down.

"Is that enough?" she asked politely. I assured her that it was quite enough and announced that she had totally wiped out the Galloping Glutton and his Philadelphia Fillups.

"Well," she said, "just to make sure," and she casually ate two more hot dogs, running her total to seventy-eight. She didn't look a bit green or overstuffed. In fact, she looked as if she could have kept right on eating. She asked me to announce a challenge to the crowd: She would outeat any five people in an oyster-eating contest at Bookbinder's Seafood Restaurant after the game. I announced it, but no one volunteered. I was told she went to Bookbinder's anyway and enjoyed a big meal.

A few days later, we got the bill for Arlene's hotel stay. One of the items was a full roast beef dinner she had consumed about an hour before the contest at the Spectrum! Where did she put it?

I would like to be remembered as a good sports executive, a businessman, a team builder, a motivational speaker, an author. Odds are, when it's all said and done, I will be remembered for big Victor and Little Arlene. I can live with that. If it weren't for promotions like the big bear and the hungry little lady, the ball-clubs I've worked for wouldn't have had any money for me to manage, I'd have been out of a job, and I wouldn't be remembered for anything.

## A Willing Convert

I may not be a circus clown, but there's no question: Clowns and I are in the same business. I'd be right at home in a rubber nose, frizzy wig, and size 90 shoes. Clowns live to make people forget their troubles for a while—and so do I.

The point of everything we did at the Spectrum Arena was *fun*. If the fans had fun, the organization made money. It was as simple as that. Everyone in the 76ers organization got caught up in the fun of the season. Nothing is more satisfying in any business environment than to see the entire organization coming together with a spirit of teamwork, and with everybody taking pride in and ownership of the total product. And the product we sold at the Spectrum was *fun*.

A basketball franchise has about two hours to sell at each game. Something has to be going on all the time. It's a tough, demanding task to fill that time with rompin', stompin', rip-roarin' excitement—but the fans have to come away remembering an entire night of entertainment or they won't be in any hurry to return. We wanted the fans back—*all* of them, to *every* game. And we wanted them to bring their friends next time.

As I became closer to Irv Kosloff, I found him to be a valuable mentor. "Ask yourself two questions every hour of the day," he told me. "First: What am I doing to help the team win more games? Second: What am I doing to help draw more fans? That's all that matters. If you remember those two questions, you'll never get sidetracked or bogged down in useless details." I follow that advice to this day.

Being only six months old in my Christian faith when I arrived in the City of Brotherly Love, I knew I needed good biblical teaching and friends who would support me in my commitment to Christ. So it was a breath of fresh air to walk into my first meeting of the Philadelphia chapter of FCA. The organization quickly put me to work helping to plan special events.

I had a harder time finding a church home, comparing every church with my special experience at First Baptist in Spartanburg and every preacher with my great friend and mentor, Rev. A. C. Walker. I spent a lot of time reading Christian books, and I was befriended, discipled, and mentored in the Christian faith by FCA worker Ted Deinert, who later married Billy Graham's daughter, Bunny.

The summer months kept me busy representing the 76ers at speaking engagements around town. I found more and more opportunities to talk about Christ, even at secular sports-oriented events. Our center, Darrall Imhoff, once said in an interview that hearing me share my story challenged him to be more outspoken about his own faith in Jesus Christ. I was really humbled to hear that. The only boldness I've ever had to talk about Jesus Christ, then or now, has come from God.

After my first year with the 76ers, we had an advertisers' reception at the Spectrum. Jack Ramsay, a fitness nut, looked at me and said, "You're getting fat!" Well, that really shocked me. That night, I went out to run, and I've been running ever since. I have logged thousands of running miles in cities all over the world.

That first year in Philadelphia was thoroughly enjoyable. *The Sporting News* did a full-page story on our crazy promotions, which was a nice affirmation. Jack Ramsay was happy, and so was Irv Kosloff. I never regretted my move from baseball to basketball. I had two more years to go on my contract and was looking forward to even wilder promotions and greater crowds in the years ahead.

That's why the next twist in the road of my career came as a complete surprise.

## City of the Big Shoulders

Bill Veeck called in late July as the team was preparing for training camp in September. A friend of his, Phil Frye of Chicago, wanted to talk with me. Frye had been one of Veeck's stockholders when Bill owned the Chicago White Sox, and Frye had become one of eight owners of the Chicago Bulls basketball team. I had no idea what Frye would want to talk with me about, but I later learned that he had a summer home in Tryon, North Carolina, just up the road from Spartanburg, and he had come down a number of times to the games. He was very much aware of what we were doing there.

Frye told me that Dick Klein, one of the other Bulls owners, had been acting as general manager. The team was at rock bottom, making no money, and drawing few fans. To fans of the Michael Jordan–Phil Jackson Chicago Bulls, that must sound incredible—but this was 1968. Frye said the owners agreed that changes had to be made. "We want to know if you'd be interested in at least talking to us about being the general manager of the Bulls," he said. "This is not an offer, but it may become one. We'd like you to come to Chicago and talk it over."

What an opportunity! Chicago has always been a great sports town, and this was a chance to run a big pro sports franchise.

A wheezing, gasping, down-on-its-luck franchise to be sure, but I believed that by doing all the right things, we could put the Bulls on the NBA map. I wanted the job. But I also had two years left on my contract with Philadelphia. "Let me call you back," I told Frye.

The first person I talked to was Jack Ramsay. He was intrigued to learn of the approach by the Bulls. He had been negotiating with Chicago all summer in an attempt to get Bulls forward Jimmy Washington, whose hometown was Philadelphia. Jack thought Washington could become a superstar in the right environment—say, in the shadow of Independence Hall. Jack was willing to give up veteran 76er Chet Walker in exchange for Washington, but the talks had been stalemated for weeks.

The Bulls had never mentioned an interest in me during those negotiations with Jack. In fact, no one had ever considered such a thing before—sweetening a trade negotiation by tossing in a front office guy along with the players. But if trading his business manager and a star player to the Bulls could get him Jimmy Washington, Jack Ramsay was all for it. "Sure," he said to me, a plan hatching behind his laughing eyes. "Go ahead and talk to them."

I flew to Chicago for a four-hour interview with the Bulls' brass. One of the owners was Lamar Hunt, one of the Texas Hunts and the owner of the Kansas City Chiefs. I expected Hunt, the architect of the American Football League and the man who gave the Super Bowl its name, to be a big, loud, brash, stereotypical Texas millionaire. Instead, I found him to be more like a college biology teacher—soft-spoken, gentle, a kind and reserved Southern gentleman.

The Bulls' owners told me it was tough for basketball to compete in a town with two major league baseball teams, plus the Chicago Bears of the NFL and the Black Hawks of the National Hockey League. I suggested a few ways we could sell the City of the Big Shoulders on NBA basketball. The owners evidently liked what they heard. A week later, Bulls president Elmer Rich called me and said, "We'd like to make you an offer if you'll visit us again," and he proposed a three-year contract for thirty thousand dollars a year. I would have made the trip overnight on a pogo stick if that's what they had wanted.

I asked Jack Ramsay and Irving Kosloff to release me from my contract. "Are you sure this is what you want?" they asked.

I was sure.

"Pat," said Kosloff, "this past year, you've become more than an employee to me—I think of you as a friend."

"I feel the same way," I said. And meant it.

"And I wouldn't want to get in the way of a friend's career."

"I appreciate that, Mr. Kosloff, I really do."

"Well," added Jack, "I've got the ballclub well in hand, and as much as I appreciate all you've done here, Pat, I think we could spare you—if the Bulls are willing to deal. After all, it seems like we've got something they want—that's you—and they've got something we want."

"Jimmy Washington?" I asked.

"Bingo."

"So if the Bulls will play ball on the Walker-Washington trade . . ." I began.

"Then we'll throw in a guy named Williams for good measure," Jack finished the thought.

"Of course, I have to check with Dick Motta first," I said. Dick was the Bulls' head coach, and if I was going to take the job in Chicago, I didn't want to get off on the wrong foot by trading away one of his best players without his say-so.

So I called Motta, and it turned out that he wasn't all that eager to hang on to Jimmy Washington—and when I told him that Chet Walker was available to play for Chicago, it absolutely lit up his day. Dick had been begging the Bulls' management to trade for Walker—and no one had ever told Dick that the 76ers had offered a Walker-Washington trade. I thought that was a terrible way for the management to treat the head coach. Dick should have been in the loop on all offers involving the acquisition of player talent. He had been burned before when the front office brought in players he couldn't coach, or when some of his key players were dealt out from under him. That was one thing I planned to change. I promised Dick Motta the final word on all future trades, and he was glad to hear it.

Jimmy Washington had a no-trade clause in his contract, but he didn't press it. He was happy to return to Philly and play before the hometown crowds. And he was honored that he was being traded for a player of Chet Walker's caliber.

But we had a problem: Walker didn't want to go to Chicago. He loved the big, loud, raucous crowds in Philadelphia—and he knew that the Bulls scarcely drew five thousand tepid fans on a big night. So I brought Dick Motta out to Philadelphia and we went to Chet's apartment to talk him into going to Chicago. We knocked. And we knocked again. And we knocked some more. No answer. "C'mon, Chet!" we yelled. "We know you're in there. We hear your stereo blaring."

Finally, we went to a pay phone and rang him up. "Aha!" I said when he answered the phone. "You *are* home. Now let us in, Chet. Dick Motta's here from Chicago, and we've gotta talk."

Chet groaned and hung up the phone.

Dick and I walked back up to Chet's place and he let us in. Dick did most of the talking. He spun a beautiful, glowing vision of an entirely new Bulls ballclub built around Chet Walker. He talked about how Chet played Dick's brand of basketball—an aggressive, physical, end-to-end game. He talked about the exciting chemistry he envisioned between Chet and the Bulls' strong cast of supporting players. "Chet," Dick concluded, "you are going to ignite this team. You are going to turn this team around. We need you. I need you. And you need a team where you can be the main offensive option."

It was the most brilliant sales pitch I had ever witnessed. Chet Walker was spellbound. So was I.

And Dick Motta's prediction came true. Chet Walker came to Chicago and became the centerpiece of the Bulls' dramatic turnaround in the late '60s and early '70s. The club had a good, solid nucleus in Jerry Sloan, Bob Love, Tom Boerwinkle, and Norm Van Lier. Dick had known all along that they just needed a strong, aggressive offensive leader to go to when games were on the line. Chet was "da man," the motivator, the spark plug. When he came aboard, he took the Chicago Bulls to the next level. Thirty years later, Chet said, "Pat, thanks for bringing me to Chicago. It was the best thing that ever happened to me."

Although the genesis of that trade had been in the keen strategic mind of Jack Ramsay, to the people of Chicago it looked like I had cut a major trade my first day on the job. In the weeks that followed, as Chet began propelling the Bulls upward in the ranks of the NBA, people gave Pat Williams and Dick Motta the credit for bringing him to town.

## The One-Second Protest

At age twenty-nine, I had become the youngest general manager in professional sports. By my first day on the job, the season opener was less than a month away. I had to set up the office, hire the staff, corral all the players, line up ticket sales and promotions—all while learning the ropes of the organization. My head was spinning—but every night when my head hit the pillow (1.7 seconds before I fell deeply asleep), I thanked God for bringing me to Chicago. I had been content to stay in Spartanburg. Then I had been content to stay in Philadelphia. Each time, the Lord had opened a new door of adventure for me. The Bible says, "Delight yourself in the LORD and he will give you the desires of your heart."[3] Without my making any effort to maneuver or position myself for advancement, God had given me the desires of my heart. I was continually amazed by his goodness.

After only a few days in Chicago, I caught my first sight of Moody Memorial Church—a huge, stately, historic building just a few blocks from the Loop. Deciding that Moody Church might be a good place to begin looking for a home church, I attended worship services that Sunday—and I was sold. The pastor, Dr. George Sweeting (who later became president of Moody Bible Institute), preached straight from the Bible—and straight from the shoulder. It was the kind of no-nonsense Bible teaching that communicated clearly and forcefully on my level as a new Christian. Moody Church became a regular stop whenever I was in Chicago on Sundays. Dr. Sweeting and I became friends, and he invited me to share my story from the pulpit.

There was no Fellowship of Christian Athletes chapter in Chicago, but not long after I arrived, God led several Christian athletes into the area. Don Shinnick and Craig Baynham joined the Chicago Bears football team. Jimmy King came to the Bulls. J. C. Martin, Randy Hundley, and Don Kessinger were already in town playing for the Chicago Cubs. Suddenly there was a nucleus of Christian sports figures, and all of them wanted more outlets for exercising and sharing their faith. In the summer of 1970, a group of us got together and started an FCA chapter. Within a year or so, most of us who founded that chapter had moved on—yet it continued to thrive. God had brought us together to begin a work there, and the fact that it continued without us to this day shows that the work was of God.

My biggest challenge was figuring out how to boost attendance at the games. Our sales director, Dick Gonski, told a story that illustrates the fix we were in at the time. One evening, about half an hour before tip-off, a man came to the ticket booth with his wife and two children. He rapped on the window and woke Dick up from a sound sleep. "I'd like four tickets to the game," the man said. "When does it start?"

If the glass of the ticket booth hadn't been in the way, Dick would have kissed the man and his entire family. "Bless you, sir! You want to buy four tickets—when would you like the game to start? For four tickets, we'll come over to *your* house and play!"

As Bill Veeck always said, "The best promotion is winning," so winning games became job one during my first few months with the Bulls. Dick Motta and I made some more good trades, the team started winning games, and the fans started coming out. We dreamed up some great promotions: Boy Scouts night, merchants night, plus a lot of other stunts and events that were proven crowd-pleasers from my Miami, Spartanburg, and Philadelphia days. About a month into the season, we drew our largest crowd up to that point—more than ten thousand people. The Atlanta Hawks were visiting, and the Bulls were blowing them off the court. The crowd was thunderous. It was quite a party.

Then, in the second half, something went wrong. The Hawks caught fire, making a lot of buckets off Chicago mistakes and turnovers. By the middle of the fourth quarter, Atlanta had closed the gap. Finally, with seconds on the clock, the Hawks surged to a two-point lead. Dick Motta called a time out to talk it over.

The Bulls needed a basket to send the game into overtime. Dick set up the play in the huddle, and the team charged back onto the floor. The ball was inbounded and ended up in the hands of Clem Haskins. He lobbed a brick. The crowd moaned—then roared its approval as Tom Boerwinkle grabbed the rebound. Precious seconds ticked off as he slashed to the hole and laid the ball up.

The ball rolled . . .

And fell through the hoop. It was good! Tie game! We're going to overtime!

The fans went wild. The noise was deafening.

But down on the court, the referees were whistling and shaking their heads.

No good, they were saying. No basket. The game's over. Hawks win.

A stunned murmur replaced the momentary celebration. Then the murmur turned to outrage, Chicago-style. There was shouting and booing, and it looked like some fans were ready to get some rope and string up the refs on the spot.

The refs claimed the basket didn't count because time had run out before Boerwinkle made the shot. Dick Motta charged onto the floor, screaming at the refs and gesturing to the old hockey clock in the rafters. It clearly showed one full second left. That's an eternity in basketball.

I ran onto the floor, collaring a ref (I nearly tripped over his seeing-eye dog) and I none-too-gently attempted to direct his attention to the official clock. One second, ref! One second!

It was a scene of utter chaos. Everyone was yelling, and it went on like that for minutes.

But the officials refused to budge, claiming they had counted the last seconds off to themselves because the noise was so great they couldn't hear the final buzzer. They said they couldn't look at the clock because they would have missed the action at the basket.

So the game ended as a loss for the Bulls.

After the game, we filed a protest with the NBA office, using tape-recorded and photographic evidence to support our claim. No one had ever won a protest in the National Basketball Association, but we knew we were right. For the next two days, the sports pages in Chicago's four major daily papers were abuzz with stories about the controversy—losing that game turned out to be the best thing that could have happened to us. Suddenly the whole town was in an uproar over what had happened to its team! People who had never been to a Bulls game were outraged at the unfairness of the bad call—and they began to get behind the team.

We hosted the Boston Celtics in our next home game. I worked out a promotional deal with Kentucky Fried Chicken, so a lot of fans came hoping to get prizes and free chicken dinners. But even more fans came because of the uproar over the Hawks game. Attendance at the Celtics game was up by three thousand people—about 30 percent—over the previous game. The Celts walked into a buzz saw that night, going up against a psyched-up team and fired-up fans. We routed the Celts, and you could really sense something happening in the city.

The crowds kept growing. A few weeks later, we brought in the Harlem Globetrotters to give a preliminary exhibition before our game against the San Diego Rockets. Only six weeks into the season, we filled all nineteen thousand seats. I could hardly believe my eyes.

The following week, Kareem Abdul-Jabbar came to the Windy City with the Milwaukee Bucks and played to another full house. In December, we offered free basketballs for all the kids who came. Fifteen thousand fans arrived. After three months on the job, I was ecstatic. The Chicago franchise was buzzing with activity and excitement. The NBA commissioner's office later upheld our protest of the Atlanta game. In an unprecedented move, we were allowed to replay the game from the point of the protest. Even though we lost the game in overtime, we all felt vindicated and honored to have been a part of the first protest in NBA history to be upheld by the league. It seemed now that the Bulls were a team the NBA had to take seriously.

Jerry Krause—who is now the highly visible and controversial general manager of the Bulls—was a scout for the team in those days. He's known today in basketball circles as The Sleuth, a nickname I gave him in the early 1970s. I had seen the movie *Sleuth,* in which Laurence Olivier plays a writer of detective novels. The nickname fit Jerry's scouting style—skulking around gyms and locker rooms, listening at keyholes, and hiding behind potted palms, always stealthy and surreptitious. Almost thirty years later, the name has stuck.

## Successful—and Still Learning

Everything was promotion, promotion, promotion—and the result was that we had to jam people into the arena with a shoehorn. If it was clean, legal, and moral, if it would pack 'em in, we would do it.

Before the start of the 1969–70 season, a fan came to my office and introduced himself as Landy Patton, a go-getter real estate developer in his twenties. He loved everything we were doing with the Bulls, and before he left, he said, "If there's anything I can do to help you, just say the word."

Around that time, we created a team mascot—a red bull suit—to breathe a little extra fun into the game. We named the mascot Benny the Bull after our public relations wizard, Ben Bentley. We held a luncheon for season-ticket holders, and we wanted to unveil our mascot there—but we had nobody to wear the bull suit. I thought of Landy and his open-ended offer.

So I whipped out Landy's business card and called him. "Landy, this is Pat Williams," I said. "Remember when you told me you'd do anything to help?"

"Uhhh—"

"Well, I've got a job for you. I want you to put on a bull costume. Then I want you to come out and jump around and act crazy all over this restaurant."

Now, I really had no idea if Landy could pull this thing off, because being a sports mascot is an art—a performing art. It's not as easy as it looks. But as it turned out, Landy was good—so good, in fact, that we made him our permanent man-in-the-Benny-the-Bull-suit. He never took the suit off, and the identity of the man in the suit remained a mystery for years. To my knowledge, Landy Patton was the first team mascot in the NBA.

We also were the first team in the NBA to feature cheerleaders. I revved up a four-girl dance team, put them in costumes, and had them perform at halftimes. The fans loved them, but the girls got tired of it after a few weeks and quit. We never even had time to come up with a name for them.

We were on a constant search for new acts and shows for home games. We heard of one hot, young musical group from Gary, Indiana, so we brought them in to sing the national anthem. The group was completely unknown, but in a short time they would explode on *The Ed Sullivan Show* and elsewhere. So in March of 1970, the Jackson Five—including a very young Michael Jackson—performed on the floor of our arena.

I encountered another famous Jackson a number of times at the games—Jesse Jackson. He was a young Chicago-based social activist who also happened to be a huge basketball fan. He loved to come to the games, go into the locker rooms, and visit with the players.

Gradually, NBA basketball began to capture the imagination of Chicago sports fans. Some of that resulted from our promotional ideas—but a lot of it was due to the improvement of the product on the floor. Chet Walker and Bob Love made a terrific forward combination, Tom Boerwinkle was very effective at center, and Jerry Sloan—one of the most fiercely competitive athletes I've ever known—was the heart and soul of the team. Whenever anyone expressed surprise that the Bulls were finally winning, Dick Motta would say, "Never underestimate the size of Jerry Sloan's heart."

It seemed that everything we did worked. Well, almost everything. There was the matter of the first college draft I had ever been involved with—the 1970 NBA draft. Jerry Krause was the college scout, and he had zeroed in on a promising guard from

New Mexico State, Jimmy Collins. We spent a great deal of time studying and talking to Collins, and we had a good feeling about him. But in late March, as the draft was about to take place, Motta came back from an NCAA regional game all excited about a guard from Texas El Paso. "The guy is brilliant, absolutely brilliant! I want that guy playing for the Bulls!"

"What's his name?" I asked.

"Nate Archibald," said Motta.

"Okay," I said, "let's talk to Archibald and see if he looks like a good fit for the Bulls."

So we got in touch with Archibald the day of the draft, and we told him to wait in his college dorm room for a call. We were interested in him, and we would be in touch with him. Then Dick, Jerry, and I had a meeting and planned our strategy for the college draft: We would take Collins on the first round, and if Archibald was still there when our second round pick came up, we would take him, too. Dick wasn't happy—he *really* wanted Archibald—but he went along. Near the end of our meeting, I said to him, "Dick, tell me this: What happens if Nate Archibald is not there on the second round?"

His reply has haunted me for years: "Then we'll play against him."

The draft began, and we took Collins in the first round. We anxiously awaited our second-round pick—and Archibald was snatched up by Cincinnati just a few picks ahead of us. Dick Motta groaned.

Jimmy Collins never panned out. Two years after we chose him, he was out of the game for good. Nate Archibald went on to have a brilliant fifteen-year career in the NBA and is enshrined in the Basketball Hall of Fame. So that was a learning experience—one of many. A key lesson from that experience was to never look back and let failures get me down. I learned to stay focused on the next challenge, the next opportunity, the next triumph.

Despite all the success we enjoyed with the Bulls, I discovered that the more success came my way, the more I had to learn. Every new level we reached as a ballclub meant new challenges and problems. As the team got better and the crowds got bigger, the job grew bigger. That meant I had to learn to delegate more responsibility to others so I could concentrate my efforts where I was needed most.

Delegating responsibility has never been my strong suit. I learned how to manage a minor league baseball organization by doing it all myself. There were several reasons for that. I didn't have a staff to assign tasks to, I didn't have a budget to hire staff, and I didn't understand that success is a team effort, and if you try to do it all yourself, you wind up as a smoking hole in the ground. So I became a one-man band. I had the keys on my belt, so I had to unlock all the doors. I did all the selling, I did all the game-night promoting, I did all the publicity work. I took the gate receipts to the night deposit at the bank. I even got out the brooms after the game so the cleanup crew would be all ready the next morning. I was afraid to delegate anything, for fear it wouldn't get done right.

But I was also killing myself. Sure, I slept soundly at night—who wouldn't, being so exhausted? But I paid a high price in stomach lining. I knew I should be delegating—but I couldn't bring myself to hand off responsibility. I took those same bad habits into the NBA. I had graduated to the big leagues, but my thinking was still bush-league. For years, I continued banging out press releases and writing promotional materials that easily could have been handed off or farmed out.

It gradually dawned on me that, as the basketball business got bigger and bigger, I had to deal off pieces of my growing job description to other people. I learned I had to push a lot of tasks and decisions down the chain of command. I had to trust people to get the job done, even if it wasn't exactly the way I would do it. I began to realize that, in some cases, the job was getting done *better* than I would have done it. I had hired some pretty competent people, and they were happier and more motivated because they finally felt that I had confidence in them, and they were making a contribution.

I made another big discovery. As I delegated less important stuff, the more important stuff began to come my way. Since I was no longer bogged down in details, I was able to handle larger issues—the kind of stuff only I could handle, the big decisions and tasks I was brought to town to handle in the first place.

A delegator still has to be aware of the details. He has to get reports, stay on top of what's going on, and hold people accountable for their performance. But I'm sure glad I don't have to do it all. I think, to some degree, a fear of delegating is a sign of insecurity and fear. If you trust others to carry out their assignments, you begin to wonder if you might make yourself expendable. The more secure and confident I felt in my job, the more comfortable I became with delegating responsibility.

## Victor and Me

In February 1970, I brought Victor the Wrestling Bear to Chicago. Our publicity man, Ben Bentley, thought he had a great idea for a teaser line in our press release. He wrote, "Though the bear is muzzled, it has not been fed for a month." Wally Phillips, the crazy-man disc jockey on radio station WGN, saw the release and decided to embellish it. He called housewives on the air and told each one that her husband was going to wrestle the bear at the Bulls game. Once he got the poor women worked up and believing his hoax, he'd ask questions like, "Is his insurance paid up?" and "Where would you like the body delivered?"

Of course, it was only a matter of time before the good people at the Anti-Cruelty Society got wind of it. Calls poured into the ACS office and the Bulls office, and people demanded to know what kind of fiends would trap a bear and starve it to death. On game day, we received a telegram from the head of the Humane Society in Chicago, informing us that bear-baiting is illegal in Illinois. The ladies and gentlemen of the press came pounding on my door, demanding to know why the Chicago Bulls were starving a bear.

I wasn't sure how to handle the situation, so I called my mentor, Bill Veeck, and his advice was, "Have fun with it." In other words, since the bear isn't really being mistreated, treat the flap as a joke, string the press along, and milk it for all it's worth. So I went before the reporters and said, "You know, you guys are all worried about the welfare of this big bruin. Don't you think you should focus a little of that sympathy on the poor basketball fans who are putting everything on the line to wrestle that hungry bear?" Veeck's advice was brilliant. The PR we got from that story was like money in the bank—it was all over the papers and broadcast press.

By the time Victor made his appearance, the fans didn't know what to believe. We offered free tickets and prizes for anyone who dared to wrestle him. You didn't have to win, you just had to get out there and rassle. But our publicity had been too effective. Everyone in the stands, every last red-blooded American he-man in that arena, was cluck-cluck-cluck-chicken. We got zero volunteers. Funny what a little publicity can do. Hundreds of people had wrestled that 700-pound pussycat without injury—but that night we had no takers.

The show had to go on, so Ben Bentley and I flipped a coin to see who would go out there first and tackle the bear like Dan'l Boone. I never win coin tosses—never. So I slipped off my jacket and glasses, and stepped out on the floor. I walked up to Victor, praying, "Lord, if you're rooting for this bear, then please make his first blow swift and painless. And Lord, if you're rooting for me, then please send a little miracle my way. But Lord, if you're just not taking sides tonight, then please let these people witness some kinda bear fight tonight, and make this the best promotion of my probably short-lived career."

The hoots and whistles of the crowd rang in my ears as I squared off with the old bruin. I eyed him up and down, mentally taking his measure. He only outweighed me by a quarter-ton or so—I could take him. Sure, I could. It's all a matter of leverage. You just have to—Oops!

Somehow, faster than the speed of thought, I was flat on the floor. I looked up, and there was Victor. I swear that, muzzled as he was, ol' Victor was grinning at me. And his breath! It was as if something had crawled into that bear and died—a few days ago.

I clambered painfully to my feet. "Okay, big guy," I said through clenched teeth, "let's make it two out of three falls, okay?"

He must have understood me, because in the very next instant, he whipped me back onto the floor. As I lay there, wheezing for wind, the bear stood over me and danced a victory jig. So that's why they called him Victor! The crowd loved it. They were yelling for that fuzzball to pin me. Well, that made me mad! That big bruiser had turned my own Chicago fans against me.

I jumped to my feet—

And found myself back on the floor again. The entire bear fight had lasted all of twenty seconds.

"Okay, buster," I groaned, crawling away, my dignity in tatters. "You win."

Ben Bentley went out after I did, and fared no better.

By the end of my first year in Chicago, average attendance had risen from about three thousand per game to easily more than ten thousand. Best of all, the team was winning. The Bulls made it to the playoffs, though the Hawks knocked us out in the first round.

That season was a great confidence-builder. I found out I could run an NBA club. I could even have a hand in taking a bad ballclub and turning it around (working with a great coach, Dick Motta, and a great team, of course). At the same time, I became active at Moody Church and in the FCA, and I had more speaking engagements than I could handle. At each event, I had a chance to talk about my faith with people from all walks of life. I thought, *Man, it doesn't get any better than this!*

We made even more progress in the 1970–71 season. For coaching the club to fifty-one victories in eighty-two games, Dick Motta was named Coach of the Year by the NBA. He earned it. Unfortunately, we were eliminated from the playoffs in round one by the L.A. Lakers. Over the next two seasons, the Bulls would twice make it to the playoffs with fifty or more wins, only to be knocked out of the postseason by the Lakers.

The Bulls really came into their own during the 1971–72 season. Everything seemed to be working on the floor. The team rolled up fifty-seven victories, finishing second in the East to the Milwaukee Bucks. By playoff time, however, injuries had taken their toll, and the Lakers swept the Bulls four straight in the playoffs. Even so, it had been an exciting season. Our winning play and promotions were packing them in, turning the Chicago Bulls into the Cinderella story of the NBA.

It was a fabulous year for me. I was growing deep in my faith and deep in my friendships with other Christians. My life had taken so many unexpected, serendipitous turns lately—it was really an adventure. I wondered what could possibly happen next.

Little did I know the surprise that was just around the corner.

# 6

# Hour of Decision

Forty thousand people! Forty thousand human souls!

I had spoken in churches and civic group meetings, but I had never spoken in front of so many people. I was in awe as I stepped up to the lectern, following the inspired music of Ethel Waters and a gracious introduction by Cliff Barrows. I had been invited to speak at the Billy Graham Chicago Crusade at McCormick Place in June 1971—and it was hard to believe that God had provided such an opportunity to tell others what he had done in my life.

Since the spring of that year, I had been working with the organizing committees for the crusade, helping out with publicity and event planning. I had been content to let God use me behind the scenes, and I could scarcely believe it when the crusade organizers asked me to speak at one of the big stadium events. I felt God had entrusted me with a great responsibility, and I wanted his Spirit to speak through me.

Even now, I can close my eyes and recall the sights, sounds, and feelings of that night at McCormick Place as if it were yesterday. As I began to share my story, I was amazed at the serenity I felt. I talked about the peace of mind and joy Jesus Christ had brought into my life the moment I trusted him that day in Mister R. E.'s office in Spartanburg, South Carolina—and I truly felt a supernatural peace and joy within as I spoke. I talked about how God had turned a driven, self-centered Pat Williams completely inside-out. He had forgiven my sins, taken control of my will, and redirected my life.

I was unaware of one young lady in the choir behind me— but I would soon become aware of her in a big way. Jill Marie Paige had read about me and seen me at Bulls games. She had made up her mind to meet me. Because of the crowds, she didn't get close enough to introduce herself that night—but she was persistent.

Months later, Jill learned I was going to speak at a special Thanksgiving service in Moody Church. I was sitting in the front row, signing autographs for some kids after the service, when this lovely young woman approached me. She was a tall, stunningly beautiful brunette of twenty-two. She was recently graduated from Sterling College, a small Presbyterian school in Kansas, and had just started her first job as an elementary school teacher in a Chicago suburb. "Would you mind signing my program for my third-grade class?" she asked. I was instantly captivated by her luminous eyes and brilliant smile.

I stood and said, "I'd be happy to sign your program—if you would sign mine. Oh, and while you're at it, could you put your phone number by your name?"

I thought I was being so suave, playing my cards so cleverly— and I didn't have a clue that she had actually planned our meeting with that very outcome in mind. Mission accomplished! And Jill Marie Paige wasn't alone in this enterprise. I later found out that her entire family was praying for our first meeting to be successful.

I would also later learn what a gifted, talented young woman she was—a finalist in the Miss Kansas pageant while in college, and a gifted musician. In years to come, she would also display enormous talent as an author, speaker, artist, and home decorator. She remains, in fact, one of the most skilled and capable women I've ever known. Small wonder, then, that eight months later I would want to make Jill my wife.

## Gotta Make a Good Impression

A few days later, I phoned her—but she wasn't home. I gave my number to her mother and asked her to give Jill the message. Her mother wrote down on the telephone pad, "Guess Who called," along with my phone number. When Jill returned my call, she apologized for being tied up all weekend at a Christian youth seminar. Though I didn't like being put off, I was impressed that she was serious about her faith.

Over the next few weeks, I got caught up with work and the usual hectic activity of the Christmas season. I thought about calling Jill—but I was so short of time that I never seemed to get around to it. I got a Christmas card from her, and she wrote a good-luck note inside. Around New Year's, I got another nice card from her.

Finally, a few days after receiving the New Year's card, I called her and asked her out. Using my best Bill Durney sales techniques (and completely unaware of how carefully she had planned all of this), I gave her a choice of options designed to close the sale. "I'd really like to take you out this weekend," I said. "What's better for you—Friday or Saturday?"

She chose Friday, but I'm afraid her dream date turned out more like a nightmare. It was a game night for the Bulls, so I was going to be busy during the game—our date would technically begin after the final buzzer. I left a ticket for Jill, and she came to the game. The Bulls lost, and I am never sanguine about losing, so I was in a down mood. I think Jill was walking on eggshells around me—nervous and insecure. My stormy mood only served to shake her confidence in herself and the relationship. She went home that night and told her mother that our first date had gone badly. "He was just upset about the game," her mother told her. "Just have faith."

A few weeks later, the Bulls played a Sunday afternoon game. Afterward, I came out and found Jill waiting by the gate. "I just came by to say hi," she said, flashing a brilliant smile.

Still feeling guilty about our inauspicious first date, I said, "Well, I'm on my way to an FCA meeting at a church in Evanston—they asked me to speak there. Would you like to go with me?"

"Sure."

I liked her, though I didn't feel anything serious toward her. Still, I was intrigued by the way she kept showing an unabashed interest in me. Later, I discovered that Jill even kept a scrapbook highlighting each step of our growing relationship.

That was late January 1972. For the next few months, right through the summer, I continued to see her about once a month. Clearly, this was not starting out to be a red-hot romance. It was that awkward, tentative, gee-I-gotta-make-a-good-impression stage. When you're too self-conscious to relax and be yourself, you just can't connect. But Jill was persistent, and around May and June, we began to see more of each other. We began to talk about feelings and issues, and I began to look forward to seeing her and talking to her. Soon, I was calling her every day.

## Hour of Decision

Hindsight, they say, is twenty-twenty. Looking back, I can see that the seeds of the problems that would shatter our marriage were present from the beginning. Jill had her plans and her romantic, idealistic expectations of what our marriage should be like—and I don't think those expectations wavered throughout all the years we were married. I have always been very career-oriented and success-driven, and I never pretended to be otherwise. Though Jill undoubtedly wanted me to be successful, she also expected me to be devoted, attentive, and at home every evening and weekend. My career obsession rankled Jill—but her attitude seemed to be, *We can fix that. He can be changed.*

Years later, after Jill and I were divorced, my mom told me, "If Jill thought she was going to change you, I could've told her *that* would never happen." And that's true. Although people do change and grow in many ways over time, a person's fundamental, core personality is usually set at an early age. I was fundamentally a success-oriented workaholic from the time I was quite young, and it was unrealistic of Jill to think she could convert me to a nine-to-fiver.

Today, my advice to people who are considering marriage would be: Take a good, hard, clear-eyed look at each other. Sweep away all the misty, gauzy, romantic illusions, turn off the violin music, and make a list of the things that bother you or nag at you about this person. Ask yourself if you are willing to accept and live with these characteristics and flaws, both the good and the bad, for the rest of your life, day in and day out. Don't ever think you can fix the flaws and that he or she can be changed—that's a prescription for disaster down the road.

If you can accept this person in his or her entirety for a lifetime, then you may have a basis for a lifelong marriage commitment. If you really don't want to spend a lifetime putting up with those differences, then don't put yourself, this person, and any eventual children through that kind of grief. If people would view their relationship with that realism, there would be a lot less pain and a lot fewer divorces.

I would also recommend that people take time to get to know each other well before marriage. Looking back, I realize that Jill and I didn't really know each other well when we got married. For example, I was acquainted with Jill for several months before I learned that she had been in several beauty contests. Raised in a talented and musical family, Jill had won the Miss Western Cook County pageant, which qualified her for the Miss Illinois competition. When she entered the week-long Miss Illinois contest, I sent her flowers and a telegram of good wishes. I went to the pageant in Aurora and watched her perform—and was amazed at how accomplished she was as a violinist and vocalist.

On the last night of the pageant, I sat with her parents as the pageant's emcee, former Miss America Phyllis George, announced Jill as one of ten finalists. When she made the next cut to five finalists, then two, it suddenly hit me: *Ohmigosh, Jill's going to be named Miss Illinois! When that happens, I'll hardly see her for a whole year.* Suddenly, my emotions became mixed. For Jill's sake, I wanted her to win—but for my sake, I was hoping she would come in second.

Phyllis George opened the envelope containing the decision of the judges—

And announced Jill's name as first runner-up.

I was bitterly disappointed for Jill, but she was content with the decision. She took it with a calm acceptance that I never could have felt in those circumstances. "I'm just happy to be involved," she told me.

The next morning, I was shaving while listening to Billy Graham's *Hour of Decision* on the radio. Graham's soloist, George Beverly Shea, was singing in those deep, rich, rolling tones of his: "I'd rather have Jesus than silver or gold; I'd rather be his than have riches untold." I was humming along with the music, and God seemed to reach into my soul through that song. Suddenly, I just felt overcome by emotion, and tears welled up in my eyes.

In that instant, I felt a sense that God was speaking to me, saying, *Okay, big fella, face facts. It's over. She's the one, and you know it.* At that moment, God's will seemed crystal clear: I had found a wife—and I hadn't even been looking.

I didn't exactly propose to Jill. A few days after my *Hour of Decision* revelation, she and I were sitting in the car and talking about our goals in life and our plans. Though we had been spending more time together, the subject of marriage had never come up. So I just casually slipped it into the conversation: "Well, I guess we'll end up getting married." And she just casually took what I had said as a given. Without me asking a question, without her actually answering, I had proposed and she had accepted. I bought her a ring and told her she could go ahead and plan the wedding.

In the time since Jill and I have been divorced, I've often puzzled over that time in my life. I had such an unmistakable sense that God had brought Jill and me together, that Jill was the one woman I would love forever, that this was literally a match made in heaven. Was I wrong? Did I mistake my own emotions for the voice of God? Was I somehow misled into marrying the wrong woman?

Christians sometimes look at the whole issue of marriage from a deterministic rather than free-will point of view. We think that God has one person picked out for us, and our job during the dating years is to sift through all the possibilities until we find that one life partner. That was certainly how I viewed the process when I was a young man.

I realize now that God gives us a lot of leeway—360 degrees of free will, including the choice of whether or not to marry a certain person. Once two people decide to marry, it is up to them to carry out the commitment they have made before God, day after day, year after year, until they are parted by death.

That's why I fought the divorce so hard. I believed that we had made a commitment before God, that he had joined us together, and that we didn't have the right to terminate that commitment.

I believe it was a complex, mysterious fusion of God's assent and human free will that brought Jill and me together—but it was human free will alone that tore us apart. I also believe that God truly did speak to my heart that day as George Beverly Shea sang on the radio. God could have helped us make our relationship work for life—but I also know that God has created the world in such a way that human free will often functions outside the perfect, loving will of God.

When we take it in our hands to run counter to God's will, we make a mess of things, no question. God, in his grace and mercy, will sometimes pick up the pieces of our lives and put them back together in new and surprising ways. It happened in my life. But before I got to the point where God put my pieces back together, I had to go through the most intense emotional pain and struggle of my life. Anyone who can avoid the pain of divorce should do so, because until you've been through it, you have no idea how much it hurts.

Three months after the Miss Illinois Pageant, in October 1972, we were married in Wheaton Bible Church. The wedding date was determined in large part by the fact that I would be free because the Bulls had just started a road trip; my busy times were during home games. I invited all the Bulls fans to come, and nearly a thousand guests showed up. Fortunately, it rained or we might have had a few thousand more. And in case you're wondering, no, we did not have a halftime show.

We honeymooned on Aruba. The fracture between the way I viewed marriage and Jill's perspective showed up right away. Sports is my life, always has been, always will be. I have never gone twenty-four hours without reading a sports page, so I was pleased to find a newsstand at the hotel that carried newspapers from the States. Each night of our honeymoon, I went to the newsstand and bought a paper—and Jill was practically destroyed by that. She wanted 100 percent of my attention on the honeymoon, and she felt that if I showed an interest in sports on the trip, I wasn't interested in her. I figured I could attend to both a bride and the box scores. Taking away sports news was like depriving me of food, water, and air. So it was a difficult adjustment for both of us.

Some of the differences between our expectations were due to the fact that Jill's father had a structured career that allowed him to be home at five every night. She wanted me to keep the same hours. But that was not what my career was about at all. The life of a freewheeling sports exec has its perks, but there is no structure to the job, there are no set hours, and the phone rings day and night. It was something of a culture shock for Jill to come out of her *Leave It to Beaver*–type family and abruptly enter the world of professional sports. Also, when we married, I was thirty-two and she was twenty-three. A big difference in ages can produce a difference in outlook, expectations, perceptions, and maturity.

On the plus side, Jill and I communicated well on a spiritual level. Though I was only a few years old in the faith and she had been a Christian since childhood, we had a lot in common in terms of our spiritual walk. We were both very solid and committed to our faith, yet we considered ourselves learners and fellow strugglers in the Christian walk—not experts or spiritual giants by any stretch of the imagination.

I had waited many years to even consider marriage, and despite some adjustment pains, I felt Jill was worth the wait.

## "Let Him Eat His Contract!"

Some of the best days of my life were spent in Chicago. I loved the city, I loved the fans, I loved the team. I had enjoyed incredible success during my first three years with the Bulls. Working alongside Dick Motta and the rest of the organization, I had a hand in turning a dying franchise completely around, propelling it to the forefront of the NBA.

I don't think Jill really understood the intensity and passion I felt for sports until one night in December 1972, just a couple of months after we were married. The Bulls were playing the Lakers in Chicago Stadium when a ruckus broke out between the two teams over a malfunction of the game clock. I don't recall all the details, but I remember that the call went against the Bulls. Everything broke loose on the floor—including a young general manager named Pat Williams. I jumped out of my seat and waded right into the middle of the court—something I have never done before or since. As my bride looked on in amazement—wondering, *Who is this madman I married?*—I got in the face of referee Mark Mano and expressed my disagreement with the call at the top of my lungs. Looking back, I'm glad David Stern was not the league commissioner at the time—I probably would have ended up being the first NBA exec in history to be fined and suspended from the game.

In 1972, the Bulls were sold to new owners, one of whom called me every day from Cleveland. He ran a company called American Shipbuilding, and he insisted on knowing every decision that was made and why we made it. His name was George M. Steinbrenner III. He was intensely interested in the game of basketball, and he really wanted to be a hands-on owner. The following year, 1973, I read that an ownership group headed by Steinbrenner had purchased the Yankees from CBS. Suddenly, the calls stopped—he never called me again, even though he kept his ownership in the Bulls for years. Today, George lives in nearby Tampa, and I see him from time to time. He's a good friend.

After the new group took over the Bulls, I began to see that my days with the organization were numbered. The owners never expressed any dissatisfaction with my work, but I could see that their philosophy of management and promotion differed from that of the previous owners. Moreover, as we began to experience contract disputes with players and their agents, the headaches of my job began to outweigh the fun. Worst of all, the strain of these disputes eventually ruptured my friendship with head coach Dick Motta, with whom I had enjoyed a great three-year working relationship. Dick and I had worked out a good partnership which protected his coaching relationship with the players. He kept me posted on which players he thought were valuable and deserved more money, and I kept the exact figures from him at his request. But all that was coming to an end.

I always tried to be fair with the players. Unfortunately, there is often a gap between what the front office thinks is fair and what a crowd-pleasing point guard or center (and his commission-hungry agent) thinks is fair. One of the biggest tests of this principle came in our negotiations with star forward Bob Love.

Bob led the Bulls in scoring, and I thought we should pay him accordingly. Though he had signed a contract for $22,000 with us, I went to him six weeks into that season and said, "Bob, I'm tearing up your contract. I'm going to write you a new contract at $5,000 more a year, with another $5,000 raise for the following year." I know that sounds like peanuts in today's market—but remember that this was in 1969. The kind of money I was talking was actually fairly generous then.

The following season, as Bob started his third year with the Bulls, I saw that he was playing with such brilliance and fire that he easily deserved much more than even the raises we had given him. So I scrapped the prior contract and worked up a new five-year pact that jumped his pay to nearly $150,000 a year, including deferred payments and benefits—very good money for an NBA player in the early 1970s.

In the summer of '72, as the club was being sold, I was approached by Bob Love's new agent, who had convinced Bob that he was worth superstar money. Well, maybe he was. I reviewed his contract in light of his accomplishments on the court and said, "Okay, maybe we can work something out." Bob had acquired some debts, and I thought the best solution might be for the Bulls to help pay some of his obligations. The process bogged down as the change of ownership went through, and Bob began to get antsy.

While I was in Chicago, getting close to a deal with Bob's attorney, Bob was in Hawaii, playing an exhibition series with the team. Since he hadn't heard any news on his negotiations for a while, Bob sat down with some sportswriters and blasted me. Soon, the story hit the Chicago papers that Bob Love was accusing Pat Williams and the Bulls organization of foot-dragging and reneging on promises. Meanwhile, Bob was turning in a lackluster performance on the court, compared with previous seasons. Dick Motta asked Bob what was wrong with his game. Bob replied that he was distracted by all the bad feelings he had because Pat Williams had "lied" to him. He wasn't playing well, he explained, because he wasn't "happy."

Dick exploded—righteously. If there's one thing Dick won't forgive in a ballplayer, it is allowing personal problems to affect the team. It didn't matter if Bob was "distracted" or if he was deliberately dogging it to send a message to me—either way, it was inexcusable.

When the team returned to the mainland, Dick came to my office, furious with Bob Love. "Let me take over the negotiations with Love," he said. "I'll tell him he has a choice. He can fulfill his present contract and play like a man, or he can sit on the bench. And if he thinks any other NBA team will touch him after he pulls this crybaby stuff, he's got another think coming." (Dick was right about that. Bob had shot off his mouth in the papers, and all the other teams were leery of hiring a player who would publicly attack the front office. We later tried trading him, and we didn't get a nibble.)

"Dick," I said, "you don't want to insert yourself in the negotiations. You can't go out and coach a guy you've had to haggle with. Let me finalize the deal I've been working on with his agent, and—"

"No way!" Dick hotly insisted. "Why do him any favors, Pat? Haven't you gone out of your way to give him a big raise every year? And didn't he repay you by blasting you in the papers? Look, if that's the kind of gratitude he's going to show, if that's the way he's going to treat this team, then let him eat his contract as is—no new deals."

"I can't do that, Dick," I said. "I promised him a new contract, and the deal is almost finalized. Just let me handle it and get back to coaching, and everything's going to work out fine."

Dick was furious. He wanted Love to pay a price for his disloyalty to the team—and he felt I was coddling him instead. But no matter how Bob Love had behaved, I figured a promise was a promise. I considered it a matter of my personal honor and the honor of the team that we complete the negotiations we had begun. So we did, and Love was temporarily happy. (The following year, after I was gone, Love would again return to the well, with yet another new agent in tow, demanding still more money.)

After this episode, Dick Motta was very cool toward me. We had been good friends and had forged a great partnership that had turned the Chicago Bulls organization around. I was terribly disappointed to see the Bob Love fiasco cause damage to our friendship and our working relationship. Things only got worse when I gave a sizable raise to Clifford Ray, our second-year center. We had signed Cliff for little money, and his bonuses and fringe benefits bumped his rookie-year salary to about $42,000—not bad for your average rookie in 1972, but Cliff was not your average rookie. He deserved better, and I wanted him to get it. Dick didn't see it that way.

Cliff's agent, Richie Phillips, wanted a four-year contract at $500,000. Dick thought it was outrageous, and he didn't want the Bulls to pay it. I thought it was a little steep for the first couple of years, but possibly a real bargain in the out-years if Cliff continued to develop his skills and crowd appeal. With our starting center, Tom Boerwinkle, experiencing knee problems, I thought it wise to nail Cliff down to a fixed amount for four years. If Tom's knee went out, Clifford Ray could name his own salary—and we would have to pay it. So I gambled and signed

Cliff for half a million—and it turned out to be a bargain. Sure enough, Tom Boerwinkle reinjured his knee in training camp, and we relied heavily on Cliff to carry the game in the paint. With Cliff at center, the Bulls never won fewer than fifty games in a season.

Lester Crown, one of the main investors of the new owners' group, gave me a strong vote of confidence. He told me on two occasions that the main reason he had bought into the franchise was because of Dick Motta and Pat Williams. "The day you leave," he said, "is the day I sell my interest in the team." It was the highest compliment I could have received.

Our promotions continued to click with the public, the Bulls continued to win games, and the gate receipts kept climbing. But Dick wasn't happy. Sportswriters kept predicting his departure, right through to the playoffs. It was clear that he was, in fact, shopping for a new job—and the static electricity that was building up in our working relationship was about to discharge with a clap of thunder.

## Demoted and Demeaned

The Milwaukee Bucks and the Los Angeles Lakers ended the season with identical records. Since the Bulls were to play the club with the best record, L.A. and Milwaukee had to meet in a one-game championship. The Lakers balked, claiming that their contracts called for eighty-two regular season games, no more. They refused to play another game before the playoffs. So the league decided to settle the matter with a coin toss to determine which team would play the Bulls. Had the toss gone in favor of Milwaukee, the Bulls would have made the short hop to Wisconsin for the ball game the next night. Instead, the toss went to the Lakers.

I was shocked when the commissioner's office called and told me the Bulls were to drop everything and fly to L.A. the following night for the first game of the playoffs. "You're kidding!" I said. "You can't expect our ballclub to play on the West Coast on one day's notice. We need time to travel, get rested, and practice. This is totally unfair. You're giving the Lakers a huge home court advantage, and guaranteeing that our ballclub will not be in any shape to play."

"Well," said the commissioner's representative, "you don't have to play. You could forfeit."

Infuriated by the take-it-or-leave-it option that had just been handed us, I called Dick Motta and gave him the news. He was silent for several seconds, but I could feel his white-hot (and completely justified) anger radiating from the phone. "This is insane!" he rumbled. "How are we supposed to play our best game under those conditions? While they're at it, they oughta just tie our shoelaces together and cuff our hands behind our backs. I'm getting awful tired of getting kicked around in this league. Why didn't you refuse?"

"I *did* refuse," I replied. "Look, Dick, they told me it was play or forfeit. You want to forfeit?"

"You coulda been tougher, Pat," he snapped. "Don't you ever get tired of being pushed around?"

I tried to cool him down, but it was no use. Finally, I simply wished him well and got off the line.

So the team went to Los Angeles the next night. Ben Bentley, our director of public relations, tried to keep Dick from the press, but there was no stopping him. Dick told the press that the Chicago management was "spineless," that we hadn't backed him in his opposition to the league's decision. The Bulls lost that first game in L.A. but forced the series to seven games before being eliminated by a last-second rally in a heart-stopping finale. It was a tough defeat.

A few weeks later, in May 1973, I was called into Lester Crown's office. I could see he had something on his mind, and he wasted a few minutes with small talk before he got to the point. "What would you think," he began, "of giving up player negotiations so you could concentrate on your promotional specialties?"

I frowned, suddenly suspicious. "Who would handle the negotiations?" I asked, though I already knew the answer.

"Well," said Crown, "since Dick is so close to the situation on the court—"

"I want you to know," I said, "I think that's a terrible mistake. I can't imagine a worse situation for a ballplayer than to have to go out and play for the guy he haggled with about money. There should be a layer of insulation between the coach and the player negotiations so the coach can maintain rapport and respect with the team. Besides, the job of acquiring talent shouldn't be left in the hands of any one person. It's important to keep checks and balances in place. The system's working—why change it?"

Crown sighed. "I see," he said. "Well, thanks for letting me know your views. I'll think it over and get back to you."

A few weeks passed. Then Crown sent word through an intermediary that I was to make an announcement to the press. The announcement was that Dick Motta was taking over the duties of director of player personnel. I would remain in charge of promotion, public relations, and ticket sales. I was stunned, and I was angry. I believed Dick had undermined me and talked the owners into taking away half my job description. It was a demotion—and I felt demeaned and betrayed.

*Okay*, I thought, *the decision is made. It's humiliating—but I still have a job to do.* So I went out and made the announcement without comment. Inside, I felt crushed. Sportswriters questioned me daily about how I felt about the change. I tried to pretend it didn't bother me, but I was angry, and I know it showed despite my denials.

## On the Winning Side

I prayed every day, asking God for victory over my bitterness. I asked my closest friends for their counsel, and wrestled intensely with the situation. I avoided making any decisions or statements until I had my feelings sorted out and under God's control.

I wondered why I was going through this shakeup in my life. I went through weeks of self-pity and soul-searching before it finally hit me: Why *shouldn't* I have some obstacles in my career? Why *shouldn't* I go through testing and refining? I had enjoyed three successful years with the Bulls. Should I feel unfairly treated now that my four-lane highway had turned into a detour through an obstacle course? What about people who *really* had it tough in life—people who had cancer, or who lost their careers, a spouse, or a child? God had been good to me far beyond my deserving. Now things were a little tough— should I stop trusting him? No way.

I realized God's Word had plenty to say about dealing with disappointments and problems. I spent a lot of time with passages such as, "Give thanks in all circumstances, for this is God's will for you in Christ Jesus,"[4] and, "We know that in all things God works for the good of those who love him, who have been called according to his purpose.[5]

I've often been asked if I believe the Christian faith is relevant to the world of professional sports. Isn't religion irrelevant to the issues and problems people face today? No. To me, Christianity is not a religion. It's a person. Christianity is Christ. And he is relevance personified—he is gutsy, contemporary, strong, and real. He is the friend I depend on in my ups and downs.

When I felt undercut and betrayed in my final year with the Bulls, I had a choice as to how to respond. The old Pat Williams would have told off a few people, smashed the glass on top of his desk, ranted and raved, and found some way to get even. But this was the new, changed Pat Williams. I can't take an ounce of credit for the improvement. It's all due to Jesus.

One factor that changed the way I react to difficult circumstances is the assurance that comes from knowing Christ. That assurance enabled me to get through my trying days in Chicago—and, years later, through the calamity of my separation and divorce. That assurance comes from knowing that God is in control of my life. I may not know how all the circumstances will play out tomorrow or the next day, but I know that God has a happy ending planned for me someday. I already know how the game is going to end, so I don't have to worry so much about one bad shot or a foul or a turnover. When the final buzzer sounds, I'm going to be on the winning team.

I remember one night when the Bulls were playing in Phoenix and the game was aired live on a Chicago radio station. Instead of listening to it, I decided to watch a delayed telecast. I have never been able to listen to my own teams on the radio—it's too nerve-racking. For some reason, I feel less nervous and helpless if I can *see* what's happening.

So the evening of the game, I settled in and turned on the delayed telecast. Early in the second half, the game was close and I was enjoying the tension. Soon, I was shouting and carrying on, just as I do in the arena for a home game. Even though I knew the game was over in Phoenix, it was still playing out in front of me on my TV, and it was as good as a live experience.

Then the phone rang. I answered, and it was my secretary. "Pat!" she burbled joyously. "We won! The Bulls won!"

"Thanks, Cathy," I said, trying not to let on that I was disappointed she had spoiled the suspense. I halfheartedly thanked her, then went back to the game.

As I continued watching, I noticed something interesting: Yes, the ending had been given away and the suspense had been dispelled—yet I still found myself enjoying the game. In fact, I was enjoying it in a new way. It was like watching an adventure movie. You know that Indiana Jones is going to win in the end, but it's still fascinating and exciting to see how he does it. The game even had a rousing, nail-biting climax.

What a great feeling to know how the game ends. I know how the game of life ends. I know that God will accept me at the end of my life because I have placed my trust in Jesus Christ. I know that no matter how bad things get, Jesus will return one day and set everything right. Job hassles, personality clashes, anger, hate, bigotry, violence, crime, political corruption, scandal, economic uncertainty, natural disaster, war—none of these things matter in the final analysis. They are painful, they cause us anxiety and fear, but they are not the end of the story.

Jesus is on the way. He'll beat the final buzzer—of that I have no doubt. So I can't lose. I'm on the winning team. That's the source of my confidence and assurance, even in tough times.

Is the truth of God relevant to the world of sports? No question. Is the Christian faith an essential part of my life, including my life in the NBA? Absolutely. It was proved to me during the waning days of my tenure as general manager of the Chicago Bulls, and it has been confirmed to me again and again ever since.

As the truth of God's Word began to work its way into my spirit, the bitterness I felt toward the Bulls' ownership and Dick Motta began to drain away. I was able to look at my situation with greater clarity. I began to see that it was time to move on—not because I was bitter and angry over being mistreated, but because God had something else planned for me. I just needed to open my eyes to what he wanted to do next in my life.

Soon after I had this realization, a sportswriter asked how long I would be happy as a "ticket salesman." I smiled and said, without any bitterness or resentment, "Not long." And it felt good to finally voice it out loud. I had promised the Bulls my loyalty for as long as I was a part of the organization—but it was clear that my days with the organization were coming to an end. I was approaching yet another hour of decision.

# 7

# Gone with the Wind

Multimillionaire Arthur Wirtz, the Bulls' principal owner, was asserting himself more and more intrusively as the year went on. That, of course, is an owner's prerogative—but history has shown that the owners of successful teams know how to hire good people to run the organization, and they trust those people to do a good job. I had proven I was good at what I did, and so had the other people in the Bulls organization—but, despite our successes, Art Wirtz didn't trust us to do our jobs.

Wirtz was an intimidating, all-business workaholic. His business and real estate investments were wide-ranging, and included the Chicago Stadium and the Chicago Black Hawks hockey team. Though well into his seventies, he worked fourteen hours every day. At 6'6", 300 pounds, he was a dour, imposing man who thought that all the halftime hoopla I came up with week after week was just a lot of baloney. He raised prices, which caused attendance to drop even while the Bulls were enjoying their best season ever. His philosophy of running a ballclub violated everything I had learned from people like Mister R. E., Bill Veeck, and Bill Durney—and it violated all the successful experience I had enjoyed in my short but meteoric career.

I once asked Bill Veeck about Arthur Wirtz, and he replied, "Wirtz wouldn't give you the right time of day if he had twenty wristwatches on."

## Whistling Dixie

Around this time I received calls from two people who had heard about my situation in Chicago. One was Frank Cashen, president of the Baltimore Orioles. Right on the phone, he offered me the general manager's job with the Orioles. It was a chance to get into major league baseball—and it was very tempting.

The other was Tom Cousins, president of the Omni group, which owns the hockey and basketball franchises in Atlanta. I had known Tom when he was principal owner of the Hawks for a few years before joining Omni. I knew he was a smart businessman, a genuine sports enthusiast, and a dedicated Christian. "I've been following your situation there in Chicago," he said. "You haven't said much, but I can read between the lines. You're not very happy about it, are you?"

"No, Tom, I'm not."

"Would you be interested in talking with us about joining our organization?"

I liked the city of Atlanta—and I like the idea of a new challenge. "Tom, I would definitely be interested—and I'm honored that you asked."

So I had two very interesting possibilities on the table. Baltimore had a great championship team. These were the Orioles of Brooks Robinson, Frank Robinson, Earl Weaver, and Jim Palmer. Though the team was doing well, it was struggling with the promotional side and not filling the stadium. I called Bill Veeck, and he cautioned me about Baltimore. "It's always been a tough place to promote baseball," he said. "Even with a winning team, you might find it tough to succeed there."

I went to Atlanta and met with the Omni group—and made up my mind quickly. This hour of decision only lasted a few minutes. They offered a three-year deal with good money— $55,000 the first year and $5,000 escalators each additional year. It meant an opportunity to work in a new city, a new arena, with a lot of growth potential. I grabbed it. Little did I know that I was walking into another buzz saw.

I called Frank Cashen in Baltimore and thanked him for considering me for the job with the Orioles. "My time is ended here in Chicago, but there's an offer in Atlanta that I've decided to take. I feel I want to remain in the NBA." He wished me well, and the decision was set. I didn't even go to Baltimore for an interview—though there would be times in Atlanta when I would wish I'd at least looked at the Orioles job.

Once the decision was made, I went home and said, "Jill, we're packing and leaving. We're going to Atlanta."

Jill was stunned. She didn't know what was going on. I had never talked with her about my problems with the Bulls organization. She knew I had pressures, but she thought it was the normal stuff that went with the territory. Suddenly, we were moving—and she hadn't had a clue that this was coming. I explained the situation, and she said, "Well, I'm your wife. I'll go wherever you go."

Next, I went to the office and tendered my resignation. Soon after that, Arthur Wirtz summoned me to his palatial office at the Furniture Mart on Lakeshore Drive. When I walked in, he had a document laid out, waiting for my signature. It was a lot of cold legalese about the termination of my relationship with the Bulls. Everything was in order, so I signed. If I had expected Wirtz to shake my hand or thank me for all I had done or even say, "Good luck," I would have been disappointed. But I expected none of that, and he did none of that. He simply picked up the document, turned his back without a word, and walked away.

Thus ended my association with the Chicago Bulls.

Just before I left town, I got a call from the fabulous Harry Caray, the voice of the Chicago White Sox. "Pat," he said, "you can't leave town without talking to everybody. Come out to

Comiskey Park and let me interview you." So my last act in Chicago was to be interviewed on live TV at the White Sox ballpark by Harry Caray—then I was off to Atlanta.

It was a good time to move on. I had a few weeks to prepare for the opening of the basketball season in Atlanta, and I was looking forward to the challenge. As we packed our belongings for the move to Georgia, I had a big, silly grin on my face, and I couldn't keep from whistling, "Oh, I wish I was in Dixie, away, away."

## Hit the Ground Running

During our first week in Atlanta, we found a beautiful three-bedroom apartment and began furnishing it. I immersed myself in getting acquainted with the Atlanta Hawks organization and setting up my office. I began lining up promotions, getting player negotiations under way, and checking out my new surroundings. We liked the Atlanta weather and the Atlanta people. We quickly found a church home, First Baptist Church, where a young Bible teacher named Charles Stanley had just begun his ministry as pastor.

There was also time to take in some memorable Braves games. We saw Hank Aaron increase his lifetime home run total to 713 by the end of the 1973 season—and the following year, we would be sitting in the stands when Hank broke Babe Ruth's record. I was invited to share my story at a number of pregame chapel services for visiting teams who came to play the Braves. Soon after I came to town, I found myself heavily booked with speaking engagements before civic groups and community organizations. I never passed up an opportunity to go someplace and promote the Atlanta Hawks—and to promote Jesus Christ. I usually found some way to share my faith, no matter the gathering.

One of my greatest honors was to be invited to speak in chapels for such teams as the Cincinnati Reds and the Houston Astros. Sparky Anderson, manager of the Reds (and a friend from my Spartanburg days), would close the locker room doors and call everybody together. For Sparky, chapel was mandatory. Everybody sat in front of their lockers and Sparky introduced me and gave me ten minutes. I talked about God's love and concluded, "I challenge you with the adventure of having Jesus Christ in your life as your lord and friend. When you play the game for God, you'll be a better ballplayer. But best of all, when you know him, your past is forgiven and your future is sealed. All you need to concern yourself with today is doing your best for God."

At the chapel service for the Houston Astros before the last game of the regular season in Atlanta, I met pitcher Jerry Reuss, who had served up the pitch for Hank Aaron's 713th home run, and Dave Roberts, the left-hander who had the forbidding task of facing Hank Aaron on the last day of the season.

I spoke on Mao Tse-Tung's "Four Absolutes," his plan for capturing the world for atheistic communism. Now, you might think that's a pretty weird choice for a sermon text—but I think those four absolutes make a great basis for living out the Christian faith: absolute acceptance, absolute dedication, absolute discipline, and absolute action. If Christians would be as serious about Jesus as the Chinese communists were about their ideology, maybe Christianity would be a stronger force in the world.

I made a lot of friendships in Atlanta that are still important to me. I quickly became good friends with our broadcaster for the Hawks games, a young man named Skip Caray. Skip went on to become one of the most prominent baseball announcers in the nation—and we later hired his son Chip as a broadcaster in Orlando. One of my first interviews in Atlanta was with a young Christian broadcaster who was just starting out, working from a studio in a little Quonset hut on the edge of Atlanta. Little did I realize that the young broadcaster would eventually become the host of TV's "700 Club"—Pat Robertson.

I was also invited to speak at a chapel service for a new company that had been founded by a man named Cecil Day. Today, that company is a worldwide hotel chain—Days Inn. At a luncheon in a downtown Atlanta club, I was introduced to the owner of a small UHF television station in Atlanta—a brash, bombastic young man with big plans. Today, that man—Ted Turner—is one of the biggest forces in broadcasting worldwide.

For our first game of the season, I invited Gov. Jimmy Carter to the Omni to give the opening prayer, which he was happy to do. That night, as the governor stood at center court and prayed, Jill and I sat in the stands behind the basket with the governor's five-year-old daughter, Amy. Less than three years later, Amy and her parents were living in the White House.

To this day, some of my happiest memories are of my exciting, whirlwind days in Atlanta and the many friendships I made in that city. The gracious Southern hospitality we experienced reminded me so much of the hospitality of Spartanburg and made the transition to our new home smooth and enjoyable.

## Pistol Pete

In 1973, the Atlanta Hawks were in transition. I wasn't coming to resuscitate a dying team as I had in Chicago. I had been hired to add some extra horsepower to a team that had never reached the top, but which had been an annual playoffs contender for more than a decade. When I came aboard, the team seemed poised for a promising season.

So it was a shock and a disappointment when, just a few games into the season, the team began to unravel. During my four years in Chicago, the Bulls had never lost more than three straight games. The first time the Hawks lost four in a row, I went into a blue funk. We lost sixteen of our first seventeen road games after New Year's Day. How could this happen? We had a lot of talent, and the players were coached by a brilliant motivator, innovator, and strategist, Cotton Fitzsimmons. But for some strange reason, the team just didn't jell. The players couldn't get in sync to win. And my "brilliant" ideas for promoting the team only backfired and made things worse.

My plan was to televise all of the road games to the Atlanta fans. I figured if enough people saw Lou Hudson, Walt Bellamy, and Pistol Pete Maravich in action on their TV screens, they'd come out to cheer them on the home court. Problem was, out of our first twenty-four televised games, we won four and lost twenty. That didn't exactly inspire the good people of Atlanta to line up at the ticket window.

Fitzsimmons found losing hard to swallow. He tried every conceivable way to psych up his players, but nothing worked. One night, he focused his pregame pep talk on the word pretend. "Guys," he said, "I want you to *pretend* that you're the greatest basketball team in the world. And I want you to *pretend* that this game is for the NBA championship. And I want you to *pretend* that instead of a three-game losing streak, we're on a three-game winning streak. Now go get 'em!"

The Hawks raced out onto the floor—

And took one of their worst whippings ever from the Boston Celtics. Fitzsimmons was shattered. As he trudged off the floor, our all-star guard, Maravich, dashed past him and slapped him on the back. "Cheer up, Coach," he called. "Just *pretend* we won!"

Near the end of the '73–74 season, I was talking to Fred Rosenfeld, an L.A. attorney who was also one of the owners of the New Orleans Jazz, a newly created NBA expansion franchise hungry for top-drawer talent. "We need to talk about Pete Maravich," he said. "You know, Pete went to Louisiana State, and our fans just love him. It would sure help us get this team off the ground if we could put a hometown legend on the home court."

Rosenfeld was dreaming. "You don't have enough money to acquire Pete Maravich," I said, laughing. Fact is, we really did want to trade Maravich—but to the Jazz? What did they have that the Hawks would want? Pete was a great player, but he had been suspended by the team for a couple of games during the season because of some bad behavior at a Houston hotel (Pete later became a Christian and cleaned up his act). With Pete or without him, the team wasn't winning many games.

Cotton Fitzsimmons had his hands full with Pete Maravich. He had a tough time keeping him under control and playing within the team's system. Pete was a marvelous talent, an exciting player to watch, but he was not coachable, he was not disciplined, he didn't listen. He was a thrill-a-minute wonder—but he made life hard on those around him.

The losses we experienced that season showed that we didn't have a well-balanced, well-harmonized team—just one red-hot, run-and-gun performer plus four other guys who ran up and down the court and watched him shoot. If we could get a couple of more talented players, we believed we could ignite the entire team—but no other teams in the NBA were willing to offer two starters in trade for Pete.

In the weeks after that conversation, Rosenfeld kept calling, wanting to make a deal for Maravich. As an expansion franchise, the Jazz could choose one player each from the rest of the teams in the league before the college draft. But because each NBA team had the right to protect its seven top players, the best New Orleans could do was field a team of eight men—the kind of talent the rest of us in the NBA would consider substitute players. We weren't about to trade Pete for any amount of money and a couple of subs. But Rosenfeld kept calling, and each time he called, his offers got more creative. In exchange for Pistol Pete, he offered players, draft picks, cash, trading stamps, baseball cards, jazz trumpeter Al Hirt, and a lifetime supply of crawdad gumbo and catfish meunière.

Finally, Rosenfeld called with a suggestion that was the perfect yes-yes solution to his problems and mine. As I listened, I realized we were on the verge of making one of the biggest deals in the history of professional sports. I had Cotton sit in as we negotiated over the phone. I wanted our head coach to have the final say on any talent we acquired or lost. So in one ear, I had Cotton telling me what he needed, and in the other ear, I had Rosenfeld telling me what he could offer. I ran Rosenfeld's offer by John Wilcox, president of the Omni ownership group, and he said, "Don't take any more from them. If New Orleans gives you one more concession, we'll bust their franchise and those draft picks won't be worth anything."

It was a sweet deal for our side—yet I also knew that Rosenfeld could hardly believe his own good fortune: he had landed

Pete Maravich! Yes, the price tag was steep, but the deal would be a big money-maker for New Orleans in the long run.

In exchange for Pete, we got the right to draft the first guard and forward in the expansion pool, which gave us Dean Meminger from New York and Bob Kauffman from Buffalo. We also got New Orleans' first-round draft choices in '74 and '75, their second-round choices in '75 and '76, and—in '76 and '77—the option of using their first choice or ours, whichever was most advantageous. In effect, we got eight top draftees who could, over four or five years, be worth an entire franchise. And we had an added advantage: By taking so many top New Orleans draft picks, we made sure their club was bound to finish low in the standings for a few years, which meant their draft picks (which we were acquiring) would be among the first and most valuable each year.

I was nervous as I drove over to Pete's apartment to give him the news. His contract included a no-trade clause, so we couldn't trade him unless he approved. I hesitantly laid out the deal we had made. Pete listened, frowning. Finally he said, "What did you get for me?"

I listed all the concessions New Orleans had made—the players, the draft picks, the money, Al Hirt, the gumbo, everything. It was the deal of the century—but Pete Maravich was insulted.

"That's it?" he complained. "That's all you got for me?"

He resisted the deal at first. He said he should have been informed during the negotiations—an understandable reaction. But I pointed out that it was in everybody's best interests to keep the talks secret. If the deal had fallen through, the Hawks organization would have looked silly and Pete would have been offended for nothing. In the end, Pete negotiated a new, more lucrative contract with New Orleans and everyone was happy—and nobody was happier than me.

There's a postscript to the story. The Atlanta Hawks never realized the benefits of the incredible deal we made. After I left the Hawks organization, my successors inexplicably failed to sign all the draft picks we had gotten from the Jazz. The Hawks could have become one of the dominant NBA teams of the late

1970s. I've never understood why they let the opportunity slip through their fingers.

## Baby Makes Three

The private line in my Atlanta office rang at around noon one fall day in 1973. I picked up the phone and heard Jill's emotion-filled voice. At first I was concerned—I couldn't tell if she was laughing or crying. As it turned out, she was laughing *and* crying! She could hardly speak—then I made out three words. "Happy anniversary, Daddy!" she said.

"Jill," I stammered, "do you mean—are you—are we—I mean—really?"

"Dr. Harrison told me I'd better get out my knitting needles," she said. I started laughing with joy, and Jill continued to cry with joy. We had prayed for months about starting a family. This was the Watergate era, a tense and pessimistic time. We weren't sure exactly what kind of world we were bringing a child into, but the Lord knew best. We hadn't picked the time for this baby's arrival in the world—but he had.

That weekend—our first anniversary weekend—we took off for Orlando and Walt Disney World. We celebrated our first year together and the approaching adventure of parenthood. Come June of 1974, when that baby was to be born, we would no longer be able to just pick up and take off, but we didn't care. This couple was going to become a family. Little did I imagine how large a family we would eventually become!

On the job at the Omni Arena, I continued to promote my brains out. We showed off a 130 pound pumpkin during a Halloween costume contest. We gave discounts to the fans with the biggest feet when the Detroit Pistons' Bob Lanier (and his size 22 gunboats) came to town. When the little shooting guard, Nate Archibald of the K.C. Omaha Kings, came to play, we had Mighty Mite Night. For contrast, we had Sky High Night for the tall folks. One night, we even gave a free ticket to a fan who claimed he had been discriminated against because he was "too average!" We honored two of our players, John Wetzel and John Tschogl, with a Wetzel-Pretzel, Tschogl-Bagel Night where we gave every fan the choice of a pretzel or a bagel.

But we needed more than fun promotions to bring in the fans. We needed to win games—and we were losing more than we won. As the crowds continued to dwindle, I became terribly frustrated.

Even worse, I discovered that my job situation in Atlanta was even more tenuous than it had been during my last year in Chicago. If I had done my homework a little better, I would have learned that the Hawks organization was a revolving door for marketing, sales, and managerial people—they were hired and fired in rapid succession. I began to realize that, even though I had a three-year contract, the skids were greased— the owners didn't have confidence in me. They made me feel like I didn't know how to put one foot in front of the other. That year in Atlanta turned out to be every bit as unpleasant as my final year in Chicago.

Still, I could be thankful for many things. I was eager to meet my new son or daughter—I didn't care which as long as he or she was a sports fan. It was one of the thrills of my life to go with Jill to the doctor's office and hear that little heartbeat for the first time. No frustration in my job could quench the joy of knowing that our first child was on the way.

Also during this time, I authored my first book, working with Jerry Jenkins. *The Gingerbread Man* was my autobiography as the youngest executive in the NBA. It was a relatively short book—but, of course, I had lived a short life by that time.

Our son was born at 5:13 P.M. on Monday, May 27. I was there from labor to birth, and it was the most awesome worship experience I'd had up to that point. I would relive that experience three more times when our birth children were born, and I had a different but equally profound feeling when we received our fourteen adopted children into our lives. I can't imagine how an atheist can watch a baby being born without going through a spiritual conversion on the spot.

When the doctor said, "We've got a boy here," I thanked God for his goodness. We named our little boy after my two fathers—

my birth father, Jim Williams, and my spiritual father, R. E. Littlejohn, who was largely responsible for bringing about my second birth as a Christian. James Littlejohn Williams was born on the day of the NBA draft, so I decided to get my little son off to a good start in pro sports.

In the tenth round of the draft, as execs from the league office and the other clubs listened via a conference-telephone hookup, I announced the next choice of our team. "The Atlanta Hawks select James Williams," I said.

"James Williams?" someone cut in. "You mean Fly?" Jim "Fly" Williams was a junior at Austin Peay, and drafting him would have been a rules violation.

"What school?" asked Si Gourdine, assistant to the commissioner.

"Piedmont Hospital in Atlanta," I replied. "He's nineteen and a half inches tall, seven and a half pounds." There was a moment of surprised silence on the line.

Then Gourdine deadpanned, "Disallowed."

## Warning Signs Ignored

Though I didn't see it at the time, the next few days foreshadowed the eventual breakup of our marriage some twenty years later. Because I was so busy with the draft and other activities with the team, the only time I spent with Jill at the hospital was a brief visit on the way to the office each morning. I didn't appreciate how much Jill was suffering from postpartum depression and how isolated and abandoned she felt. Fortunately, Jill's mother came down from Chicago and helped with the baby.

For several weeks, I got the silent treatment from Jill. When I asked her what was wrong, she answered, "Nothing's wrong," in a tone that conveyed, *"You* figure it out."

Clueless, I persisted in trying to open a dialogue with her. Finally, she told me, "You should have visited me more in the hospital."

*Oh, so that's it. Didn't she know what I was up against at work?*
"You know I was very busy," I replied defensively.

"Too busy to visit your own wife when she's just had your child?"

"Okay," I admitted reluctantly—and halfheartedly. "I should have spent more time with you."

"So you realize you were wrong?"

*Hey, anything to keep the peace.* "If you say I was wrong, then I was wrong."

"That's not good enough," she returned coldly.

"Whatever you say."

I passed it off as one of those new mother things. Jill would get over it. She just didn't understand the magnitude and complexity of my job.

Over the next few years, Jill and I settled into a pattern in which she would feel neglected and respond by giving me the silent treatment or badgering me about something I had done or failed to do. My part of the pattern was to say whatever was necessary to keep the peace. We didn't honestly and respectfully discuss our relationship. If she was upset, I'd say, "Tell me what you want me to do." She'd tell me, and I'd do it for the sake of tranquility.

Neither of us was solving the root problem, and neither Jill's way nor my way was a healthy way to deal with conflict in a marriage.

## Gone with the Wind

I had a difficult time with the man in charge of the Omni group, John Wilcox. He was a career lawyer, and he didn't really understand the sports business—especially the entertainment aspect. Wilcox was in charge of the arena and the basketball and hockey teams. He was a demanding personality, and a lot of people in the front office had their struggles with him.

The turning point for me came in February 1974. I had come up with a Saturday night halftime promotion with a guy named

Uncle Heavy and his Pork Chop Review—a hilarious trained pig act. Uncle Heavy's porkers could sit up on command, whoosh down slides, jump through hoops, just like a trained seal or dog act. Best of all, it was funny. Sure, it was belly-laugh stuff, not highbrow humor by any stretch, but the fans loved it. Uncle Heavy got more laughs and applause than just about any act we ever brought in. I thought it was one of our best promotions ever—but there was one man who didn't share that opinion.

The following Monday morning, I went into the office feeling very pleased. On my desk was a note summoning me to John Wilcox's office. I went in and found him not merely angry but beside himself with rage. "That pig act," he said, "was the most embarrassing fiasco anyone has ever inflicted on this arena! It was an absolute disgrace!"

Apparently, Wilcox had invited some of his friends to the game, and they had all been offended by Uncle Heavy. Well, Uncle Heavy would have been right at home at every other team I had managed, from Spartanburg to Philly to Chicago. Somehow, my trained promotional instincts told me that, given a choice between Uncle Heavy and a string quartet performing a Mozart concerto, most of our fans would have gone for the pigs. A basketball game is supposed to be fun, not a culturally uplifting experience.

From that moment on, I was in deep trouble with John Wilcox. The season continued in dismal fashion, with more restrained and "tasteful" halftime shows—and a losing ballclub.

It was a difficult experience for me, undergoing severe opposition and even failure, first in Chicago and then in Atlanta. From Spartanburg to Philly through my first three years in Chicago, I had been on a steady rise, enjoying success after success. Then—two failures in a row. At this point, I had been a Christian for only six years—still a youngster in the faith. Failure had not been a part of my theology. I had assumed that being a Christian meant being protected by God against falling on your face. I was wrong—big-time.

As unsettling and painful as they were, my troubles helped take me to the next level of spiritual maturity. I went through a time of asking God, "What are you doing with me, Lord? Why is all this happening?" And I emerged from it with the realization that God was using these tough circumstances to produce something good in me—a realistic toughness for times of trial. After that experience, I was able to go into one-on-one encounters with people or speak before crowds and say with authenticity, "Until you go through the fires, God really can't use you."

I discovered that God wanted me to learn to be more dependent on him. I learned more about him during those two years of adversity than in all my years of success and good times. One of the Scripture verses that came to mind often through my trying experiences was 1 Peter 5:6–7: "Humble yourselves, therefore, under God's mighty hand, that he may lift you up in due time. Cast all your anxiety on him because he cares for you."

One day, my office phone rang, and it was Irv Kosloff, owner of the 76ers, calling from his daughter's home in Phoenix. The general manager's slot at the 76ers was open—was I interested?

Was I ever! I was ready to pack and go in a heartbeat. So I arranged with Kos to interview for the job. Irv knew me well, he knew how I worked, and he trusted me to get the job done. Philly was like home to me, and I told him I was ready to come home.

Throughout our year in Atlanta, I had not told Jill anything about the problems, pressures, and frustrations I was laboring under. She had the impression that everything was going along smoothly. I thought I was protecting her. But when she learned that I had been keeping my feelings and problems from her for months, she felt hurt. We were not openly sharing with each other, which is what intimacy in marriage is all about.

I didn't tell her I was thinking about a move back to Philadelphia until I had nearly finalized my decision. In the summer of 1974, I boarded a plane for Philly to visit the front office and interview for the job. I told Jill that if anyone called, she should not tell anyone where I was going or why. Sure enough, while I was gone, Philly sportswriter Phil Jasner called and asked Jill if I was talking with the 76ers about the general manager position. "You know, his mother lives close by in Delaware," she said. But the writer wasn't fooled. He took it as a yes.

I accepted the job in Philly, and I had no trouble breaking my contract. John Wilcox was no more happy with me than I was with his organization. So we were finally out of each other's hair. A year or so after I left, so did John Wilcox and much of the front office staff. The entire Atlanta organization was dismantled and rebuilt from scratch. As much as I loved the city of Atlanta, I was never more glad to get out of any job as I was to escape that one. I felt fortunate to get out when I did and land on my feet in Philly.

So after only one year in Atlanta, I was gone with the wind. I was on my way back to the City of Cheese Steaks, Soft Pretzels, and Brotherly Love.

Here I am at age twenty-two in the dugout at Miami Stadium. June 1962, my first day on the job in professional athletics.

Miami Stadium, 1962. Bill Durney, the general manager of the Marlins, my first pro team. Bill was a great friend and teacher.

In 1967 we won the Larry MacPhail Promotional Trophy for the top promotional job in minor league baseball. I caught up with the great baseball executive himself to pose for this photo in 1968. I was twenty-eight at the time.

1967. A publicity shot with Paul Anderson, the Strongest Man in the World. This is the photo Paul signed, "From your friend in Christ."

Bill Veeck, my hero. I really modeled my sports executive style after his.

Mr. R. E. Littlejohn, the owner of the Spartanburg Phillies and the man who had such a powerful impact on my life.

This is Dr. J, one of the classiest athletes I've ever known.

Billy Cunningham took on the 76ers coaching duties in 1977.

A dream week event in Florida. What a treat to be behind the plate catching the great Bob Feller.

In April 1987 the NBA awarded us an expansion franchise and the Orlando Magic was born. Stewart Crane, Jimmy Hewitt, and I join the celebration in downtown Orlando.

We tried to bring major league baseball to Orlando in 1991. I'm back on the stump again hustling tickets, trying to rally the community.

July 1998. We announce Carolyn Peck as the coach–general manager for our new WNBA franchise. Our president, Bob Vander Weide is on the far right. Cari Coats, vice president of marketing, is on the far left.

April 5, 1997. There haven't been too many wedding pictures that look like this one.

May 1998. Just before selling WNBA tickets to a women's group, I donned a hairpiece and hat to get a few laughs. Anything for the cause.

This photo is my pride and joy. I was invited to Ted Williams' eightieth birthday party in Ocala, Florida, summer of 1998.

Ruth and I have a nice chat with one of my heroes, the late Og Mandino. This was at a convention in Orlando in 1996.

# 8

# The Rainbow Chasers

When I returned to Philadelphia in August 1974, it had been five years since I had left the 76ers organization—and a lot had changed. It was hard to believe that this was the same team that had won an NBA championship and finished the '66–67 season with a 68-13 record. The team I found in 1974 was ready for last rites.

The Sixers' win-loss record in the '72–73 season was 9-73. No, that's not a typo. I said 9 wins and 73 losses. When the team had back-to-back days off, they called it a winning streak. The team was so bad, it was nearly impossible to recruit new players. Marvin Barnes, who was an All-American at Providence, refused to sign when he was drafted by the Sixers in 1974. "I'll work in a factory before I'll play ball in Philly," he said. He ended up going to the NBA's rival league, the American Basketball Association. The Sixers were devastated.

Coach Kevin Loughery and general manager Don DeJardin left Philly after the '72–73 season. Gene Shue was brought in as coach—but they didn't even bother filling DeJardin's slot. Gene tried to handle both positions, and he did a good job, under the circumstances. In the '73–74 season, the Sixers finished with a 25-57 record—still abysmal, but a definite improvement over the previous season.

As I arrived in town with my wife and six-week-old son, I was excited about this new direction in my life. The situation was much like the one I found in Chicago. Philly is a big, loud, brawling town with a rich sports tradition—just like Chicago. And like the 1969 Bulls, the 1974 Sixers were down, demoralized, and defeated. There was no place to go but up! I love a challenge—and that's exactly what awaited me. There are few sports jobs as demanding as rebuilding a team from rock bottom. So my work was cut out for me—both in rebuilding the team and in rebuilding the promotional and entertainment side of the organization.

One interesting memory of those days is of Halloween 1974. As we were getting ready for a home game with the New York Knicks, I was swamped with details for our Halloween Night promotion, such as the apple-bobbing and pumpkin-pie-eating contests. The phone rang, and it was Barry Abrams, a record promoter who worked part-time at our games. "Pat," he said, "There's a young recording artist I'm working with who has just recorded a song. Could you play it at the game tonight?"

"Gee, Barry," I said, "that's not the kind of thing we usually do—"

"You'd sure be doing the young man a favor, Pat—and you'd be doing me a big favor, too."

"Okay," I said. "Have him look me up tonight before the game." I hung up and completely forgot about it. Later that night, a skinny guy with a mop of hair came up to me. "Are you Mr. Williams?" he asked. "Barry Abrams told me to ask for you." I stared at him blankly, vaguely remembering I had talked to Barry, but unable to recall what we had talked about. "I brought my tape," the fellow continued, holding up a cassette. "Can you play it at the game tonight?"

Then I remembered. "Oh, yeah," I said. "You're the guy with the song." I instantly regretted my promise to Barry. "Kid, are you sure you want your song played in a basketball arena? The acoustics are horrible, and people don't come to a basketball game to hear music."

186

"I take these tapes everywhere," he replied, "to radio stations, baseball games, basketball games, school dances, birthday parties, anyplace. If I get enough people to hear my tapes, some are gonna want to buy my records."

"Okay," I said. "See those guys in the sound booth? Tell 'em you talked to me and I said it's okay to play your tape."

"Thanks!" the young man said brightly, then dashed off toward the sound booth. I promptly forgot about it and went back to work.

That night, during one of the time-outs, I noticed a song on the PA, a smooth easy-listening ballad. When it was over, there was a smattering of applause—I figured the guy had brought his mother and a couple of cousins for a rooting section. The next time I heard that song, it was on the radio. The song was called "Mandy," and it was zooming to the top of the charts—and a young mop-haired singer-songwriter named Barry Manilow was on his way.

## A Bunch of Einsteins

We began rebuilding the 76ers by bringing Billy Cunningham—"the Kangaroo Kid"—back to Philly from the ABA. He joined us in the fall of '74, and the fans really loved him. Though Billy C. was no longer in the prime of his career by this time, he had good instincts that compensated for his slowing reflexes. He knew the intricacies of the game, still was an unerring passer, and fired a laserlike jump shot. He had the raw physical ability and sheer ferocity to power the ball to the hole.

To get Billy, we had to go through his New York–based agent—stocky, fast-talking, cigar-chomping, diamond-studded, hard-nosed Irwin Weiner. Irwin drove a hard bargain, and Billy cost us plenty—but he proved to be worth it, both as a player and as a crowd draw.

We tried to cut deals for George McGinnis of the ABA's Indiana Pacers and former Philadelphian Earl Monroe of the Knicks, but both deals fell through. Fortunately, however, Doug

Collins stepped forward that season. Though Collins—a guard from Illinois State—had been the Sixers' number one draft choice in '73, he missed almost all of his rookie year with a foot injury. In fact, the doctors had to transplant a piece of bone from his hip to his foot—and no one could say if he would be able to play after the surgery. Fortunately, when Doug rejoined the team in '74, he exploded onto the court, demonstrating all his old moves, plus a lot of star potential. He would go on to make the Eastern All-Stars team five times.

By the middle of the 1974–75 season, we were clearly improving, but we needed a big man at center. All the promising big men in the college ranks were sophomores and juniors. The previous year, the best high school center in the country, Moses Malone, had signed with the ABA franchise in Utah, passing up his basketball scholarship at the University of Maryland. That got us thinking in a new direction. If we couldn't trade or draft a center, why not just rob the cradle?

We got word of a monster 6'10" high school center in Orlando, Florida, named Darryl Dawkins. I went to Florida in March 1975 to see him play—and I could scarcely believe what I saw. Darryl was all of eighteen years old, with his head shaved and shined, a body sculpted of pure protein, and moves that really ignited the crowd. I expected to see a tall, gangly high school kid. I was wrong. This was a *man*—a big, powerful man—playing basketball with kids. He stood a head taller in size and ability than anyone else on the floor.

Gene Shue went to Jacksonville and saw Darryl play in the state tournament finals. I called him at his motel to get his impressions. Gene didn't hesitate an instant. "Let's go with him," he said. Our owner, Irv Kosloff, also gave thumbs up to "the kid."

Signing "the kid" to a contract, however, turned out to be tricky and expensive. I called Chicago attorney Herb Rudoy to present our offer and make himself available to represent Dawkins in the negotiations. We wanted to make sure Dawkins was well represented so there could be no accusation that our organization had taken advantage of a naive high school kid. Herb went to Orlando and phoned me with Dawkins' reply.

"Mr. Dawkins would be pleased to join the Philadelphia 76ers," he said, "for two hundred thousand dollars a year for seven years, plus a hundred thousand dollar signing bonus." While most of his buddies were getting jobs at the local car wash or McDonald's, Darryl was angling for six figures.

The asking price was steep, but we could afford it. All we had to do was keep Darryl under wraps long enough to draft him. Let me tell you, it's not easy keeping a 6'10", 250-pound center under wraps. We had to keep him out of the postseason high school tournaments so other NBA scouts (not to mention about two hundred college scouts) wouldn't stumble onto him and try to steal him out from under us. That meant we had to hire his high school coach to baby-sit him. In return, the coach became our official Florida scout (at five thousand dollars a year for seven years).

When Herb Rudoy and I went to Orlando to finalize the contract, up popped Darryl's "financial advisor," the Reverend Mr. Judge, who was there to look out for Darryl's interests— and to take away a large piece of Herb's commission. The deal threatened to come unglued even before we got to the NBA draft. I convinced Herb to hold the deal together and take a smaller commission—half a loaf being better than no loaf at all. Barely mollified, Herb turned to the Reverend Mr. Judge and growled, "This isn't right! You're not a financial advisor— you're a reverend!"

The Reverend Mr. Judge smiled and replied with holy smugness, "Mr. Rudoy, there are many kinds of reverends—and I am a *financial* reverend."

We had fifth pick in the first round of the 1975 draft, and we held our collective breath through the first four picks, hoping that no one had gotten wind of our plan. When we announced our selection, you could hear the murmurs go around the hall: "Darryl *Who?* What college does *he* play for?" Soon word got around that we had drafted a guy straight out of high school— and the murmurs changed to laughter. Though Moses Malone had been drafted out of high school by the ABA, it had never happened in the NBA. People thought we had lost our minds.

But a few months later, when they saw Darryl Dawkins play, everyone thought we were a bunch of Einsteins.

The cost of acquiring this high school kid was $1.5 million for seven years, including signing bonus, plus $35,000 over seven years to appease his high school coach. A lot of money, especially for a rookie player in the mid-1970s. But we never begrudged a nickel of it—he was that good.

Darryl Dawkins had a serene confidence and self-assurance that he carried with him, on and off the court. This was no shy, self-conscious teenager, but a young man who knew what he wanted and where he was going. I remember phoning him at his apartment one time shortly after he moved to Philadelphia. He answered in a deep, booming voice, "Hey, this is The Dawk, and I'm ready to talk."

If I'd been a little quicker with a comeback, I'd have said, "Hey, this is Pat, and I'm ready to chat."

## "Meet Your New Owner"

We followed the Dawkins acquisition with players like high-flying Lloyd Free and the mighty George McGinnis—a burly blacksmith of a player with muscles in places most guys don't even have places. The signing of McGinnis was a big media story.

We had the NBA draft rights to McGinnis, who was then playing for Indiana in the ABA. In the spring of '75, in a completely audacious and reckless move, Mike Burke, president of the New York Knicks, signed George McGinnis to a Knicks contract in spite of our draft rights on McGinnis' services. Apparently, Burke thought he could take advantage of the transition while Walter Kennedy was leaving office as NBA commissioner and Larry O'Brien was coming onboard.

We immediately obtained the best legal counsel to represent us—the legendary New York trial attorney Louis Nizer, who earned his fee and won the case. Commissioner O'Brien overthrew the Knicks contract, returned McGinnis to us, slapped the Knicks with a heavy fine, and took away their number one draft choice.

After we signed McGinnis to the 76ers, I went to New York for a half-hour interview with Howard Cosell in the ABC studios. I had never met Cosell, and it was fascinating to see him in person. I was surprised to see that, although he looked rather short and stooped on TV, he was actually quite a tall man. I was also surprised to find him the most insecure man I'd ever met. Many people have the impression that Cosell was an egotist, but I found him to be quite the opposite. After we finished the show, he asked me, "What did you think? How did I do? Was it a good enough interview? Did I ask you the right questions, Pat?" He totally confounded my expectations.

We opened the 1975–76 season with a pair of big wins—a road win in Chicago and a home win over the Lakers. Immediately, attendance at the Spectrum Arena jumped from around seven thousand to over twelve thousand a game.

Then, one Friday night in December 1975, disaster struck. We hosted the New York Knicks before a big, loud home crowd. Billy Cunningham had the ball. At the top of the key, Billy put the ball on the floor and attempted to fake Butch Beard, the Knicks defender, with a crossover dribble, then slash to the hole. But as he pushed off to get around the defender, Billy's knee buckled. He never even made contact with the other player—he just went down. You could hear Billy's knee coming apart, like the sound of a celery stalk breaking in half.

Billy shrieked with pain, a howl that echoed in the arena, ringing out over the noise of the crowd. He writhed, holding his knee, his face contorted in agony. Dr. Joseph Torg, the team physician, later told me, "Everything that could be damaged in Billy's knee has been damaged." Despite a lot of surgery and an attempted comeback, the Kangaroo Kid was finished as a player.

When they carried Billy off the Spectrum floor that night, a pall descended on the Sixers team and fans. Billy C. had been the heart of our team and the centerpiece of our planned comeback from the humiliation of the previous two seasons. Yet even without Billy's leadership, the team continued to battle might-

ily through the season, finishing with a 46-36 record. We tied
Buffalo for second place in the Atlantic Division—just behind
the Boston Celtics. Despite the early loss of Cunningham, we
achieved the turnaround we had promised our fans and made
the playoffs.

In the best-of-three first round of the playoffs, the Buffalo
Braves beat us at home, 95-89, then we beat them in Buffalo,
131-106. In the final game, we suffered a heartbreaking 124-
123 loss at home in overtime. I remember walking down Broad
Street on a warm windy day, a week after that bitter loss. A yel-
lowed newspaper swirled past me and lodged against the curb,
flipping open. My eye was drawn to the page as if by a magnet.
There was a photo of Buffalo's most valuable player, Bob
McAdoo, going up for a crucial play that forced the game into
overtime. Above the photo was a blaring, mocking headline:
"Braves Edge Sixers out of Playoffs." A week after the game,
that loss continued to haunt me.

A few days later, I was summoned to a meeting in an office
on the nineteenth floor of the United Engineering Building. I
didn't have a clue whose office it was or what was up. Arriving,
I was met by Sixers owner Irv Kosloff, who looked like a pall-
bearer at a funeral. As I stepped into the conference room, Kos
indicated another man in the room. "Pat," he said, "I want you
to meet your new owner." He said it without even a how-do-
you-do. That was Kosloff's style—direct and to the point.

I was stunned. There had been no hint that a sale was in the
works. I turned to the other man and was introduced to Fitz
Eugene Dixon, heir to the Widener transportation fortune and
a former part owner of the Philadelphia Phillies baseball team
and the Philadelphia Flyers of the National Hockey League. He
was a short spectacled man, and he was beaming. I met Dixon's
son, George, and one of Fitz's young executives, a smug and
vaguely unpleasant sort. He seemed to relish the fact that I had
not been told of the impending sale. He would later make other
remarks of a "we are in charge now, just stay in your place"
sort. I've never quite understood the pompous satisfaction some
people seem to take in lording it over others.

Fitz signed me to a five-year contract shortly after he purchased the club. He was a very different sort of owner from Irv Kosloff. He had enormous financial resources—and he was willing to commit those resources to the job of building a championship team. More than anything, Fitz Dixon wanted to win.

## Is There a Doctor in the House?

The summer of '76, the American Basketball Association folded and four ABA teams were merged into the NBA—Denver, San Antonio, Indiana, and New Jersey. A lot of talent came into the NBA from the four teams that were dissolved, including center Caldwell Jones, who joined our team. We purchased Henry Bibby, a guard from New Orleans, for ten thousand dollars, and added rookie draftees Joe Bryant, Terry Furlow, and Mike Dunleavy. Suddenly we were awash in talent. That crop of 76ers talent produced a notable second generation of talent—Joe Bryant's son Kobe is a star guard for the L.A. Lakers today; Henry Bibby's son Mike was a star college player for the Arizona Wildcats, and was the number two draft pick in the '98 NBA draft, going to the Vancouver Grizzlies; and Harvey Catchings' daughters became outstanding college basketball players—Tauja at Illinois and Tamika at Tennessee.

Then came the *big* news: Julius Erving—the legendary Dr. J—was about to become available. He believed his team, the New York Nets, was welching on his contract, so he was getting ready to boycott the Nets training camp. I called the Nets' general manager, Billy Melchionni. "If things deteriorate to the point that you have to trade Julius Erving," I said, "please let me know."

A few weeks later, Billy called. "Looks like Erving isn't going to report," he said. "If you want to acquire his contract, we can talk—but we want cash. Our owner, Roy Boe, is in a real financial bind."

"How much cash do you want?" I asked.

"Three million."

"Three million *what?*"

"Uncle Sam–type dollars."

I whistled. "Let me get back to you."

But that was only the beginning. The three million was just the money we would pay to the Nets to buy Dr. J's paper. How much would Erving himself want? In the end, the package to Erving and the Nets totaled a cool six million.

I told Fitz Dixon that we had an opportunity to get Julius Erving. The moment I mentioned Erving's name, I expected Fitz to come out of his chair with excitement. Instead, his response was, "Now, tell me, Pat—who is this Erving fellow?"

I couldn't have been more surprised if he had asked me who was George Washington or who was Abraham Lincoln. Fact is, Fitz had only become a fan of the game shortly before buying the team, and he had not been following the sport.

But Fitz understood the kind of talent Erving represented when I described him as "the Babe Ruth of basketball." When I told Fitz what it was going to cost to get Julius, he asked, "Are you recommending this deal?" I replied that Erving was worth it. Fitz leaned back in his chair, smiled benignly, and replied, "Fine and dandy."

Imagine that! Making a decision to spend six million dollars with three words: Fine and dandy. To his credit, Fitz Dixon knew a great player when he saw one, and he never regretted a nickel of the six million he paid for Dr. J. "We were right in getting Julius Erving," he told me a couple of years later, "and I'd make the same decision today."

The Sixers announced the signing of "The Six Million Dollar Man" at the largest press conference in Philadelphia history on the day of our fourth wedding anniversary. That evening, as Jill and I drove to a restaurant to celebrate, she asked, "Are you ready to be a daddy again?" Our second child was on the way, scheduled to join the Williams clan in June.

Julius Winfield Erving II was the Muhammad Ali and Michael Jordan of the 1970s and early '80s, the most recognized athlete of his time. During his glory days with the Sixers, fan mail poured into our office from around the world. The letters were addressed to Dr. J, or The Doctor, or simply Doc.

At 6'6", Julius Erving was built like a greyhound—long and lean. His arms seemed telescopic. His hands were so large, a basketball to him was little more than a tennis ball would be to you and me. Shake hands with Doc, and your hand was swallowed up in his. More than once, I saw the Doctor take the ball at midcourt, put the ball on the floor, dribble once, then sail through the air for a slam dunk. Clearly, Julius Erving had the power to repeal the laws of gravity. A master of improvisation, Doc instinctively found openings where lesser players would have been stopped in their tracks.

Much of Doc's greatness no doubt came from his unyielding work ethic. The man worked hard in practice, and he set the tempo for the rest of the team. His attitude was contagious—and that was why he was such a leader. He never let up, he never allowed himself an off night, he always gave 110 percent to the game, to the team, and to the fans. Doc once told me, "When I first started playing basketball, I couldn't hit the backboard from twelve feet. Everything I acquired as a player came through hard work."

Of all the athletes I've known, Doc is the most humble, honest, and genuine. Sure, he has an ego—a healthy ego, the kind of straightforward self-appraisal that sees himself as no better or worse than he truly is. Just as there is no false modesty in him, neither is there the false conceit or swagger that marks so many sports superstars. His style of play was businesslike and professional—his game face was an expressionless mask. It is impossible to imagine Dr. J doing a Merton Hanks chicken dance or trash-talking an opponent—he was simply larger than any such theatrics.

Though Doc is physically imposing, he is even more impressive when he opens his mouth to speak. He is thoughtful, soft-spoken, and articulate. He chooses his words carefully. He is passionate about causes he believes in and gives his time to: the Special Olympics, the Hemophilia Foundation, the March of Dimes, the Lupus Foundation, literacy and education, keeping kids off drugs, and more. He has a big heart—and it has been broken. In 1969, when he was a freshman at the University of Massachusetts, his older brother, Marvin, died from lupus. It was a devastating loss and gave Doc a profound and sober outlook on life.

When he was near the apex of his NBA career—approaching the age of thirty and having fulfilled most of his life goals—he realized there was a terrible void in his life. He mentioned these feelings in a couple of interviews, and he soon got mail from people who told him this void was due to the lack of Jesus Christ in his life. During the summer of '79, he attended a family reunion and learned of a strong heritage of faith dating back many years in his family. At around the same time, a pastor told him, "Julius, the Lord done laid a mighty big blessing on you."

Doc thought it over and considered the wonder that, out of millions of people, he should have the gift of unparalleled brilliance on the basketball court. He realized he could no longer avoid the Giver of that gift. He made a commitment to Jesus Christ, and invited the Lord into his life. At that moment, he found the peace that had eluded him.

One of the great thrills of my life came in the summer of 1997, when all of us in the Orlando Magic organization welcomed Dr. J to O-town as the new vice president of the Magic. It's a great joy to be working alongside the Doctor once again.

## The Best Team Money Can Buy

We opened the '76–77 season at home against the San Antonio Spurs. Dr. J led the charge, closely followed by a whole roster of marquee names: George McGinnis, Doug Collins, Darryl Dawkins, Lloyd Free, Caldwell Jones, Joe Bryant—a team that sports reporters instantly dubbed "The Best Team Money Can Buy." Amazingly, however, the best team money could buy went out and lost its first two games.

Coach Gene Shue and I sat down to talk about the disappointing start. We decided that our win column was empty because our roster was too full. We didn't have a basketball team—we had a flying circus. We had too much talent—everybody wanted twenty shots a night. We had Lloyd Free proclaiming himself the Prince of Midair. Darryl Dawkins, adopting a moniker that could not be topped, proclaimed himself All-Universe. Joe Bryant and Steve Mix continually elbowed each other for more court time—and the chemistry between Dr. J and George McGinnis was always touchy.

We moved quickly to correct the situation, trading a couple of players, putting a couple more on the injured reserve list, and waiving a few others. Once we had pared the team back, Gene was able to get this expensive collection of talented egos under control—and the 76ers began winning games. We went on to win fifty out of eighty-two games, taking the division title. We came close to taking it all but lost the NBA championship series to the Portland Trail Blazers, four games to two.

In an amazingly short time—1974 to 1976—we had taken the 76ers from laughingstock to blue chip status. Every postgame press conference was a media circus, full of laughs, swagger, and jive talk. Best of all, we were filling seats at the Spectrum, averaging over fifteen thousand per game.

We began the playoffs with a seven-game series against our old nemesis, the Boston Celtics. We battled our way through the series, winning the finale at home, 83-77. That win was largely due to Lloyd Free, who lobbed incredibly accurate long-range artillery shells at the hoop all game long.

Then it was on to the Eastern Conference finals against the Houston Rockets. I didn't travel with the team, because Jill was due to deliver our second child any day. In Houston, our team faced a powerhouse in the pivot by the name of Moses Malone—a name that would come to mean a lot to the fans in Philly. The last game of that series ended with an official's decision in the closing seconds that easily could have gone either way—an offensive charge against Houston or a defensive foul against the Sixers. Miraculously, the Sixers got the benefit of the call, much to the disapproval of the hometown crowd in Houston—and we won the game, the series, and the Eastern Conference championship.

So it was on to the NBA Finals—and again, I stayed in Philly, waiting for our second child to arrive. Our opponents were the Portland Trail Blazers, led by a big red-headed vegetarian and all-around nice guy, Bill Walton, and coached by my old friend, Jack Ramsay. The Sixers, featuring Julius Erving, were favored to win, despite the egos, bickering, and dissension that had come to mark the team. By this time, the 76ers had come to be viewed as the ultimate playground team—no real teamwork, no system, just tons of talent and endless improvisation. Though the oddsmakers favored us to win, a lot of fans across the country hoped we would lose. Americans like to root for underdogs—and the 76ers were the ultimate overdogs.

We opened the series at home and took the first two games. The second game was raucous and ugly, and typified what many fans had come to dislike about the Philadelphia ballclub—controversy, ego, and lack of team play. At one point, Portland's power forward, Maurice Lucas, got into a minor fistfight with Darryl Dawkins, and both players were ejected. Darryl dealt with his frustration by going into the locker room and ripping a door off a toilet stall—then, following the game, he ripped into his teammates in the press for not coming to his aid during the fight. Just what we needed.

The series moved out to Portland and the Blazers won both—easily. More than ever, the Sixers just weren't playing as a team. Dr. J carried everyone. George McGinnis, his self-confidence eroded, apparently wanted so badly to play well that he played—well, badly. Knotted at two games each, Portland and Philly returned to the Spectrum—and the Trail Blazers took us to school on our home court. Reeking of desperation, the Sixers went to Portland for game six. They battled uphill all the way. Trailing by two as the clock wound down, George McGinnis took one last shot in quest of a reprieve—but the shot refused to fall. The Trail Blazers celebrated their championship, and the Sixers flew home wrapped in a gloomy silence.

In the press, the team (with the exception of the Doctor) was depicted as a collection of egotistical ball hogs who deserved to lose. The most unkind skewering was reserved for George McGinnis. In the previous year's final game loss against Buffalo, McGinnis had been heavily criticized by fans and reporters for a foul-out in regulation play. It had been a stupid reach-in foul, and many who saw it accused McGinnis of deliberately fouling out just to get out of the game—a game the Sixers lost in overtime by a single point. A year later, in the finals against Portland, he simply seemed to freeze—and the fans and reporters again placed a lot of the blame on him for the play-off loss.

Fair? Unfair? Who knows? The press and the Philly fans weren't the only ones who had decided enough was enough where McGinnis was concerned. The day after the team limped back home from Portland, Gene Shue stormed into my office. "McGinnis is through!" he roared. "I want him off of my team and out of my sight."

For days, I tried to deal George McGinnis to another team—but no deal. The whole world had seen him apparently folding in two straight playoff years—and no one wanted to hire a guy who seemed to freeze in the clutch. So I went back to Gene and said, "I've been on the phone for days. Nobody wants McGinnis."

"C'mon!" Gene shot back. "You're not trying hard enough. You just don't want to get rid of him. You'd sabotage this team to keep that broken-down—"

"Now, hold it right there, Gene," I interrupted. "That's not fair, it's not true, and you know it. This is my team as much as it is yours—why would I want to sabotage it? No one wants to win more than I do, but if I can't arrange a trade, I can't arrange a trade."

"Somebody's got to want him. Just sweeten the pot enough and—"

"Oh, really, Gene? Let me ask you—if McGinnis was playing for the Lakers or the Bulls, and they called up and wanted to deal him to the Sixers, what would it take to get you to say yes?"

"They couldn't pay me enough to—" He stopped, realizing he had just made my point.

"Bingo," I said. "Gene, I can't trade him."

He scowled and ruminated darkly. Then he growled, "Well, just waive him, then."

That was ridiculous. Whatever McGinnis's flaws, however he may have let us down in those two playoff games, he was still a great player. You don't put a player of his caliber on waivers. I knew Gene was speaking out of the emotion of the moment— and I knew he was under a lot of pressure. He had recently negotiated the biggest coaching salary in the NBA; the talks had been acrimonious and had stretched his relationship with the owner to the breaking point. Gene was under a lot of pressure to prove he was worth his fat paycheck, and the only way he could prove it was with wins, especially playoff wins.

This loud, brash, egomaniacal organization called the Philadelphia 76ers was a three ring circus—and Gene, whip and chair in hand, was fighting for his life. Fitz Dixon didn't hesitate to put the screws to him. After one regular-season loss, I saw Fitz confront Gene, arms crossed in front of his chest, face flushed with anger and pinched into a big scowl, demanding, "Well, Gene, what are your excuses tonight?"

For all its talent, victories, good press, and acclaim from the fans, the Sixers was not a happy family. There was tumult on the court, tension in the locker room, and frayed nerve endings in the front office. Moreover, Fitz Dixon had become a controversial figure in Philadelphia. Instead of parking in the super-boxes, he carved out a reserved-seat section for himself on the floor, behind the basket nearest the Sixers' bench—apparently to keep a close eye on Gene Shue. He hired a former Secret Service agent to head up a goon squad of security guards to surround him wherever he went. The guards always made the fans detour around Fitz so he always had an unobstructed view of the court. Fans quickly grew to resent the apparent high-handedness of the Sixers' owner.

## Enter Bobby Williams

Right after the playoffs—on the night of June 9, 1977—I was at a summer league game in McGonigle Hall at Temple University. As the game was about to begin, I was walking along the end of the court behind the basket when I heard a muffled ringing sound. It came from a box on a post behind the basket. Curious, I lifted the cover and found a phone inside. So I answered the phone—

And almost fell over in astonishment.

The voice on the line belonged to Jill!

I ask you: What are the odds that Jill would call Temple University's basketball arena, trying to find me—and I would just happen to walk by and answer the phone? Incredible.

"It's time to go to the hospital," she said in a tense voice.

"I'm on my way," I said.

The labor was long and hard. At eleven-thirty the next morning, Bobby Williams was born in the Burlington County Hospital in Mount Holly, New Jersey. That was exactly an hour and a half before the collegiate draft was due to start. I watched my new son come into the world, then rushed to Philly to take part in the draft. Once again, we had a son being born on the day of the NBA draft.

We ended up drafting two players I'm sure you've never heard of, and who, as it turned out, added little to the prospects of the Philadelphia 76ers. I later thought I should have stayed at the hospital with Jill and the baby.


## "We Owe You One"


The 1977–78 season was a year of intense pressure for the 76ers. The NBA Finals the previous season had been a deep and bitter embarrassment for the team. With talent like Dr. J and Co., we should have won it. The loss in the finals was widely (and justifiably) perceived as a triumph of pure basketball—preparation, strategy, fundamentals, and teamwork—over Sixers-style, one-on-one hot-dog antics.

Though the 76ers had put together a season that would have been the envy of most teams, to the Philly fans we were bums because we hadn't won it all. We knew we had to do something to get the fans back on our side. During the summer of '77, we met with a couple of creative advertising men, Jerry Selber and Vic Sonder, and asked, "How can we resell this team to the fans?" They came back with a brilliant ad strategy combining an apology for last season's finals loss with a promise of great things to come. The theme—we blew it, but we're going to make it up to you—was expressed in a slogan we plastered all over town: *We Owe You One.*

The campaign cost us a cool half-million dollars. Julius Erving was our spokesman in radio, TV, print, and billboard ads. We burned the image of Doc, holding up one index finger, into the public consciousness, along with those four words. We really crawled out on a limb with that campaign. Could we deliver? That was the question that haunted us and drove us. We had set a very high standard for ourselves.

As the season began, our crusade turned into a humiliating retreat. The Sixers lost four of the first six outings—and it was clear that we were playing tight, nervous, hesitant. Perhaps there were tensions among the players, or between the team and the coach. Perhaps the "We Owe You One" hoopla was just too much pressure. Whatever the reason, the Sixers were not delivering. Soon we began to hear taunts from the stands: "You owe us *two!*" No doubt about it, the Philly crowd can be tough.

The fourth defeat was at home against the Chicago Bulls—a lackluster ballclub at that time. Even before the game ended, Fitz Dixon was red-faced with fury. He was entertaining friends and business associates at the game—and his team was stinking up the joint. Finally, he had seen enough. He jumped to his feet, wagged his finger in my direction, then pointed menacingly at Gene Shue. Gene was too busy coaching the game to see Fitz's gestures, but it didn't matter. Fitz wasn't trying to get Gene's attention—he was signaling to me that Gene Shue was through. Because of Fitz Dixon's conspicuous seating under the basket near our bench, everyone in the arena could see what was going on.

Immediately after the game, I joined Fitz and his attorney, Peter Mattoon, in the lounge. Fitz raved nonstop. Personally, I didn't know if the breakdown of the team was Shue's fault or not—but it didn't matter. Gene had lost the confidence of the only Sixers fan who counted at the moment: Fitz Dixon. "That man is out of my organization as of five minutes ago!" Fitz roared. "Now, who can you get to coach this team?"

I didn't have to think about it. "Billy Cunningham," I replied.

It had only been a short time since Billy had worn a 76ers jersey, and he was still visible to the fans as a color commentator for CBS. A ferocious competitor, Billy knew what it took to win. He was still close to his old teammates and had their respect. Plus, the people and press of Philadelphia loved him. There was bound to be some backlash after word of Gene's firing got out—but if we could announce Billy's hiring in the same breath, it would probably keep the fans happy.

I knew Billy had been at the game that night, so I phoned him at home around midnight and set up a breakfast meeting for the next morning. We got together at ten-thirty, and I laid out the offer to him. Billy wanted the job. While we were working out the contract, our office tried to find Gene Shue, but he had simply disappeared. Though none of us wanted Gene to find out about his firing in the press, it was beginning to look as if he already knew and just didn't want to be around when the story broke. I didn't blame him.

We finally reached Gene ten minutes before the morning press conference when we were scheduled to introduce Billy as our new coach. I talked to Gene, and he already knew. The conversation was terse and not overly warm, just as you might expect under the circumstances. Thanks to Billy C.'s popularity with the fans and the media, the press conference went well.

Billy made his coaching debut that same night in a road game against the New Jersey Nets. He didn't even have time to run one practice before coaching the game—but the Sixers won. It was a close, tight battle, largely decided by some big plays down the stretch by the Dawk. Billy was a wild man—striding the sidelines in a sweat-soaked three-piece suit, jumping, shouting, and firing up the players with his manic enthusiasm. He coached just like he used to play—flat-out. The reignited 76ers came home for the next game and thrashed a good Denver team before a sold-out house.

Billy knew the game inside out—from a player's perspective. But he quickly realized he needed help from a coach's vantage point. He already had one solid assistant coach in Jack McMahon, who had been Gene's assistant. Next, Billy brought in Chuck Daly from the University of Pennsylvania, a master of the xs and os of the game. Twenty years later, Chuck and I would cross paths again when he signed on as the head coach of the Orlando Magic in June 1997.

The Sixers went on to rack up an impressive 55-27 record, five games better than the previous year. It was one of the best years in the history of the franchise. We were well on our way to paying off on our promise.

## Bottomless Cup

Came the Eastern Conference finals that spring, and the Sixers found themselves facing the Washington Bullets—a wild card team that hadn't even been expected to make the playoffs. The smart money said the Bullets' bubble was about to burst. The Sixers had superior talent and momentum on their side. Sure, Washington boasted the presence of rebound king Wes Unseld, jump shot triggerman Elvin Hayes, offensive strongmen Kevin Grevey and Bob Dandridge, and fiery, feisty coach Dick Motta—my old team-building partner from Chicago Bulls days. But everyone knew that the Bullets on their best night were no match for the Best Team Money Can Buy.

Unfortunately, someone forgot to tell the Bullets.

Time and time again, Washington's situation seemed hopeless—then Motta would remind his team that it ain't over till it's over. He'd send his men back out on the court, and they'd find some way to win. They took the first game of the series in overtime on our own court. The surprised Sixers came back for game two at home and won—but now would have to play the next two games on the road.

Our guys were stunned by the ferocity of the Bullets. Lloyd Free was playing with heavy distractions because his sideline business—Lloyd's Free Throw shoestore in Philly—was going bust, and Lloyd figured his agent was cheating him. Elvin Hayes was eating George McGinnis's lunch, then crowing about it in the papers. Even the invincible Dr. J was looking surprisingly vincible in his matchup with Bob Dandridge. The Sixers were destroyed in games three and four at the Capital Centre. They crawled back to Philly, down three games to one.

Back home in the Spectrum, the Sixers won game five—a glimmer of sunshine. The fans kept reminding us that we owed them one. The pressure was on as we approached game six in Washington. We had only one focus: Win game six so we could force a seventh. It was a tight, hard-fought contest all the way to the final seconds. With less than ten seconds left, Wes Unseld tipped in an offensive rebound and the Bullets went up by two. Billy C. called a time-out and set up a final play, intent on sending the game into overtime. The plan was to get the ball to Free. Free would then slash through the Bullets' perimeter defense, dish off to Doc—and the Doctor would perform his buzzer-beating magic.

The play started off exactly as planned. Free got the ball and penetrated. Doc was right in position to receive the pass. But as Free elbowed past Elvin Hayes, he was called for an offensive foul. That gave the ball to Washington and sealed the game.

It was yet another numbing elimination from the playoffs. Again, we drank from that bottomless cup of frustration. Again, the Philadelphia 76ers went home feeling like bums, incapable of getting the job done even against a team like the Washington Bullets. We had come to the end of the season, and we still owed the fans one—with interest. We knew they wouldn't let us forget it.

## Rebuilding—Again

Again, it was time to rebuild. Billy Cunningham saw the same weak spot in our lineup Gene Shue had seen the previous two seasons: George McGinnis. So Billy came into the front office and sang the same tune we had heard from Gene: "We've got to get McGinnis out of here." For the third year in a row, George—a productive player in regular season—had let us down in the playoffs. In a strange way, it boiled down to the fact that George was not all that enamored with the game of basketball. He had great agility, strength, and skills, and the game had been good to him—but he wasn't intense in his approach to the game. He didn't have a good work ethic, and he hardly ever touched a basketball in the off-season. George's mind was just not in the game.

"The regular season is important," said Billy, "and it's great to win fifty-five games. But the NBA playoffs are everything. If we come up empty in the playoffs one more time, this team is going to be ridden out of town on a rail."

Billy had a point. I heard that a bunch of the townsfolk were starting a tar-and-feather concession in front of the Spectrum—and they were expecting to make a fortune.

"I think one problem with this team," Billy continued, "is that we're a running team without a really fast guard to run the break and orchestrate the tempo. Our guards—Doug and Lloyd and Henry Bibby—are primarily shooters. We need speed."

So we began to deal. We spent weeks trying to get rid of McGinnis. We tried to deal him to Indiana and Kansas City but couldn't come together on the terms. Then, out of the blue, I got a call from Carl Scheer, the general manager of the Denver Nuggets, and he offered to accept McGinnis if we would take Bobby Jones and Ralph Simpson—and hand over our number one draft pick. That hurt—but we really needed to unload McGinnis, and we all knew that Bobby was a fast, smart, coachable player, the best defensive forward in the game.

"Tell you what," I countered, "we'll do the deal you laid out, including giving you our first-round pick—but we also want a future first-rounder from you. Make it any draft from 1980 through '84. You choose."

"Okay. Make it '84."

"Done."

We still needed that running guard. Thanks to the shrewdness of assistant coach Jack McMahon, we found him: Maurice Edward Cheeks of West Texas State, the thirty-sixth pick overall in the 1978 college draft. Jack always went on scouting sorties while the team was on the road, and he had visited West Texas State while the Sixers were in New Orleans. Though the team he saw was generally lead-footed, one player stood out as a guy who could play fast-break basketball: Maurice Cheeks. Fortunately, other NBA scouts didn't see what Jack saw, and Cheeks remained our little secret until the draft. Quiet and shy offcourt but dominant on, Cheeks completed our lineup, giving us the leadership and quick tempo we needed at guard.

So Bobby Jones and Mo Cheeks came aboard, and we said good-bye to George McGinnis. It was a bittersweet parting. For all of his shortcomings and the times he left us flat-footed in the playoffs, he had been a major part of the resurrection of the Sixers when I first came back to help rebuild the team. We had worked hard to bring him to Philly, and we had worked even harder to get him out of town. But once he was leaving, I was sad to see him go. George had grown to love Philly, and he didn't want to leave, either.

## Mo and the White Shadow

A gaunt Ichabod Crane of a player, Bobby Jones was quickly nicknamed "the White Shadow." A product of North Carolina, where he had played under the mentorship of the great Dean Smith, Bobby paired up at forward with Julius Erving much better than George McGinnis had. He was a complete player—terrific on offense and terrifying on defense, a great passer, and an ambidextrous shooter. When you met Bobby and watched him play, you were immediately impressed by his self-effacing attitude combined with an intense playing style. But perhaps the most amazing thing about Bobby was that he played every game knowing he could collapse with a seizure.

Bobby is an epileptic, and he has used his position as a basketball star to inform the public about his condition. He has done many commercials for the Epilepsy Foundation. "It's such a misunderstood disease," he once told me. "I've only had a few seizures, and then when they're over, for me it's been like taking a nap. I wake up and it's all over. It's my wife or whoever is around that faces the real ordeal. She knows to take something, like my wallet, and stuff it in my mouth so I don't choke or swallow my tongue. Once, she tried to use her hand and I almost bit off her finger. Anyway, I take my medication, get my rest, take care of myself, and I haven't had that many problems."

Bobby had met his wife, Tess, in college, and she had helped reawaken a neglected commitment to Jesus Christ. One of the first things Bobby did when he joined the Sixers was come to me about starting a chapel before Sunday afternoon games. I thought it was a terrific idea, and we began holding team chapels. The speaker at our first chapel in February '78 was Melvin Floyd, a black inner-city youth worker. Three players showed up—Bobby, Julius Erving, and a Milwaukee player, Kent Benson—plus our assistant coach, Chuck Daly. From that small and inauspicious start, the idea of team chapels has spread throughout the NBA. One of the greatest joys of my career was helping launch a chapel service at the NBA All-Star weekend in 1981, which continues to this day.

Bobby filled the role vacated by George McGinnis—and he filled it to perfection. The next role that needed filling was the tempo-setting guard position—and Maurice Cheeks more than filled that bill.

We held preseason training at Franklin and Marshall College in Lancaster, Pennsylvania. From the moment he set foot on the floor, Maurice Cheeks took charge. Instead of showing the tentativeness you would expect from a rookie, Mo immediately began running the break, igniting the offense, and setting the tempo—exactly what Billy wanted. When the season began, Maurice Cheeks was a starter—an amazing feat for a first-year player.

Mo's personality and his style of play are one and the same: low-key, economical, fundamental. Mo never talked much, and when he did, he spoke softly. When he played, his face was furrowed in concentration. A wad of gum was forever in one cheek. Playing the most visible position on the floor—that of the ball-handler and ball-distributor—Mo nevertheless shunned the spotlight. His quick hands made him a leading ball-stealer. His unselfishness made him a leader in assists. He knew all the subtleties of the game.

They say that opposites attract, and Maurice Cheeks was the attractive opposite that perfectly balanced the chemistry of the Philadelphia 76ers. In a locker room full of big, brash egos and media hogs, Mo stood out by his very quietness and camera-shy demeanor. Unlike the rest of the team's starters, Mo would just as soon play the game, hit the showers, and go home. He was just what our team needed.

As coach Billy Cunningham saw the rookie guard from West Texas becoming a strong leader, he grew increasingly disenchanted with Lloyd Free. Lloyd (who would later legally change his name to World B. Free) was an immensely talented offensive player—but he was not a role player. He was selfish with the ball, and while he often could be productive as the Lone Ranger, his approach to basketball interrupted the flow of Billy's game plans. When Lloyd had the ball, he put on a show—and the other four guys on the court were reduced to spectators. They were watching Free instead of staying in sync, getting in position to rebound, or getting back on defense.

"I'm determined to rebuild this team around coachable players," Billy told me. "Lloyd just isn't going to fit in with the new structure. How about seeing what you can get for him?"

"I'll look into it," I said. We tried shopping him around, but there was no interest in him. All the other teams saw Lloyd for what he was: a great individual talent, but not a team player. Finally, as we were approaching our final roster cuts before the start of the '78–79 season, San Diego called. The new coach of the San Diego Clippers was Gene Shue. The Clippers needed more offensive power in their starting line, so Gene was willing to take a chance with Lloyd. In return for Free, the Sixers got San Diego's first-round draft choice in 1984. We were so eager to move Lloyd out to San Diego that we even paid a portion of his salary.

Free flew straight from Philly to Phoenix for the Clippers' season opener against the Suns—and he proceeded to score twenty-one points. Well, that's what he loved to do, and with the Clippers he could launch the ball at the hoop all night long without messing up the game plan. Free was happy, and so were we.

## Potholes in the Road

Around this time, I took up serious running. I had always been a jogger, but I wanted to be a runner—that is, six or more miles a day, full speed ahead. I would get up early every morning, take out a memory verse on a card, and run and read the verse, run and memorize the verse, run and say the verse aloud (or as aloud as possible between gasps). I'd spend about eighty minutes or so every morning, running and memorizing verses, building my heart, my lungs, my legs, and my soul. I became obsessive about what I ate. If you are what you eat, then I am 100 percent whole grain, with no added sugar, salt, or preservatives.

Jill became pregnant with our third child, and we decided we needed a big house in which to stash all the young'uns. We located a huge two-hundred-year-old colonial farm house on a tree-lined lot in Moorestown, New Jersey, near Philadelphia. It was a wonderful house, full of bedrooms, spare rooms, bathrooms, nooks, crannies, attic space, the works. Best of all, the place needed work, and Jill was looking forward to the remodeling project.

I was absorbed with rebuilding and promoting the Philadelphia 76ers. We began the season flawlessly, winning our first nine games. The Sixers were no longer Gene Shue's All-Star Flying Circus but Billy Cunningham's Well-Oiled Winning Machine. Strangely, even though we were now winning consistently, attendance began to slip—an apparent contradiction of Bill Veeck's rule, "The best promotion is winning." At first, I was mystified—then I realized what was wrong. Many of our fans had come to see the old aerial pyrotechnics and to breathe in the carnival atmosphere of the Flying Circus. Instead, they were witnessing precision basketball, skillfully and flawlessly performed—and some fans just weren't as excited about the new 76ers.

I decided not to worry about it. As the season wore on, as we got closer and closer to the playoffs, the excitement would mount and our adrenaline-addicted fans would be back. All that mattered was that we were again on the road to the playoffs.

We didn't count on the potholes in that road. The first pothole came in January, when Doug Collins developed a painful stress fracture in his foot. A relentless, explosive 110 percenter, Collins had simply blown out his foot with too many jarring starts and stops, abrupt cuts, and spin moves. His feet were being hammered and eroded by all that beautiful sneaker-squealing that is music to every basketball fan's ears. Doug was sidelined from January till March, then he returned for a few weeks—then the foot blew out again and he was grounded for the duration.

We shored up our line the best we could, picking up guards Eric Money and Al Skinner from the New Jersey Nets in a trade that sent Harvey Catchings and Ralph Simpson to the Nets. The Sixers ended the season with a creditable (if unspectacular) showing of forty-seven wins and thirty-five losses, just a dozen games over .500. We finished second in our division, seven games behind the defending world champion Washington Bullets. We went into the opening round of the playoffs and handily knocked out the Nets.

After just one day off, it was on to the semifinals against the San Antonio Spurs. Facing the likes of George "Iceman" Gervin and Larry "Special K" Kenon, we lost our first two in Texas, split the next two at the Spectrum, and headed back to Texas with a 3-1 deficit hanging over our heads. The pundits counted us out, but—surprise!—we beat the Spurs on their home court, then beat them again in Philly. Now we were tied at three games each.

I went with the team for game seven in San Antonio, and the arena was a big, noisy pressure cooker. It was loud, it was raucous, and the Spurs were egged on by a mob of beer-soaked Neanderthals who called themselves the Baseline Bums. They were rude, crude, and full of attitude. The nicest thing you could say about them is that they were intimidating.

In the first minute of play, our big center, Darryl Dawkins, was sent hobbling to the locker room with a sprained ankle. He tried to come back later, but it was no use. Despite our depleted roster, the team continued to battle, holding the lead right into the last three minutes of the game—and that's where it started to slip away from us. While the Sixers were focusing on keeping the Iceman and Special K contained, the rest of the Spurs bench stepped up and began to hammer away. San Antonio won the game 111-108—and the Sixers were bounced from the playoffs again.

I went out for a midnight run after the game, and it was like Mardi Gras—there were horns, sirens, and music and dancing in the streets. My running shoes beat out a mocking rhythm on the pavement: "We owe you one, we owe you one, we owe you one."

It was tough going home and facing the task of rebuilding once more. I wanted that championship so much I could taste it. That desire was fueled in part by a competitive desire to win, in part by a sense of obligation to our fans, and in part by fear of failure. I think most sports execs, and maybe even most players, are driven to excel by the fear of failure. In the sports world, you are completely exposed, eminently visible. Every move you make is watched, discussed, and dissected. Your mistakes are magnified in *Sports Illustrated* or on ESPN. Foul up a draft or muff a trade, and everyone—owners, colleagues, players, reporters, and fans—instantly knows about it. Don't get me wrong, I love the job and all the challenges that go with it—but it takes intense concentration to stay on top of the game.

On July 28, 1979, Jill gave birth to our third child—and first daughter—Karyn. While Jill was in labor, there was a power failure in the area, so the hospital had to switch to auxiliary power. Karyn was born under a light supplied by a backup generator. Instead of staying in the hospital for several days as she had with Jimmy and Bobby, Jill brought Karyn home from the hospital a mere nine hours after the birth.

## Chocolate Thunder and the Train

In the summer of 1979, we began sifting the ashes of defeat once more, looking for some way to redeem ourselves. We had some strong assets—Doc, Bobby Jones, Henry Bibby, Mo Cheeks—especially Mo, who had averaged 18.8 points a game and shot 54 percent. But Eric Money and Al Skinner were stopgaps, not starters. We didn't know if Doug Collins would return from his foot injuries.

Jack McMahon put us on to Billy Ray Bates, who had played guard for Kentucky State, then was drafted by the Houston Rockets, then cut. He had been playing for the Continental Basketball Association in Maine, yet Jack was convinced he had the makings of an NBA starter. So we signed him to a two-year contract. In the draft, we took Jim Spanarkel of Duke and Clint Richardson of Seattle, two smart, coachable guards. We hoped the three of them would give us depth in the back court. During the exhibition season, Bates and Spanarkel did not pan out as hoped and were not long with the team. Even Clint Richardson came close to being waived.

But then, in an exhibition game in Pittsburgh against the New Orleans Jazz, Richardson came alive. I was sitting in the stands that night with a plane ticket in my pocket—a ticket back to Seattle in Clint's name. I don't know if he ever knew how close he came to being exiled on the spot. His brilliant performance saved his position with the Sixers—and he went on to be a very productive player for us.

As the 1979–80 season began, Doug Collins was back from surgery and playing with his old relentless drive. It turned out to be a glorious year for the Sixers—we won fifty-nine games, losing only twenty-three. It should have been our year, the year we'd been waiting for. Problem was, it was an even better year for Boston. After floundering for a few seasons, the Celts had acquired a rookie phenom by the name of Larry Bird. His presence generated a complete turnaround in Boston. They went from a record of 29-53 the previous year to an astonishing 61-21—two games ahead of the Sixers.

Early in the season, we had a game in Kansas City. Our center, Darryl Dawkins, had the ball and went up for a dunk, crashing the hoop from the right side. The only Kansas City defender under the hoop was Bill Robinzine. Seeing that the dunk was a done deal, he made no move to block the shot or foul. Darryl smashed the rim with such force that the backboard exploded, showering both players with millions of pieces of glass. It was an awesome sight—something that had never been seen before in the NBA (though others, such as Shaquille O'Neal, have since repeated the feat). The game was halted for about forty-five minutes while the floor was mopped up and the backboard replaced.

The incident sent shockwaves through the sports community, and made Darryl an instant celebrity. The Dawk, who claimed to come from the planet Lovetron and who was rappin' before the term even existed, had already coined a name for each of his various dunks, including the Yo Momma, the Left-Handed Spine Chiller Supreme, the In Yo Face Disgrace, the Hammer of Thor, and the No-Playin' Get-Outta-the-Wayin' Backboard-Swayin' Game-Delayin' Super Spike. He claimed his speciality in life was "interplanetary funkmanship," and showered himself with a plethora of nicknames, including Sir Slam, Chocolate Thunder, and Master of Disaster. But the exploding backboard feat tested the limits of even Darryl Dawkins' poetic prowess. He finally settled on this description of his demolition dunk: "Chocolate-Thunder-Flyin' Robinzine-Cryin' Teeth-Shakin' Glass-Breakin' Rump-Roastin' Bun-Toastin' Wham-Bam-Glass!"

The dunk was replayed over and over on TV, and the nation was electrified. The NBA office, however, was not amused—as I learned in a frosty phone call from New York. "That," commissioner Larry O'Brien informed me, "is not to happen again."

"I understand," I replied. "It won't happen again."

Three weeks later, it happened again.

We were hosting the San Antonio Spurs in the Spectrum, and Darryl went up for a dunk and came down in a shower of glass. Being the promoter I am, I dashed out onto the floor with a paper bag and scooped up all the glass I could. Then we announced that we would give away souvenir pieces of that backboard at the next home game—a promotion that was quickly scotched by the league office.

The next morning, Darryl and I were summoned to the commissioner's office in New York for a meeting. Our walk up Fifth Avenue turned into an impromptu parade, with people waving, pointing, and calling out, "Hey, Chocolate Thunder! Wham-Bam-Glass!" The cheering ended abruptly as we entered the solemn, library-quiet office of the commissioner.

We took our seats and Darryl was asked to explain himself. The shattered backboards, he explained, were accidents.

"There will be no more 'accidents,' Mr. Dawkins," said Larry O'Brien. "Is that clear?"

"Yes, sir."

Then O'Brien turned to me and gave me a fifteen-minute tongue-lashing. The long and the short of it was that there would be no giveaway of backboard glass souvenirs, not at the next home game, not ever.

Out of those incidents came the so-called Dawkins Rule: Any player who shattered a backboard would be automatically ejected, fined, and made ineligible to play the following game. Those incidents also gave rise to snap-back rims, which are now universally used in the NBA because they put less stress on backboards. Even with snap-back rims, however, we still see a backboard explode now and then.

As the season progressed, the Sixers were locked in a duel with the Boston Celtics. Midway through the season, Doug Collins again went down with a foot injury—this time the other foot. Rookie Clint Richardson took his place as starter, and we began a search for more talent to give us more depth at guard. One intriguing possibility that surfaced was Pistol Pete Maravich, the White Globetrotter, the very same guy I had traded to the Jazz when I was in Atlanta in '74. In the twilight of his career, he was still a marquee name—and we needed someone with a neon name to boost our sagging attendance.

So we brought Pete to Philly for a talk. Though he had held a grudge against me for several years because of that trade, our reunion was warm and filled with laughs. Billy, Pete, and I met for dinner and explored the possibility of putting Maravich in a Sixers jersey. Near the end of the meeting, my heart sank when Pete mentioned he was also on his way to Boston to talk to the Celtics—our biggest rivals.

The story of our meeting slipped out to the press—and the papers made it sound as if we had already signed Maravich to a contract. When Pete popped up in a green Celtic uniform, it appeared that Billy and I had botched the opportunity to get Pete Maravich to Philly. Even Fitz Dixon thought we had bungled it. The fact is Pete had taken a look at both teams, then jumped to the team he felt most likely to go all the way to an NBA championship.

So we didn't get Pete, but we did acquire—at great expense—Lionel "The Train" Hollins from Portland. Fitz wanted a championship, and he was willing to spend big to get it. From his first game as a Sixer—against the Lakers at the Spectrum—Train made a big impact on our team. Train and Mo started as guards, backed up by Henry Bibby and Clint Richardson. Billy used Darryl Dawkins and Caldwell Jones as his "twin towers" up front. After a few weeks, Doug Collins came back. Suddenly we had enormous depth at the guard position—and it showed in the way we were winning games. It was a great team.

In March, while playing against Washington, Doug twisted his knee, resulting in his third trip under the surgeon's knife in two years. He was done for the season—maybe more. But something good came out of this. All of his travails and frustrations that season confronted him with the need to think seriously about his life. As a result, he made a decision to allow Jesus Christ to be Lord of his life. His newfound faith sustained him through the tough days ahead.

## Cruel Magic

As the regular season drew to a close, the stage was set for the big confrontation everyone wanted to see—Boston versus Philadelphia, winners of 121 regular season games between them. We went into the first round of the playoffs against Washington, and easily blew the Bullets away. Next, we went up against Atlanta, and the Hawks fell in five games. We split the first pair of games in Boston—then we wowed the world by beating the Celts three straight. Heavily favored Boston was trampled in only five games.

Again, the 76ers were in the finals—this time against the L.A. Lakers. The series got off to an auspicious start as the Sixers split the first two in L.A. But then they came home and split the next pair at the Spectrum. Tied at two, we went back to L.A. for game five. Early in the game, Kareem Abdul-Jabbar sprained his ankle and limped off the court. He returned in the fourth quarter, favoring the injured ankle, playing through the pain. Somehow, he threw down a basket, drawing a foul, and sank the free throw. That three-point play was the difference, giving the game to the Lakers.

Game six was in Philly, and Kareem's ankle was so bad, he stayed home. The Sixers made the mistake of thinking that the Lakers without Kareem were no longer a threat—we could mail this one in. We failed to account for a rookie from Michigan State named Earvin Johnson—a.k.a. Magic. That night, Magic Johnson played every position, collecting 42 points, 15 rebounds, 7 assists, and 3 steals. At the end of the day, the score was Lakers 123, Sixers 107. Our championship hopes went up in a puff of smoke, thanks to the cruel hoop sorcery of Magic Johnson.

Since my return to Philly in August 1974, we had spent six years chasing the rainbow, six years battling our way into the playoffs—and every one of those seasons had ended in playoff disappointment and frustration. I began to wonder if this team was doomed to always have the NBA championship dangling just beyond reach.

We were continually haunted by that phrase—"We owe you one." Would we ever be able to pay off that debt?

# Moses and the
# Promised Land

By a blinding stroke of good fortune, we landed Andrew
Toney in the 1980 draft. With Doug Collins hurt again, the team
sorely needed an outside shooting threat, and Toney—a stand-
out guard from an obscure school in basketball, Southwest
Louisiana—was the answer to our prayers. The only problem
was that Toney had a rather exaggerated opinion of his worth
to the team. He hired high-powered attorney Bob Wright to
conduct contract negotiations, and held out during rookie ori-
entation camp. His story was that he wasn't sure he really
wanted to join the NBA—he was thinking of going to grad school
instead.

I had never dealt with a holdout before, and I wasn't quite
sure how to handle the situation. Clearly, Toney was good at
the game of basketball. I decided to see how good Toney was
at another game: poker. Just a few hours before the start of
training camp, I called his attorney and asked if I could speak
directly to Andrew. The attorney okayed it, and I got the young
man on the line. "Andrew," I said, "I was really looking forward

to welcoming you to the team, but I can see that you are really serious about going to grad school. So I just called to wish you success with your studies, and I hope you have a great life." I did most of the talking. Andrew did most of the stammering.

I hung up and didn't even have time to walk away from the phone before it rang again. It was Andrew's attorney. "I don't know what you said to Andrew," he said, "but whatever it was, it worked. We're flying in to Philly in the morning to sign on the dotted line."

Quite a game, poker.

Andrew had unbelievable speed in running the court and unbelievable concentration in shooting. He was even more spectacular under pressure, covered by three defenders, than when taking a wide-open shot. Best of all, he was one of the most coachable, least temperamental players I ever met (which surprised me, given the holdout episode). We again had a solid, strong-shooting guard line—made even stronger when Doug Collins returned for his umpteenth comeback. We had such depth at guard with Mo, Lionel, Clint, and Doug that, even when Andrew Toney was out for the first month of the season with an ankle sprain, we were in good shape.

Doug played a dozen games, then his feet went out from under him again just before Thanksgiving. This time, he retired from basketball and went into broadcasting. Today, he is the NBA analyst for NBC and is generally considered the best in the business.

## Razor-Thin Margin

It was a phenomenal season—sixty-two wins against twenty losses, a three-game improvement over the preceding season. Julius Erving had one of his career best seasons, averaging almost twenty-five points a game and winning the league MVP award. At the postseason banquet in Doc's honor, Commissioner Larry O'Brien called him "a national treasure to be admired and savored."

We ended the season with a photo finish against the Celtics—they, too, had a 62-20 season. We went to Boston Garden for the game that determined who got the first-round bye and home-court advantage in the playoffs. Despite an incredible thirty-five-point performance by Andrew Toney, the Celts won 98-94. The Sixers became one of the few teams in NBA history to win more than sixty games in a season and still end up facing a first-round playoff miniseries. One off-night can torch a golden season into molten slag.

Our first-round opponent was the Indiana Pacers—and we handled them with ease. In the Eastern Conference semifinals, Boston breezed through Chicago in four straight while the Sixers battled through a bitter seven-game grind against the Milwaukee Bucks. The final game of the series was an end-to-end thriller, which the Sixers won 99-98. Oddly, the Spectrum was less than half full—only seven thousand seats occupied. The only explanation I can imagine for the low turnout is that the game was on Easter and everybody was in church all day.

Fitz didn't care if the game was on St. Swithens Day, he figured there should have been a sold-out house that day. Upset, he made an offhand remark that he ought to sell the team—and a reporter carried the comment in his newspaper. Out in Huntingdon Valley, a businessman named Harold Katz read the remark—then called his attorney. "I want you to get in touch with Fitz Dixon and find out if he's serious about selling the Philadelphia 76ers."

Out on the left coast, meanwhile, the defending champion L.A. Lakers were upset by the Houston Rockets, powered by Moses Malone. Houston went on to beat Kansas City and San Antonio. Sports pundits agreed that Houston was fortunate to get that far—and the next NBA champion would be the survivor of the contest between Boston and Philadelphia.

So in April 1981, we went to Boston Garden for the first of seven—and we won it, 105-104. The next night, a vengeful Boston got even by a nineteen-point margin. For games three and four, the scene shifted to our home court—and we won both. We went back to Boston with a three to one edge. We needed only to win one of the next three—then we could take on the relatively easy challenge of the Houston Rockets in the finals.

In game five, we were leading big-time as the clock wound down. Hundreds of disheartened Boston fans left the arena to beat the traffic. A few good sports stopped to shake my hand. "Good luck against Houston," they said. "Hope you win it all now." They did not suspect that the Sixers would come unglued, suffering an epidemic of turnovers. When the final buzzer sounded, everyone in that arena was stunned at the numbers on the scoreboard: Celtics 111, 76ers 109.

So we returned to the Spectrum for game six. The Sixers exploded to a huge lead by halftime. We were ready to celebrate. When we took the court for the second half, the lead slowly, possession by possession, began to crumble. More turnovers, more missed shots, more struggling to stay in the game as the Celts finally edged past us. The last two points belonged to Boston's Cedric Maxwell, who made a pair of free throws with only two ticks left in the game. Final score: Boston 100, Philadelphia 98.

Two days later, we were back in Boston for game seven. It had all come down to this: we would have to battle hard to win in the loudest, most difficult sports arena for any visiting team. Again, the Sixers exploded and took command of the game in the first half—and again, the lead evaporated in the second half. I can't sit in the stands or on the sidelines at games like these— I have to pace the concourse. As I paced, I sneaked an occasional peek—just enough to see that the Celts had ignited for a final surge in the closing minutes. With the roar of the Boston crowd going through my head like a freight train, I went into a broom closet to pray. I think it's the only time in my life I ever actually asked God for victory in a game.

Finally, with only one second left, the Sixers had the ball at the sidelines, trailing by one point. I could no longer stand it. All those rebuilding years, all those hundreds of games, all those trades and haggles and organizational battles had brought us to these precious few seconds in Boston Garden. The Sixers must inbound the ball and score in a second or less—nearly, but not quite, impossible. Bobby Jones launched a long alley-oop of an inbound pass from midcourt to Julius Erving. If Doc could just slam the ball down the throat of that basket . . .

But Doc had plenty of company under the basket. The ball bobbed from fingertip to fingertip as the final buzzer sounded—and the Sixers again went home empty. The score: Boston 91, Philadelphia 90. We had lost the last three games by a combined total of five points. That's a razor-thin margin of only 1.6 points a game!

Billy Cunningham was in agony, unable to speak. The Sixers were dazed, barely able to comprehend that the season's biggest prize had slipped from their grasp yet again. Numbly, like robots, they showered and dressed and boarded the charter bus for the trip home. Before they went just a few blocks, the bus was surrounded by delirious Celtics fans who beat on the bus and rocked it from side to side, adding insult to injury. We went back home to lick our wounds and rebuild.

Again.

In the championship series, the Celtics beat Houston in six games.

## Beware the Crab

We needed more depth at forward. Our existing lineup—Steve Mix, Julius Erving, and Bobby Jones—was still strong but not getting any younger. We knew most of the top college prospects would be gone by the time our pick came around in the draft—but one player looked promising, and there was a chance he would be available when our turn came. His name was Danny Ainge, and he had enjoyed an outstanding college career at Brigham Young. His big moment of glory occurred in the NCAA tournament when, in a game against Notre Dame, he dribbled from one end of the court to the other through all five Irish defenders, putting up the winning basket at the buzzer.

That year, Ainge became one of the first athletes to take advantage of a new rule that allowed turning pro in one sport while retaining eligibility and amateur status in another. He had played baseball in parts of two seasons with the Toronto Blue Jays while playing basketball in the NCAA. He insisted publicly that he was heading for a full-time career in baseball, but some of my friends in baseball told me they believed Danny's baseball skills were limited. My sources projected a better future for him in basketball.

I set up a meeting with Ainge in Cleveland on May 15—he would be there for an Indians–Blue Jays game. We had a long talk. Finally I said, "Danny, we'd like to see you play for the 76ers, but we don't want to waste a draft pick if you don't intend to play basketball. So you tell me: If we draft you, are we just wasting a first-round pick?"

"Yes," he said. "I want to concentrate on baseball. In the off-season, I need to practice my hitting, so I just don't see myself playing basketball."

The trip to Cleveland was not a complete waste. I also met with another prospect, a guard from Cleveland State named Franklin Edwards (who we eventually drafted)—and I went to the ballpark that night to watch the Indians and Blue Jays play. I sat behind the third base dugout and kept score on the program, something I don't normally do. Danny Ainge was playing second base, and even though he had turned down an offer to be drafted by the Sixers, I wanted to keep track of him as a baseball player.

As the game unfolded, Len Barker, the Cleveland pitcher kept retiring Toronto batters. By the third inning, I noticed he had retired nine hitters. By the fourth inning, twelve hitters. Fifth inning, fifteen hitters. I thought, *This is getting eerie.* By the top of the ninth inning, Barker had retired twenty-four straight batters, and a hush descended over the ballpark. The crowd sensed that history was being made.

I don't think anyone in the stands drew a breath while Barker faced the last three batters. He put them away, one after the other. Purely by chance, I had been fortunate enough to witness one of the rarest events in baseball—a perfect game. I got into the locker room and had Barker sign and date the program for me. It's one of my favorite baseball keepsakes.

After I got back to Philly, I called Danny again—just to make sure. "I'm sure," he said. "I'm sticking with baseball. Thanks anyway."

Came the day of the draft and Boston picked Danny Ainge in the second round. I was surprised—but assumed that Boston simply hadn't done its homework. Danny was going to play baseball—and if the Celtics wanted to blow a draft pick, that was fine with me. Imagine my surprise when Danny Ainge signed with the Celts! He left baseball to play basketball in Boston.

Not long after that, I testified on behalf of the Toronto Blue Jays in their suit against Ainge for breach of contract. The Blue Jays felt Danny had misled them—and I could certainly testify that he had misled the 76ers.

We were happy to sign Franklin Edwards as our first pick. We flew him to town so he could begin practicing that summer. He signed the contract in the afternoon, and that evening I took him to dinner at the hotel owned by Billy Cunningham. We all had seafood—Franklin had flounder stuffed with crabmeat. After dinner, we went to watch a Baker League basketball game. Halfway through the game, Franklin collapsed right in front of us. His eyes swelled shut, and his body puffed up grotesquely. I thought he was dying.

He was taken out of the arena on a stretcher and rushed to Temple Hospital. The doctors stabilized him and determined that he had experienced an extreme allergic reaction to shellfish. The crabmeat stuffing in that flounder had nearly killed him—and on the same day we had signed him to the team. I made a mental note: Henceforth, all new players are served prime rib, not seafood.

## Fitz and Katz

Ever since Fitz Dixon had taken over as owner of the 76ers, I had been in close contact with him, talking to him at least two or three times a week about team operations. But during the spring and early summer of 1981, Fitz retreated into invisibil-ity. I thought it was odd that he no longer called and odder still that he didn't return my calls. But as summer came, I became very busy with a Word of Life camp in the Adirondack Moun-tains of New York and had little time to wonder about Fitz. I happened to be out on an island in the middle of Schroon Lake when I got a phone call from Fitz's attorney.

"It's in your best interests," said the attorney, "to come back to Philadelphia as soon as possible."

"What's going on?"

"Sorry, I can't say."

I couldn't pry any more information out of him over the phone, but I detected a note of warning, so my next call was to former owner Irv Kosloff. Though he no longer had an owner-ship interest in the team, he usually knew what was going on around town. "Kos," I said, "have you heard anything lately that I ought to know?"

"Yeah," he said. "Fitz is selling the 76ers."

I whistled. That was big. "So who's the new owner?" I asked.

"Ever hear of a guy named Harold Katz?"

"Nope."

"Well, you've seen him around a lot. He's a season-ticket holder."

I hung up and caught the next plane to Philadelphia. I arrived at the Sheraton Hotel only fifteen minutes before the start of the press conference that would introduce Harold Katz to the world. It was the first time I had ever met him—but Irv Kosloff was right, I had seen his face countless times at the games. I had even chatted with him a time or two, little realizing I would one day work for him. The moral of the story is to always be kind to your season-ticket holders—they could own you someday.

Katz is a self-made multimillionaire, a street kid from South Philly turned financier and basketball enthusiast. He made a fortune acquiring Nutri System, building it into an empire, and then selling it. The acquisition of the 76ers was the fulfillment of a lifelong dream for Harold Katz. Having just met him only fifteen minutes earlier, I was appointed to introduce him to the media. It went well.

Days later, the papers carried rumors that I would be leaving the Sixers and moving to Chicago to be general manager of the White Sox or the Cubs. There was nothing to the rumors—at least as far as I knew—except that I had gotten an exploratory phone call from Eddie Einhorn, one of the owners of the Sox, but it didn't lead anywhere.

A week later, Katz and I sat down for a five-hour meeting in which we sized up each other. I found him to be loaded with ideas and strong opinions. But then he had a right to be opinionated. He had done his homework on the team, and he was conversant with every player's abilities and role. He also had an extensive grasp of marketing and promotion. "I'm a salesman, a street-hawker, a carny-barker," he told me, "and I know you are, too. I've been watching your promotions for years. So I'm going to give you a free hand in promoting this team—with just one stipulation: No pigs."

Katz wasn't referring to the act I had introduced in Atlanta, Uncle Heavy and his Pork Chop Review. No, he had another stinker of a promotion in mind. In 1974, after I first joined the 76ers, I got a call from a man who said he had a surefire half-time promotion for me—The Ham 'n' Egg Review. It allegedly included a trained chicken and a singing pig named Pepper. I couldn't help it—I liked trained pig acts. So I hired the act, and I really played it up in the press. We got a lot of advance publicity for The Ham 'n' Egg Review—though I would later regret it.

Came the day of the halftime show, and I was wishing I had auditioned the little swine. The supposedly singing pig belonged in a BLT. The handler got Pepper to "sing" by holding him and punching him in the spareribs. As any stupid pig would do when punched, Pepper protested, squealed, grunted, and tried to get away. I didn't consider that singing. Neither did anyone in the stands. The crowd booed Pepper and the pork-puncher off the floor. It was the worst promotional disaster in 76ers history. The next day, the headline of the Philly sports page read:

> 76ers Lose to Knicks—Pig Booed
> Pat Williams Has His Own
> Bay of Pigs Fiasco

Harold Katz had been in the stands that day—and he wanted to make sure there would never be another Bay of Pigs.

Near the end of our five-hour meeting, Harold asked me how I would set up the organization. I replied that the best structure was one man in charge, reporting directly to the owner. "I agree with you," he replied, "*if* that one man is right for the job. I'd like to see you in action."

The next day, Harold Katz picked me up in his block-long limo and we went to meet with Philadelphia Mayor William Green, seeking help regarding the exorbitant Spectrum lease and the need for better police security at the games. On the way, Harold showed me the morning headline—his wife was divorcing him and suing him to block his purchase of the team. He wasn't worried. In fact, when we walked into Mayor Green's office, Harold presented the newspaper to hizzoner with a flourish and said, "Mister Mayor, just look at the favor I'm doing for you—keeping you off the front pages."

When the mayor called him "Harry," Katz quickly corrected him: "It's Harold, Mr. Mayor, Harold."

As the day went on, I began to get a feel for Katz. Yes, he was tough, aggressive, and blunt—but he was also lovable in his own way. And I began to relax. Harold Katz and I were going to get along just fine.

A press conference was set up to announce that I was staying on as general manager of the 76ers and that John Nash was coming aboard as business manager. Since this was "silent summer," the year of the baseball walkout, there was not a lot of sports news to cover, so the press conference got a lot of coverage. I was aware of that, so I decided to take a bit of a chance and either score real big with Katz—or go out in a blaze of glory. Prior to the press conference, I called my friend Dave Bailey, who owned a farm in nearby Alloway, New Jersey, and arranged a surprise for Katz. If Harold had as good a sense of humor as I suspected, it was going to be fun. If not, I was probably out on my ear.

The day of the press conference arrived and Katz had just begun to address the reporters. On my cue, the door at the back of the room opened, and in came Dave, dressed in bib overalls

228

and a straw hat with a freshly scrubbed, squealing pig under his arm. Harold was dumbstruck as Dave walked up the center aisle and presented the pig to the Sixers' owner.

Then I stepped to the microphone and told the reporters, "You've asked about the details of my contract. Well, Harold has instructed me not to reveal those terms—he's as ashamed of that contract as I am. I can say, however, that it is a multi-day deal, and that I have received a signing bonus that will allow my mother to work for the rest of her life. I'm looking forward to a long association with Mr. Katz, a truly good and decent man whose idea of an obscene gesture is reaching for his checkbook."

I went on like this for a few minutes, and I watched Katz out of the corner of my eye. Was I writing my obituary with the Sixers? No. He stood there, holding the pig, and laughing with everyone else. He loved it.

From then on, whenever we did any public appearances together, Harold always begged me, "Go ahead! Rip me, rip me!" I felt like Don Rickles—with my boss begging me to call him a hockey puck.

A few weeks after that press conference, the NBA gave Harold Katz its approval as a new owner, and the sale was finalized. Though I believed Katz would be good for the organization, I was sad to lose Fitz Dixon as our owner. He just dropped out of sight—he didn't attend the press conference or return to the 76ers office. I called him at his estate in Maine, told him I was sorry about the playoff loss, and that I was sorry he was getting out. I meant it. Fitz had been a good owner, he had backed and trusted his management team, he had never tried to meddle in matters with which he wasn't conversant, and he was always willing to open his checkbook to acquire the resources we needed to win.

I knew it had been as discouraging and frustrating for Fitz Dixon as it was for the rest of us to get so close to the NBA championship so many times without attaining the prize. Finally, sadly, he bowed out. But he was a good owner. If only there were more like him in professional sports.

## "Will the Sixers Choke?"

Just before training camp in 1981, after years of injuries and comebacks, Doug Collins' playing career came to an abrupt end. True to his work ethic, Doug had been working hard all summer to get in shape for the season. During a preseason scrimmage, his knee collapsed. Doug finally decided enough was enough. With four years to go on his 76ers contract, he went to work in administration and PR with the team, as well as working in radio and TV broadcasting. He later went on to a long coaching career as an assistant at Arizona State, and as head coach of the Chicago Bulls and Detroit Pistons. He also established himself as an outstanding NBA television analyst.

Meanwhile, the Sixers continued to prepare for yet another grab at the brass ring. Throughout preseason training camp, Harold Katz walked the sidelines, dressed in sweatsuit and sneakers. He kibitzed, he analyzed plays, he shouted encouragement, he had a ball. The great thing was that he managed to be involved without meddling or interfering. Billy Cunningham and Katz got along great, and Billy enjoyed having the boss around. "Mr. Katz is an intense competitor," said Billy. "I like that in an owner."

During the season, assistant coach Chuck Daly was hired away to be Cleveland's head coach, and we all wished him well. Chuck's Cleveland stint was short-lived, but led to a head coaching position in Detroit, where he won two NBA titles, which led to his induction into the Basketball Hall of Fame. He also coached the Olympic Dream Team that took the gold medal in Barcelona in 1992. He coached New Jersey before becoming a broadcaster of NBA games, then returned to the sidelines in 1997 as head coach of the Orlando Magic.

When Chuck left for Cleveland, we brought Matt Guokas down from the Sixers broadcast booth to be Billy's assistant coach. (Matty, by the way, also went on to Orlando, serving as the first head coach of the Magic, before moving to a network broadcast booth.)

In January 1982, in a game against the New Jersey Nets, Darryl Dawkins went up for a jump shot, making only a slight contact with a defender, then went down on the floor. Though the contact didn't look serious, Darryl stayed on the floor. He was carried off the court and the X-rays revealed a broken leg. We moved backup centers Caldwell Jones and Earl Cureton up in the rotation and began shopping around for additional talent. Harold Katz even journeyed west to L.A. to meet with forty-five-year-old Wilt Chamberlain when the Stilt dangled the possibility of returning to the game after a decade in retirement—but nothing came of it.

The Sixers finished the 1981–82 season with a 58-24 record. Boston went 63-19 to claim the bye in the playoffs while Philly faced another first-round three-game miniseries. We started the playoffs by blowing out the Atlanta Hawks with thirty-five points to spare. Game two was much closer—but we prevailed in overtime.

The highlight (or lowlight) of game two was a tragi-comedic episode between our Lionel "The Train" Hollins and Atlanta's 7'1" center, Wayne "Tree" Rollins, currently an assistant coach with the Magic. It began when Tree threw a flagrant elbow at Train, who retaliated by knocking Tree upside the head. Rollins chased Hollins, Tree chugging after Train, around and around, across the court, behind the basket, up the aisles, over the seats, leaping over fans, then back onto the floor. The officials ran around blowing their whistles, and the fans roared. Unfortunately, Hollins had broken his hand on Rollins' head, so the team doctor pronounced him sidelined for the duration of the playoffs.

With Hollins out, Billy Cunningham moved Andrew Toney to the starting position. Andrew performed like a champ, and showed the stuff that ultimately made him one of the top guards in the NBA. Clint Richardson also moved up in the rotation, delivering much-needed scoring, rebounding, and defensive strength off the bench.

In the quarterfinals, the Sixers beat Milwaukee in six games. There was no time to savor the victory, however, because the team was off immediately for Boston and the Eastern Conference finals. The first game was a complete rout—the Celtics demolished the Sixers by a forty-point margin. The next night we rallied to beat the Celts on their home court. To top that off, we promptly won two more in Philly. Just as in the previous year's matchup, our team had opened up a three games to one lead over the Celtics—and everyone remembered all too well the catastrophe that had befallen us a year earlier. The joke in Boston was, "Now we've got the 76ers right where we want 'em." In games five and six, it looked like the joke was becoming a prophecy—Boston won both, one at home and one at the Spectrum. The banner headline in Boston read, "Will the Sixers Choke?"

But the Sixers didn't choke. They charged. They won a decisive victory over Boston, proving that history does not always repeat itself—it can reverse itself. The Sixers returned home to a heroes' welcome. We still hadn't won the NBA championship—but beating Boston in Boston Garden made the city of Philadelphia just as proud and excited as if we had. To make it even sweeter, after the Sixers beat Boston in their own house, the Boston fans instantly became Eastern Conference fans, and chanted to the Sixers, "Beat L.A.! Beat L.A.!"

So that was our next challenge: To face the Lakers for the championship. And the team from La-La Land was tanned, rested, and ready for us. They had blitzed their way through the first two rounds of playoffs without a defeat.

The Lakers came to the Spectrum for the first two games. In game one, the Lakers rolled to their ninth straight playoff game win—an NBA record. In game two, we bounced back and stopped them from getting a tenth. Then we flew to L.A., where the Lakers took us to school in two more games. One of the bitterest pills we had to swallow was the thrashing we took from the Lakers' Bob McAdoo, whom we had a chance to sign in December, but decided to pass on. I was dearly wishing McAdoo was playing for us instead of against us.

Down three to one in the finals, we played game five in Philly like cornered animals—with grit and ferocity—and we won it. By this point, we were locked in the longest playoffs ever. As evidence of how long those playoffs lasted, Train Hollins—who had broken his hand on Tree Rollins' head in the opening play-off game back in April, and who was pronounced out of commission by the team doctors—was back in action for the finals against L.A.

Game six on June 8, 1982, was the latest postseason game in the NBA up to that time (now the playoffs end even later in June). When it was over, the Lakers had won 114-104. Jamaal Wilkes scored 27 points, and Magic Johnson hit three lucky thirteens—13 points, 13 rebounds, 13 assists. Again, the Sixers had gotten within reach of the championship—only to watch it slip from their grasp.

## Harold Katz's Obsession

Going into the 1982–83 season, Harold Katz announced that he wanted a new style of play from the 76ers: physical. "This is a team of nice guys," he said. "We lead the NBA in helping guys to their feet. That's gotta stop. I want this team to lead the NBA in knocking guys on their can."

We drafted Mark McNamara, a seven-foot-tall center from the University of California. Mark had led the Pac-10 Conference in rebounding and scoring, a rare double threat that had previously been the province of only Bill Walton and Kareem Abdul-Jabbar. He was a bright young man with an interest in conservation and animals, and he kept pet snakes in his room. When we introduced him to the local media at a press conference, we surprised him by presenting him with a large affectionate python from the Philadelphia Zoo. We also surprised owner Harold Katz, coach Billy Cunningham, and assorted other attendees, who stampeded for the nearest exit. Mark cradled it like a kitten and allowed it to slither all around him throughout the rest of the press conference. The picture of Mark McNamara with a python wrapped around his neck made every sports page in America.

In August 1982, Jill and I joined Julius Erving; his wife, Turquoise; and five other NBA players for a two-week trip through mainland China. It was a fabulous adventure through an exotic land, but we also saw a lot of poverty and human sadness, including a number of children who had no homes. While we were in Beijing, Jill inquired of some of the Chinese officials whether it was possible for Americans to adopt orphans from mainland China. She was told that it was completely out of the question.

When we got to Hong Kong, I phoned the 76ers office in Philadelphia and asked, "Any news from Philly?"

Oh, there was news, all right. Katz and Billy C. had been busy trading our backboard-busting star center, Darryl Dawkins, to the New Jersey Nets for six hundred thousand dollars and a first-round draft pick in '83. I felt as helpless as if I were on the moon. There I was, twelve time zones away, and I was hearing that a huge talent trade had been conducted in my absence. This was not going to sit well with the fans, I realized—especially coming on the heels of a hefty hike in ticket prices.

So Doc and I hopped on the next flight from Hong Kong to New York via Tokyo—twenty-four hours in the air. While we were returning, Katz was on his way to Reno for a little R and R. Little did I know that Harold Katz's mind was whirling like the turbine blades of a jet engine. Even on his vacation, his mind wouldn't rest. If I'd known what Katz had in mind, I would have thought he was crazy: he had become obsessed with acquiring one player—the legendary Moses Malone, the NBA's leading scorer and leading rebounder and two-time MVP. Malone had spent the past few seasons in a Houston Rockets uniform. In fact, Moses Malone practically *was* the Houston Rockets.

As his plane winged from Philly to Reno, Katz had plenty of time to think. And the more he thought, the more obsessed he became with hanging a Sixers uniform on Moses Malone. Sure, Malone was a free agent, he was available—but Katz already had the biggest payroll to meet in the NBA. Surely he didn't think he could meet Malone's asking price, did he?

Yes he did.

The moment he arrived in Reno, Harold called John Nash in the 76ers offices and said, "Call my attorney, call Moses Malone's agent, call Billy, and let's all get together in New York. Now."

"I thought you were on vacation," said Nash.

"Just do it."

Nash did it.

Harold Katz got back on the jet and flew straight to New York without having taken one breath of fresh Nevada air. In New York, he hunkered down with his attorney, Laurence Shaiman; Malone's agent, Lee Fentress; plus Billy Cunningham and Moses Malone. In a marathon, all-night session in a Manhattan hotel suite, Moses Malone came to terms with the Philadelphia 76ers for six years.

The price tag: a mere $13.2 million. That sounds like chump change in today's NBA dollars, but in 1982, it was a staggering sum.

The one factor Harold Katz found most impressive about Moses Malone was the big guy's attitude. They talked right through the night, and in all that time, Malone never once mentioned money. All he talked about was his desire to win a championship—and his willingness to do whatever it took to get it done. Katz knew a winning attitude when he saw it—and he was sold.

Meanwhile, Doc and I landed at LaGuardia and I called the 76ers office. When I heard that Harold Katz was in New York signing Moses Malone, my mouth fell open. I turned to Doc and told him. His mouth fell open.

At first, I felt a little cheated. I had always been in the middle of talent acquisition, orchestrating the big deals—but I was completely out of the loop while the deal of the century was taking place. Then it hit me: This really was the deal of the century. One of the best centers in the NBA was now a 76er. Doc and I could not believe our good fortune. We finally had put together everything we needed for an NBA championship.

Inevitably, Houston, which had the right to match our offer to Malone, fought the deal. We ended up in arbitration, and we wound up giving Caldwell Jones and a first-round draft pick to Houston. It was the same draft pick we had been protecting since we got it in 1978 from the Denver Nuggets, along with

Bobby Jones and Ralph Simpson. Surrendering that draft pick hurt. Also hurt was Moses Malone. It turned out that Caldwell Jones was one of his best friends and was one of the reasons Malone was looking forward to playing in Philly. The consolation for Malone was that he could win an NBA title in Philadelphia—something that was clearly out of reach in Houston.

The team revealed the Malone acquisition at a press conference at Veterans Stadium. There was a Phillies baseball game at the Vet that night, so a lot of sports fans were lining the stadium concourse as Moses and a group of Sixers execs made their way to the press conference. Suddenly a spontaneous cheer went up all along the concourse, followed by an exuberant chant of "Mo-ses! Mo-ses! Mo-ses!" Our new star center grinned back at the fans. He later told me that in all his seasons in Houston, he had never received the warm response he got that night from a bunch of Philadelphia fans who had come to watch a baseball game.

## "I Hate This Marriage"

History books say the bombing of Pearl Harbor occurred on a Sunday in December 1941. For me, the bomb dropped on a Sunday in December 1982. That was the day Jill told me, "I hate this marriage. It's boring me to death. I just don't care anymore." All this time, I had thought I had the perfect life with a great marriage.

Sure, there were problems and annoyances. I didn't like Jill's silent treatments, her complaining that I didn't spend enough time with her, her moodiness. I had just assumed that she was a bit self-centered and emotional, that it was a "woman thing." Didn't she understand how important my career was? Didn't she know how much time it takes to manage a successful NBA team? Being a sports general manager is not just an eight-hours-a-day, forty-hours-a-week job—it's evenings and weekends and even the middle of the night. I figured if I just kept a positive attitude, she'd eventually come around.

I didn't realize that, ten years after our whirlwind courtship and wedding, Jill had not come around at all. She had given up. She wasn't considering divorce. Instead, she had resigned herself to a life of married misery and loneliness with a man she thought was too busy and too career-centered.

So when I asked her one day what was bothering her, why she was giving me the silent treatment all through church, she dropped the bomb: "I hate this marriage." I hadn't expected that. I thought she was upset over some ill-chosen words I had said before church. I assumed I could placate her with a simple "I'm sorry."

But this was no little tiff over a few thoughtless words. This was the total meltdown of a marriage. The first question my stunned mind formed was, *How do I fix this?* That's what guys do, right? If something's broken, we fix it. "What can I do?" I asked.

"Nothing," she said. "There's nothing you can do now. I don't even know if I love you anymore. I don't know if I ever loved you." The clues had been there all along, but I hadn't seen them. For months, she had been telling me there was a major problem between us, but I just hadn't seen it.

On that Sunday in 1982, Jill finally got my attention. She was telling me that she was emotionally dead—and that I had killed her with my neglect of her feelings. To this day, I believe her demands for my time and attention were excessive and unreasonable, and I tried all along to respond to her complaints as they arose. But at the same time, I have to confess that I wasn't really listening to her—if I had been, this moment of confrontation wouldn't have come as such a shock.

I turned immediately to my Bible and to prayer. "Lord, remind me of all the offenses I've committed against Jill, and show me how I can make it right." As I prayed, I began to remember specific incidences when I had probably hurt or neglected her. I wrote down everything I could recall, then I prayed over the list, asking God to heal our relationship.

I decided that things were going to be different, and I committed myself to a greater focus on my marriage. I immersed myself in a book on marriage, *Love-Life for Every Married Cou-*

*ple* by Dr. Ed Wheat, a physician from Springdale, Arkansas. Reading that book, I was astounded at how much I didn't know about the process of being successfully married. I found a whole armload of principles for rebuilding a broken marriage, and I was determined to try them all if only I could regain Jill's love. The essence of Dr. Wheat's message is summed up in his BEST theory, which I worked hard to implement. BEST stands for blessing, edifying, sharing, and touching, and it's the basis of the message of *Rekindled,* the book Jill and I wrote with Jerry Jenkins.

Blessing is speaking well of your mate, responding with good words, doing kind acts, showing verbal appreciation, and praying for God's highest blessing in your partner's life. Edifying means building up and encouraging your mate, giving verbal praise and compliments, establishing peace and harmony in the home, and avoiding criticism. Sharing involves sharing time together, interests, concerns, ideas, innermost thoughts, a spiritual walk, working toward family objectives, achieving goals, and so forth—something that does not come naturally for most men. It means opening up oneself, listening with care to feelings and needs, and developing awareness. Touching conveys that one's mate is cared for; it calms fears, soothes pain, brings comfort, and provides emotional security. We all have a deep need for the warmth, reassurance, and intimacy of nonsexual touching.

During the holiday season, I launched a courtship campaign to win Jill back, applying the BEST lessons to our marriage in massive doses. It was then that I had an encounter—at a turkey farm, of all places—that changed our lives forever.

Three days before Christmas 1982, Jill was still scarcely speaking to me. She had ordered a freshly dressed turkey from a farm in Pemberton, New Jersey, and I was to pick it up after the office party at the Sixers headquarters. I was not in a particularly festive mood at the party, though I pasted on a smile and went through the motions of celebrating with the Sixers staff. Inside, all I could think of was that my wife was barely able to speak to me or look at me.

For days, I had been praying continually for a sign from God as to what I could do to save our marriage. The first sign came at the office party—and the second would come at the turkey farm.

During the party, there was a drawing for an all-expenses-paid trip for two to Disney World and the EPCOT Center in Orlando. I couldn't believe it when my name was called—I had never won anything in my life. It hit me that this was God's answer to my prayer: *Take Jill on a vacation, just the two of you. Shower her with attention. This is my gift to both of you.* So I gratefully accepted the prize and couldn't wait to get home to tell Jill.

But first I had to drive out to Pemberton and pick up that turkey. It was dark as I left the office in Philly. Arriving at the snow-bedecked turkey farm, I found that a number of people were there to pick up their turkeys. A chilly December wind was blowing, so I gathered my coat around me and waited in line.

I noticed the couple ahead of me—the man was carrying a tiny bundle of blankets on his shoulder. Looking closer, I saw a pair of dark, almond eyes peeking out from those blankets. Here was a Caucasian couple carrying an Asian infant. Instantly, memories of all the times Jill had urged me to consider adopting an Asian orphan flooded my mind.

As a girl, Jill often had imagined herself in charge of an orphanage, giving love to children who had no one else to love them. More than once, she had told me of how she had played with her doll collection and her stuffed animals, pretending that some were her birth children and some were her adopted children, and that she would love each one exactly the same. The dream had persisted into adulthood.

I had never taken her seriously. "It's a nice daydream for childhood," I had told her, dismissing her deep yearning with a wave of my hand, "but it's a silly idea for grownups. I'm not sure I could even love a child who wasn't my own. The answer is no." Looking back, it's hard to believe I ever felt that way.

I had grown up in the 1940s, when adoption was a bad word—it carried a stigma like that of leprosy. I realize now how idiotic those notions and stereotypes were—but I bought into them at the time. I was prejudiced against adoption because I had heard all the lame arguments, such as, "Why take on someone else's problems?" Well, that's an argument for not buying a clunky used car. A child isn't a used car. A child is a human being in need of love and a place to belong. But I wasn't ready to take on the responsibility.

Jill had refused to let go of the dream. She had raised the idea when Vietnamese babies were airlifted to the States after the fall of Saigon. She had raised it again when we visited mainland China with Julius and Turquoise Erving in 1982. Every time she raised it, my response was, "Forget it, Jill, I'm not even willing to think about it."

But as I stood in line behind this American couple with the Asian baby, I realized God was giving me another answer to my prayer: *If you want to win Jill back, open your mind to her dream.* I knew it was no accident that I had just happened to step in behind this couple.

I was choked up with emotion, so I first composed myself, then asked the couple about their baby, how the adoption had been accomplished, which adoption agency they had worked with, and other questions. They told me about the costs, the long and agonizing wait, the problems and frustrations of the adoption process—and they told me it was worth it all. It turned out that they lived in Moorestown, not far from us. They invited me to bring my family over to visit sometime.

I got the turkey, threw it in the car, and drove home at something like the speed of light. I rushed in and told Jill everything that happened—winning the Orlando trip, the conversation at the turkey farm, everything. She was cool to me. She said I was always quick to jump on a bandwagon, but she didn't believe anything I said would make a difference. Besides, the way she felt about me, the thought of spending a whole weekend in Florida with me didn't hold much allure.

Even when our family visited with the Burkheimers, the couple with the Korean infant, Jill kept her emotional distance. She was baffled by my sudden fixation on adoption—an idea I had once ridiculed into oblivion. She was even more baffled the next day when I called the adoption agency, Holt International in Eugene, Oregon, and requested information and an application. "Why are you doing this?" she asked. "Why do you want to bring another child into our home? You don't even know if you have a wife anymore!"

"I was wrong before," I said. "I can see that now." I admit it. My motives were mixed. Yes, I had fallen in love with the idea that there was a child out there who needed us and we could provide that child a home. But I was also trying to win back my wife, and if I had to paddle a canoe all the way to Korea and back to do it, I was willing.

Over the next couple of weeks, Jill's desire to adopt was reawakened, especially after she saw the materials sent by Holt International. I convened a family meeting around the kitchen table. Jimmy, Bobby, and four-year-old Karyn were all present and accounted for as I laid the question on the table: "Your mother and I would like to adopt a baby from Korea. What do you think?"

Jimmy and Bobby were enthusiastic—as long as they got a little brother out of the deal. Karyn was equally enthusiastic—for a sister. "Okay," said Jill, "let's ask for one of each." By February, we had completed and returned the application.

During the late winter and early spring of 1983, Jill's attitude toward me began to thaw. She saw I was serious about becoming a more attentive husband and father. Out of this time and the lessons I learned came the books Jill and I authored with Jerry Jenkins, *Rekindled* and *Keep the Fire Glowing*, both of which became best-sellers. Even after the eventual dissolution of our marriage, I still believe in the principles in those books. I hoped and believed at the time that those principles had saved our marriage.

The lessons we learned did buy a twelve-year extension. With the best of intentions, I continued to try to apply those lessons in the years that followed. In my mind, having searched my heart and memory, I believe I did all a man in my position could do to live out the biblical and practical principles of *Rekindled*. I realize that Jill has a very different perspective from mine, but I honestly believe she asked more of me than a man could or should be expected to give.

## Moses and Mo

On the career front, the year of Moses Malone was moving forward. At 6'10", he certainly was not the tallest center in the game. There were plenty of players with bigger hands, faster legs, a higher leap, a more accurate shot. By all objective standards, Moses Malone shouldn't have been one of the best in the game—but he was.

I spent many hours watching him play, and I concluded there's only one explanation for his greatness: Moses Malone had *attitude*. The man never quit. He thrived on intense competition and physical contact. The rougher it got, the better he played. The more hands in his face, the more deadly accurate his shot. The more energy expended by the opponent to contain him, the more power he had to break free. The longer the game went, the stronger he became. In Houston, he had averaged an amazing forty-two minutes of playing time every game. In my opinion, Moses Malone was the hardest-working player in the history of the sport. Moses once put it this way, describing himself in the third person: "It's never easy for Moses. Moses got to get out there every night and work hard."

Moses was not a strong defensive player—he seemed to conserve his energy for scoring and rebounding. His lack of speed seemed to be a major mismatch for the 76ers' run-and-gun style. Billy Cunningham had been coaching the team toward ever-increasing speed and quickness, and our guard acquisitions were always designed to ratchet up the velocity of the team. Then we added Moses—a center with a slow-down style that demands the offense revolves around him. There were some who claimed Moses was really a power forward posing as a center, some who claimed he could only play a half-court, set-it-up offense, and some who claimed he couldn't coexist with Dr. J.

There was no way to know what the team chemistry would be until all the ingredients were mixed and shaken on the court.

When we introduced Moses to the Philadelphia scribes in a raucous, sweltering press conference that September evening at the ballpark, he displayed humility and a superlative team attitude. "This team is Doc's show," he began. "Doc has always been a great show, and now I've got a chance to play with Doc, and I think it's gonna be a better show. I know what I've got to do to help this team. I'm not gonna try to do what I can't do. I'm just gonna play my game—attack the boards, go to the offensive boards, look for the fast break, look to rebound."

This was not false humility. Malone knew who he was and what he could do—and he said so. "I came into the league right from high school," he continued, "a kid just like Darryl Dawkins. They tried to put labels on me. Can't do this, can't do that. I can do anything in the world with the ball." No brag, just fact.

After the press conference, which was an overwhelming hit with the media, I took Moses into the locker room. The Phillies were playing the Cardinals that night and were about to go out for the start of the game. The Phillies players went nuts when Malone entered the locker room. Pete Rose—"Charlie Hustle" himself—ran over and welcomed Moses to Philadelphia. Luis Aguayo, the 5'9" shortstop, couldn't get over Malone's height. When Moses held his arm straight out from his side, Louis could walk under it without bumping his head. Malone loved the reception he got from the Philadelphia baseball greats. It was one of many warm Philly receptions for Moses Malone.

As the season approached, we had to prune the roster to make room for Malone. Regretfully, we gave up Steve Mix and Lionel Hollins. Then, on the first day of training camp, we had one unexpected, unexcused absence: Maurice Cheeks. It turned out that Mo was unhappy with his contract, which still had four years to run.

I tracked Mo down in Chicago and persuaded him to fly to Philadelphia to meet with Harold Katz and me. So Mo flew into town and took a cab to the Bellevue Stratford Hotel in Center City where Harold was attending a black tie dinner in his honor. I met Mo at the hotel and rushed him up the stairs. I was afraid the media might get wind of Mo's dissatisfaction, and I didn't want that kind of publicity for the team. I needed a hiding place for Mo until Katz could get away from the dinner—but where do you hide a star in a building full of people?

Off one of the upper floor landings, I found a—well, you couldn't call it a balcony—it wasn't that big. It was really more of a window ledge with a couple of potted trees. When I told him where I wanted him to wait, Mo frowned and said, "Hey, what is this, Williams? You want me to wait out *there?*"

"Sure," I said. "You're not afraid of heights, are you?"

"Well, no, but—"

"Fine, then. The fresh air will do you good."

"But wait a minute—"

"It's a warm night out, so you shouldn't be too uncomfortable."

"I know, but how long do I have to wait out there?"

"Only a few minutes."

"A few minutes, huh?"

Reluctantly, he agreed to wait behind the potted plants so no one could see him from inside the building or the street below. Half an hour went by, and the banquet was still dragging on. I waited till the coast was clear on the landing and I went and checked on Mo. "You doing okay out there?"

"There's a breeze coming up—I think I'm catching cold."

"Well, Mr. Katz will be out any minute now."

"Williams, this is the stupidest—"

I shut the window.

About fifteen minutes later, the banquet broke up and Harold came out in his tie and tails. We found an empty conference room, and I got Mo off the ledge. The three of us sat down and talked about the reasons Mo had not shown up at training camp.

"I'm concerned about my future," he said. "I've seen guys get dealt away from this team, and I don't want to leave. I want to keep playing here. I want a guarantee I'll be playing for the Sixers for a long time."

Is that all he wants? He's got it! We agreed to extend his contract, and Mo reported for camp the next morning. That year, he gave us the best season of his career, including his first of four career selections to the NBA All-Star team. He went on to become the 76ers' all-time leader in both assists and steals. By the time he finished his career (playing 11 of his 14 seasons with the 76ers), he had been in 1,101 games and racked up

7,392 assists and 2,310 steals—an NBA theft record that remained unsurpassed until John Stockton broke it in 1996.

## An Injection of Hope

The 1982–83 season began for us in Madison Square Garden. A group of us set off in plenty of time from Philly in Harold Katz's long limo, but we got caught up in a traffic snarl in the Lincoln Tunnel. We arrived in time for the tip-off, without time for a leisurely New York restaurant meal. So we grabbed burgers and fries at the McDonald's across from the Garden, and we inhaled those burgers while Doc, Moses, and Co., inhaled the Knicks. Despite the heartburn, it was an auspicious beginning.

Our home opener was against ex-Sixer Darryl Dawkins and the New Jersey Nets. It was a tough, seesaw game for forty-odd minutes of playing time—and it was obvious Darryl wanted his return to Philly to be triumphant. But in the closing minutes, Moses Malone took control of the game, grabbing every rebound, and reaping a frenzied ovation from a packed house.

Any questions and doubts that greeted Malone's addition to the team were answered in the first few games. Yes, Moses could play the running game. Yes, he could dominate any center in the NBA. Yes, he could play defense. Yes, the Sixers' game was enhanced, not disrupted, by the addition of the thirteen-million-dollar man. Our previous center, Darryl Dawkins, could be a genius one night and wear a dunce cap the next. But Moses Malone gave us something at the pivot we had never had before: consistency. On his worst night, Malone could be counted on for at least twenty-five points and fifteen rebounds. And on his best nights—look out!

And durable? Malone was a board-crashing Rock of Gibraltar. When the hated Boston Celtics came to the Spectrum, the Sixers had to battle through two overtime periods. Out of fifty-eight minutes of game time, Moses played fifty-six. Best of all, we won. And in early December, when the Sixers journeyed west to play the equally hated Lakers on their home court, Moses creamed Kareem. In three straight possessions during the crucial fourth quarter, Moses turned offensive rebounds into baskets. Again, we emerged victorious—and Malone was the difference.

We once calculated that we were paying Malone something like five hundred dollars a minute. We considered it a bargain. He brought a new attitude to the Sixers. Though there was no denying that our team was mentally tough, there was also no denying that years of playoff disappointments had taken their toll on the team's spirit. When you absorb so much pain over so many years, you begin to think it's your lot in life, that the brass ring will never be within your reach. The effect is subconscious, but it's very real. Moses gave us a much-needed injection of hope and confidence.

Maurice Cheeks put it this way: "When we got Moses, our minds changed right away. Having him was an important thing for us psychologically—just as important as what he brings us on the floor."

By season's end, we had won sixty-five games and lost only seventeen—a phenomenal record. Moses, Doc, Andrew Toney, and Maurice Cheeks all made the All-Star team. Along the way, we had fortified the team, adding seasoned veterans such as forward Reggie Johnson from Kansas City and backup center Clemon Johnson from Indiana. We compiled the best record in the league while shattering all previous home attendance records. We clinched the first-round playoff bye, avoiding the risk of a miniseries. Throughout the season, the crowds chanted "Mo-ses! Mo-ses! Mo-ses!" I often had to pinch myself to make sure I wasn't dreaming. No, it was all real. The wins. The crowds. The cheers. All real.

But then, just days before the playoffs, came the nightmare.

Moses, who had been playing like some Olympian god of basketball, suddenly became horribly, alarmingly mortal. He developed tendinitis in one knee. Dr. Clancy ordered a week of rest for Moses—and though Malone had earned it, he didn't want it. He couldn't remember a time when he had gone a whole week without playing basketball.

Billy moved the team to Lancaster for a three-day refresher camp to keep the team sharp until the playoffs. When Moses arrived at camp, there was a new horror: his other knee had tendinitis-like symptoms. We rushed him to Philadelphia for X-rays, and after he struggled to get out of the car, he couldn't walk. As Moses was carried into the hospital, we stood in numb dread, both for Moses and the 76ers. Here, on the doorstep of the playoffs, on the verge of our long-sought NBA title, calamity had struck once more.

I couldn't help wondering: *Is there some sort of curse on the Sixers? Are we star-crossed? How can this be happening?*

## Nixing the Knicks

Moses Malone sat on the locker room bench after practice, unlacing his sneakers. His knees were wrapped in protective sleeves. The Sixers' first game of the 1983 playoffs was less than twenty-four hours away. Billy Cunningham sat down beside Malone. "Well, Mos'," he said, "how're we gonna do in the play-offs?"

Without looking up, Malone rumbled, "Fo' . . . Fo' . . . Fo'!"

"I believe you, Mos'," said Billy, slapping him on the back, "I believe you."

Fo' . . . Fo' . . . Fo'! It was a bold, brazen prediction: one four-game sweep, followed by another, followed by another—four, four, four. It had never been done before—a sweep of the entire playoffs. The best any team had ever done in the playoffs was twelve and two. Moses predicted twelve and zero. Mere bravado? No. Moses believed it. He sensed something good was about to happen to this team, despite the fact that both of his knees felt as if they were being used as pincushions—and despite the fact that he couldn't even make one trip up and down the court in practice.

Moses Malone's quiet confidence inspired his teammates, and his simply stated prediction became the Sixers' battle cry: "Fo' . . . Fo' . . . Fo'!"

The Philadelphia 76ers faced the New York Knicks in the quarterfinals. The first game was in the Spectrum on Sunday, April 24, 1983. Moses took to the court soon after bags of ice were strapped to his knees. It was almost four minutes into the game when the ball first went to Moses in the paint. He received the pass, wheeled, hammered his way through a defensive triple-team, and hooked a shot that rattled in the cylinder before it fell for two points. It was official: Moses could play! He gave us 38 minutes and a lot of heart that day, scoring 38 points, 17 rebounds, and zero limps. Final score: Sixers 112, Knicks 102.

Game two, on Wednesday, April 28, was another story. Bobby Jones was out of that game with the flu. Andrew Toney was sidelined with a deep thigh bruise. The Sixers were in their own house again, yet they played as if they were dead on their feet. Early in the second half, they trailed by 20. The Knicks were ready to celebrate—but a little too soon. In one astounding skyrocket of a scoring spurt, the Sixers took over the game with a 22-1 run. The stunned Knicks watched the game slip away from them. For the Philly fans, it was one of the most memorable games ever, ending in a 98-91 Sixers victory. It was the Moses and Mo show, with Malone collecting 30 points and Cheeks 26.

Even Knicks coach Hubie Brown had to admire what the Sixers did to his team. "Even though it happened against us," he said, "it was beautiful to watch."

Game three took us to Madison Square Garden on Saturday, April 30. It was a tight game from beginning to end. The score was knotted at 105 with four ticks left on the clock. The ball went to Franklin Edwards, who had subbed for Andrew Toney. Edwards darted around his defender, Ernie Grunfeld, only to find Truck Robinson rumbling over to intercept him. Edwards pump-faked and Robinson took the bait. Truck was coming down to the floor as Edwards was going up for the real shot—a sweet ten-footer that kissed the glass, then slipped through the net for two points. Final score: Philadelphia 107, New York 105.

Game four began with New York down three games to none on Sunday, May 1—otherwise known as "Mayday! Mayday!" for the desperate Knicks. The game was close until the final seven minutes. That's when Moses blocked a Knicks shot, swatting the ball into the hands of Franklin Edwards. Franklin relayed the ball to Julius Erving, who took the ball downcourt in a few long bounds, stuffed it, drawing the foul in the process, and collecting the free throw. At that point, Moses took over—rebounding, rejecting, and scoring like a man possessed. The Knicks fell in four straight. Malone—the man who, eight days earlier, had not even been able to walk into the hospital on his own—had just waged four hard-fought battles, scoring 125 points and snatching 62 rebounds.

The first third of his prediction had come true: "Fo'!"

The quick victory over the Knicks gave the Sixers a physical and psychological edge. The Sixers believed in their heart of hearts that this was their championship year at last. Moses and his battle-scarred comrades got a few extra days in the whirlpool bath before having to face the next opponent.

## Bucking the Bucks

We all expected the next opponent to be the Sixers' nemesis, the Boston Celtics. But the Milwaukee Bucks demolished the astonished Celts in a sweep. Many fans, understandably, felt cheated of a long-anticipated grudge-match between Boston and Philadelphia.

Still, the Bucks-Sixers pairing had its own fascination. It was the third straight postseason face-off for the two teams. In '81, the Sixers had survived by a single point in game seven; in '82, the Sixers had prevailed in six. Over the last three regular seasons, the Bucks and Sixers had played seventeen games, and the Sixers had won nine and lost eight. Eleven of those games had been decided by three points or less. So it was a good, tough, emotionally charged matchup.

Game one in the semifinals was at the Spectrum on Sunday, May 8. The Bucks and Sixers grappled into overtime, where Philadelphia won 111-109. Amazingly, all seven Sixers points scored in OT were delivered by Clint Richardson, who was only in the game because Andrew Toney had fouled out. That's the kind of power the Sixers were loaded with that year—most of the bench-sitters would have been starters on most other teams. They were that good.

Game two was a body-crunching physical contest between two teams obsessed with winning. The two coaches, Billy Cunningham and Don Nelson of the Bucks, had faced each other many times and knew each other's tactics well. It is a tough defensive game at both ends, as reflected in the low final score, Philadelphia 87, Milwaukee 81.

With game three on Saturday, May 14, the series moved to Milwaukee Arena. Going into the fourth quarter, the Sixers were down by seven points. The Bucks saw their lead erode and evaporate in a thirty-three-point Sixer blitz. The game ended in a big victory for Philly, 104-96. Dr. J had a big night, scoring 26 points, and Moses and Mo turned in strong supporting performances. For weeks, sports pundits had been writing off Doc as too old (age thirty-three and twelve seasons in the game) to keep up the pace of previous years. This game shut them up.

Game four was on Sunday, May 15, in Milwaukee. The Sixers stumbled defensively and lost the game 100-94. Malone's prediction of "Fo' . . . Fo' . . . Fo'!" had come unraveled. "Okay," said Moses, "so it'll be fo'-*five*-fo'."

In game five at the Spectrum, a healed and rested Andrew Toney stunned Milwaukee with 30 points, while Moses knocked down 28 and Doc hit 24. Clint Richardson dominated the Bucks on defense. Final score: Sixers 115, Bucks 103.

Dr. J summed up the 76ers' position in the playoffs: "We have the best team in basketball. Now all we have to do is go out and prove it." And the team they had to prove it against was the Los Angeles Lakers. In the final minutes of the last game against Milwaukee, the sellout crowd in the Spectrum threw up a chant of defiance: "We want L.A.! We want L.A.!"

## Parting the Waters

It's Sunday, May 22, 1983, and the Philly fans are getting their wish: The Lakers have subdued San Antonio in six games and are in the Spectrum for the first battle in the NBA title war. We've rolled out our ace national anthem musician, Grover Washington Jr., to fire up the crowd with a stirring, star-spangled opening. In this showdown, we are hosting Kareem and McAdoo, Magic and Silk, Norm Nixon, Michael Cooper, and Kurt Rambis—the defending champions.

Game one is an evenly matched, hard-fought contest through four quarters. With less than two minutes left in the game, the Sixers are up by eight—then disaster strikes. In their next four possessions, they allow three turnovers and miss a pair of free throws. Only a flurry of rebounds grabbed by Dr. J, Bobby Jones, and Moses, plus a pair of Malone free throws, manage to save the game. Philadelphia does not play well, yet manages to salvage a 113-107 win. Toney scores 25 for the night, and Moses does even better with 27.

The second game on Thursday, May 26, is unusual in that Moses plays only 31 minutes—he is sidelined for five and a half minutes in the fourth period because of foul trouble. Even so, the Sixers find they are able to win, 103-93. Lakers coach Pat Riley takes umbrage at the officiating. Noting that his players have been whistled for 29 fouls, compared with the Sixers' 16 (and, more important, that the Sixers made 23 free throws versus 3 for the Lakers), Riley singles out ref Darell Garretson for calling the game in a lopsided fashion. That accusation earns Pat a $3,000 fine for questioning the ref's integrity. The Lakers set a record in this game—the unenviable record for the fewest free throws attempted and made in a playoff game.

On Sunday, May 29, we go to the Forum in L.A. for game three. The 76ers know they are going to win an NBA title. The Lakers sense it too, and their desperation urges them to a fifteen-point lead in the second quarter. The Sixers have been in worse spots than this, and they know how to battle their way back. By the end of the third quarter, the score is tied at 72, and the Sixers are on a roll. They launch a 14-0 run that tears the heart out of the Lakers and leaves it quivering on the court. Final score: 111-94, Sixers.

Doc and Andrew leave the court with 21 points each. Bobby Jones, nine pounds lighter after a battle with strep throat, adds

17. Mo Cheeks has four steals. But the biggest gun in this game has been Moses Malone with 28 points (12 in the fourth quarter alone), 19 rebounds, and 6 assists. This is the third straight time the Sixers have overcome a Lakers' halftime lead. The Sixers are second-half gunslingers, shooting everything that moves. Billy Cunningham speaks for the entire team when he looks to the next game saying, "We want L.A. in four. We want people to remember this team."

On Tuesday, May 31, the 76ers—the rainbow chasers—return to the Forum in a quest for the pot of gold at the rainbow's end. As has become the habit of this team, they are trailing early in the second half—this time by 16 points. But the Sixers outscore the Lakers 64-43 in the second half—and win the fourth quarter by an 18-point margin. Final score: Philadelphia 115, Los Angeles 108.

We are champions at last!

The debt has been paid! Though it took years longer than anyone expected, the Sixers have finally delivered on that slogan, "We owe you one."

Best of all, it happens almost exactly as Moses Malone had promised: Fo' . . . *Five* . . . Fo'! Clearly, this prophet at the pivot is aptly named Moses. He foresaw three sweeps in a row, then parted the waters and led us to the promised land of an NBA championship.

As soon as the game is over, I rush to the Sixers' locker room to join in the celebration. Champagne sprays everywhere, on everybody, even the team execs in their Italian suits. Nobody cares. We have won the title! Doctor J, who has battled to bring an NBA championship to Philly since 1977, is elated. Lifting the trophy for all to see, he announces, "Seven years is a long time—but it was worth the wait!"

Moses Malone, who had bucketed 24 points and grabbed 23 rebounds that night, and who earned the playoff MVP award, wraps his arms around Billy Cunningham. Billy had been rumored to be considering departure from the team after the season. Over the hoots and roars of that celebration, Moses hollers in his ear, "Hey, Billy C.! You gotta come back, man! 'Cause we gonna repeat—and 'peat, and 'peat, and 'peat!" I hear that and think, *Hmm, catchy. Almost as catchy as "Fo' . . . Fo' . . . Fo'!"*

For some unknown reason, Moses is still in his sweat-soaked Sixers jersey as the celebration begins, but he has incongruously knotted a tie around his neck. As the reporters surge into the locker room to get their quotes and snap their pictures, Earl Cureton introduces Moses as "Al Capone Malone—he steals basketball games."

Moses is happiest not for himself but for Julius Erving. "This is Doc's team, not Moses' team," he tells the reporters, just as he had said at his initial press conference. "Moses is just here to help Doc win. Moses is just a player, that's all Moses is." But what a player!

The Sixers return to Philly for a heroes' welcome. The victory parade begins at 11:30 A.M. Thursday, June 2. The team gets up on a glass-walled flatbed truck and sets out at Twentieth and JFK Boulevard in Center City, winding through the heart of the business district, down South Broad Street, all the way to Veterans Stadium. Along the way they are showered with confetti and thunderous cheers of adoration from an estimated one million fans. At the Vet, 55,000 more fans fill the stands.

The outpouring of brotherly love is long and loud as Julius Erving steps to the microphone and addresses the fans. When they finally allow him to speak, he says, "I've been trying to get here for seven years. So let us take a moment and trace back a little way. On three different occasions, we almost made it. But those occasions should not be forgotten, because it wasn't just the 76ers that made it. It was the city of Philadelphia, too."

Then, as the crowd roars its approval, Doc lifts the golden championship trophy in one hand. With the other, he reaches out to Billy Cunningham and embraces him. Then, their eyes glistening with emotion, both men raise their hands and receive the acclaim they have earned. They had chased the rainbow, captured it, and brought it home to Philadelphia.

# 10

# Magic in the Air

In early June 1983, just days after the Sixers won the NBA championship, Jill and I got a call from Pat Keltie, the social worker in Trenton, New Jersey, who was helping us with the adoption process. "Holt International has combed every orphanage in South Korea," she told me, "and they can't come up with a brother-sister combination to adopt, but I do have a photo they sent showing two little sisters. I guarantee your family will just fall in love with them. These girls are really cute!"

The black-and-white snapshot showed two toddlers wearing frilly jumpers with tags pinned on them. The girls were unsmiling and appeared to need a little cleaning up. Their hair looked as if it had been cut with a weed-whacker. Both looked like they really needed someone to love them.

Pat Keltie was right—we did fall in love with those girls. Even our boys, who had demanded a little brother, took one look at the photo and asked, "When are they coming?" Their given names were Yoo Jung and Yoo Jin, and they had been abandoned on the doorstep of a Seoul police station in early 1983. We quickly agreed to take them. Then began the process of waiting while the paperwork was processed by the Korean government and the U.S. Department of Immigration and Naturalization.

Even before they arrived, we renamed them. Yoo Jung became Andrea Michelle and Yoo Jin became Sarah Elizabeth. Jill painted their bedroom a pale shade of peach and stenciled a strip of teddy bears along the upper wall. She bought dresses and teddy bears so everything would be ready when they arrived. The social worker gave us a page of Korean phrases so we could communicate while the girls learned English.

At the beginning of September, we got word that the girls would soon be put on a plane and brought to the States. We decided to grab a brief family getaway at Eagles Meer in Pennsylvania's Endless Mountains before plunging into the new routine with our expanded family. One evening, Jill decided to go horseback riding, so she drove our car from the summer home to the stable. She switched on the car radio and listened to music while she drove. As she pulled up to the stable, the news came on—and Jill was stunned to hear the announcer describe the downing of Korean Airlines Flight 007 over the Pacific Ocean with no survivors.

Sickened with fear, Jill asked herself, "Was that the plane my babies are on?" Even though her only link to Andrea and Sarah was a dogeared photo, they had already become our children—just as much as the other three Williams children. She was a mother—a panicked, distraught, terrified mother. It took us a while to get any information from Korea, but Pat Keltie finally confirmed that the girls had not left Korea—they were still waiting at the orphanage.

The girls didn't leave until three weeks later. The twenty-seven-hour flight, which included layovers in Tokyo, Seattle, and Minneapolis, reached Philadelphia on Wednesday, September 23, 1983. There were camera crews from all three network affiliates, plus reporters from every newspaper. Scores of bewildered passengers filed off the plane under the glare of the TV floodlights, wondering what all the hubbub was about. Finally, Andrea, age two, and Sarah, three, were carried from the plane by an off-duty flight attendant who had volunteered to be the girls' escort. Each girl clutched an inflatable Mickey

Mouse given them by a passenger at the Tokyo airport—though both dolls had deflated during the trip.

There was so much noise and confusion, we couldn't hear the flight attendant's question: "Where's the mommy?" But Jill could read lips, and she instantly swooped in and embraced our new daughters.

I don't think the awesome reality of what we had done really hit until we were standing there at the airport with the girls finally wrapped in our arms. Then it hit hard: These girls were now part of our family for life, every bit as much as if Jill had given birth to them. I experienced exactly the same over-whelming joy mingled with solemn responsibility I had felt when Jimmy, Bobby, and Karyn were born. We had driven to the airport as a family of five, and we went home as a family of seven. Little did I imagine how full that van—and our lives—would become.

That night, Jill put the girls in bed, and they were instantly asleep, tuckered from their long journey. At midnight, our entire household was awakened by a long, mournful wail. Jill and I rushed to the girls' bedroom to find Sarah sitting upright in her bed. Andrea, in the next bed, was rubbing her eyes and stirring. We grabbed our list of Korean phrases and tried to reassure Sarah. Finally, Jill took the girls into our bedroom and tried to get them to go back to sleep.

But the girls weren't about to go to sleep. They were still func-tioning on Korean time—so from their point of view, it was mid-afternoon. So Jill lay back while the two girls bounced and played on our big bed. Jill saw that sleep was out of the ques-tion, so she took the girls to the kitchen and asked in phonetic Korean, "Are you hungry?" Absolutely, they were hungry! So Jill gave the girls cookies, bananas, milk, whatever they wanted—and the three of them had a tea party at three in the morning.

The next day, Jill bathed Sarah and Andrea and had their hair cut. Jimmy, Bobby, and Karyn stayed home from school and got acquainted with their new sisters. And that's how our family was introduced to the adoption experience—an experience we would repeat again and again in the years to come. Later, we would add one more birth child and twelve more adopted children from around the world. Whenever people would ask me how many children I have, I would say, "Eighteen, fourteen of which are adopted—but I forget which fourteen."

## Restless Summer

That summer, I worked with Philadelphia sportswriter Bill Lyon on a chronicle of the Sixers' uphill battle to the NBA title. *We Owed You One!* was released in September to enthusiastic response from fans and reviewers. We had won a championship, and the emotions of that triumph carried us all the way through the summer and into the fall. It was time to gear ourselves up to do it again. We had a title to defend.

Several years prior to that, assistant coach Chuck Daly had said something to me that I've never forgotten: "Ours is a suffering business, because at the end of the year, everybody is suffering except one team." Until he said that, I'd never looked at our business that way—but it is true. Think about it: The best teams in the league go into the playoffs—and every team except one ends the season in a spirit-crushing loss. Only one team gets to celebrate at the end. A suffering business, indeed.

In 1983, that team celebrating was the Philadelphia 76ers. But in the 1983–84 season, we all learned that one of the toughest things to do is to come back and play again after winning a championship. When you approach game one of the new season, it doesn't matter that you won it all the year before. This is a new year, and the schedule ahead of you is a blank slate.

That year I gained a whole new level of respect for Red Auerbach, coach of the Boston Celtics in their heyday. Red coached that team to eight consecutive NBA championships. His team dominated the game for the better part of a decade. That was the Bill Russell era, and during his thirteen-year career, Russell played on eleven championship teams. So I admired coaches like Red Auerbach and players like Bill Russell who delivered championships with dominating consistency. And I gained even more respect for baseball manager Casey Stengel, who guided the New York Yankees to seven World Series championships, including a record five in a row from 1949 to 1953. I remain absolutely in awe of that accomplishment.

Instead of dominating the 1983–84 season and establishing a dynasty, the 76ers struggled. Oh, we had a good year—a regular season record of 52-30. But we didn't play with the same fire we had in the previous season. It was noticeable on the court and felt in the locker room: Something was missing.

We were knocked out of the first-round playoff miniseries by the New Jersey Nets. Can you believe it? The first round! Instead of "fo'! fo'! fo'!" we were knocked out in a five game series, losing all three games at home.

Though life around the Spectrum was punctuated with frustration, life on the home front was sprinkled with joy. We had our five wonderful kids—Jimmy, Bobby, Karyn, Sarah, and Andrea—plus news that one more was on the way. Jill and I sat down and explained what was happening inside Mommy, and there were lots of questions. One question we didn't expect: "Can we be there when the baby is born?"

Jill asked her doctor, Brian Geary, if that was okay, and he said that was no problem. Jill was four months along before she learned she was pregnant—she had gone to the doctor to find out why she was so tired lately—so the baby came along just five months later, on June 12, 1984. The whole family was there to welcome him into the world, and we named him Michael Patrick, after Phillies slugger Mike Schmidt and me.

The draft at the end of the '83–84 season went down in history as one of the most talent-laden drafts in NBA history, and we monitored the season very closely. That was the year the Sixers drafted Charles Barkley. It was also the year Michael Jordan and Hakeem Olajuwon were drafted. We had the San Diego Clippers' number one pick because of the deal we had made in '78, when we shipped Lloyd Free to the Clippers. This was in the days before the lottery, and the Clippers were having a terrible season, which made our draft pick potentially valuable. The worst team in each division would flip a coin, and the winner would have a choice between two of the top players who ever played the game, Jordan and Olajuwon. Throughout that year, the Clippers stayed in the cellar—until Houston took what appeared to be a deliberate nosedive to qualify for first pick in the draft. That led to the present lottery system, which was devised to keep a team from dying down the stretch just to grab a top draft pick.

The next to last day of the season, the Rockets fell below the Clippers in the standings to become the worst team in the NBA—and the value of our number one draft pick dropped like a stone. We went from getting Michael or Hakeem by the flip of a coin to having a mere fifth pick in the draft. Houston took Olajuwon, and Chicago took Michael Jordan. The rest is history.

With our fifth pick, we were looking at Charles Barkley, a 6'4", 292 pound round mound of rebound from Auburn. We took him and took a deep breath, not sure how Sir Charles would pan out. We put playing-weight clauses in his contract because we were concerned about his self-discipline and work ethic. Barkley also was famous for his confrontations with Coach Sonny Smith at Auburn.

As it turned out, we had nothing to worry about in any department. Though Charles Barkley has acquired something of a bad boy reputation, we found him pleasant, easy to talk to, and a team player. Sometimes he'd get upset about something and he'd sulk or pout, but he was coachable and willing to work hard. He was also fiercely competitive—he didn't take losing well—and that's what we wanted to see in a 76er. In his rookie season, 1984–85, we could see that he was going to be someone special—and he is.

That season, we again made it into the playoffs—and we again went home empty when the Celtics beat us in five games. The last game in Boston is etched in my memory. To stay in the playoffs, we needed to win game five so we could get back to Philly for game six. It was a one-point contest right down to the buzzer. We set up a play to get the ball to Andrew Toney for the final shot, but Larry Bird defended it well and Toney's shot was off the mark. It was a crushing loss. I remember sitting on the bench with John Nash and Harold Katz. The Garden had emptied, the teams were in the locker rooms, and the three of us just sat there on the bench, so devastated we couldn't move or speak for about fifteen minutes.

I need to explain something about Harold Katz. The guy is a fascinating character, a study in contradictions. Damon Runyon would have loved him, would have written dozens of stories about him. To this day, when I get together with friends from those days on the 76ers, we inevitably break out in a rash of Harold Katz anecdotes. Most of the stories revolve around what we have come to call Katzonomics—the financial approach of a man who spent money as if it were water to acquire top-drawer basketball talent but who choked on the high price of paper clips.

As we sat defeated in Boston Garden, unable to move, unable to speak—Harold Katz gave us a classic lesson in Katzonomics. He looked up at the radio booth and saw Jack McMahon Jr., the son of our assistant coach, who was helping out by keeping game stats, even though he was not on the Sixers payroll. Harold awoke from this near-suicidal gloom that enveloped all of us, pointed at Jack Jr., and said, "Who paid his way up here?"

In the summer of 1982, when Harold signed Moses Malone in New York, John Nash was with him throughout that all-night meeting. At about 2 A.M., Harold told John, "Call Al Domenico, and let him know we're signing Malone." Al was the team trainer. So John made some calls, tracked Al down at a place on the beach in the next county, and filled him in on the deal. Then John went back to Harold and said, "I called him and brought him up to speed on the deal." Harold frowned and asked, "How much did that phone call cost? Whose credit card did you put it on?" He was dead serious. In the middle of a $13.2 million deal, he wanted to make sure we weren't wasting too many nickels in long-distance charges.

When Harold took over as the owner of the Sixers, in the 1981–82 season, I came up with a God and Country Night geared to the religious right community. Though Harold was Jewish, he loved the idea and was convinced that this promotion would fill the arena. We packed the house. The next night, Harold and I were on the dais at a ceremony honoring Billy Cunningham. Harold leaned over to me and said, "That God and Country Night promotion was inspired. I'm as proud of you as if you were my own son."

A couple of weeks later, I came up with a promotion that backfired. It fell flatter than a roadkill toad. Immediately after that game, Harold came to me and said, "That was the sorriest promotion I've ever seen. I'm taking it out of your paycheck!" He never did, but I believe he was really ready to.

So that's Harold Katz and Katzonomics—not the most practical branch of economic theory, perhaps, but certainly the most entertaining.

## Visualizing Orlando

The summer of '85 was a restless time for me. I ruminated on the fact that it had taken us seven years to get to the top of the hill. We had crested the hill in '83 but couldn't stay there. We just slid right down the other side. I could see that our team was simply not going to be able to maintain that championship edge. Julius Erving and Bobby Jones were coming to the end of their careers. Moses and Mo were no longer young players. Andrew Toney was having trouble keeping his feet healthy. The team was still strong, still making the playoffs, but definitely showing its age and creaking at the joints. Billy Cunningham resigned as coach and was replaced by his assistant, Matt Guokas.

I wasn't sure I wanted to be around to watch the decline of this proud team. What's more, I needed another challenge. Katz was such an involved, hands-on owner that he had taken over most of the entrepreneurial duties of running the team, leaving me the managerial side. Though Harold and I got along well, I longed to get back on the entrepreneurial side again.

I had always admired my longtime friend, Norm Sonju. He had stood up at my wedding and was a great friend and counselor. While I was in Philadelphia, Norm left his job after the Buffalo Braves moved to San Diego. He moved his family to Dallas to build an expansion franchise from the ground up. The name of the team, the Dallas Mavericks, was typical Sonju, because he was a maverick, and I admired and respected what he had done in going his own way and building his own team. That was sports entrepreneurship at its best. I thought that was one of the most exciting things you could possibly do.

One Sunday night in August, I was home alone—Jill had gone out with the children. I picked up the phone and called Norm Sonju at his home. "Norm," I said, "have you got a few minutes for a little brainstorming? I want to talk about expansion. You know there hasn't been expansion in the NBA since you started the Mavs in 1980. I've really been thinking a lot lately about doing what you did—starting a team from scratch."

"Whereabouts?" he asked.

"Well, there's no NBA franchise in Florida."

"Florida. I like that. Yeah, I think you might have a shot in Florida. Tampa's a big sports town."

"I've been considering Tampa. But first, Norm, I want to know how *you* did it. I want to know what it takes—money, time, community participation, business and civic involvement, ownership issues, getting the arena built, everything."

So Norm laid it out for me—and as we talked, the dream began to take hold of me. It gripped me, got under my skin, and wouldn't let go.

The following weekend, I had a speaking engagement at a sports show in Orlando. I was to appear in the basketball section along with K. C. Jones, coach of the Celtics. I made the appearance, and an old friend, John Tolson, came by and renewed acquaintances. I had gotten to know John when he accompanied our NBA trip to mainland China in 1982. He had been with a church in Houston but now was one of the pastors at First Presbyterian Church in Orlando.

John and I talked for a while, and he invited me to speak the next day to his adult Sunday school class. I agreed, and I spent the morning at his church. After services, he asked, "How are you getting back to the airport?"

"I don't know. I figured I'd take a cab."

"Well, let me take you," said John. "There's a fellow I want you to ride out with. His name is Jim Hewitt." I remembered meeting Jimmy Hewitt some years earlier in San Antonio, where I spoke at a men's retreat.

Jim drove and John sat in the back seat. Sitting in the front seat next to Jim, I asked, "Do you fellas think pro basketball would ever fly in Florida?"

"Absolutely," John answered.

"Sure it would, Bubba!" agreed Jimmy Hewitt. He calls everybody Bubba. In the business world, he's a heavy hitter with a velvet touch, a short, stocky guy with a big grin—the kind who plays with business ventures the way kids play with electric trains. He's passionate about everything he's involved in—his faith, his family, his businesses, and his sports—especially Florida State University football.

"Well, where would you put the team?" I asked. "Miami or Tampa?"

They replied, almost simultaneously, "Oh, no! Not Miami. Not Tampa. The best place for an NBA team is right here in Orlando. This is where the future is in Florida."

I looked out the window at the passing scenery and tried to picture it. Orlando was a nice, growing little community—but an NBA franchise city? At the time, Orlando had Walt Disney World's Magic Kingdom going for it, but very little else. This was before the arrival of Universal Studios, the Du Pont Centre, and the SunBank Center. In those days, Orlando didn't even have a skyline. But as I thought about it, I began to visualize a shining new sports arena rising in the center of this central Florida city.

A few minutes later, my friends deposited me at the terminal. I shook hands with them and said, "Well, guys, I'm getting on that plane and heading back to Philly. There are a lot of great ideas that never get beyond the stage we're at right now. We can drop the ball—or we can make it happen. If you guys are serious about this thing, then now's the time to begin exploring, because the NBA is entertaining expansion ideas right now."

"Well, where do we begin?" asked Jimmy.

"With the NBA commissioner, David Stern," I said. I scribbled the phone number down and handed it to Jimmy.

"Bubba," said Jimmy, "I'll check it out and let you know."

End of conversation. I boarded my plane and headed home to prepare for the 1985–86 season. I didn't really expect to hear from Jim Hewitt again. Man, was I wrong!

## Rolling Down the Tracks and Gathering Speed

Jimmy Hewitt went right to work, talking to Mayor Bill Frederick, Orange County Commission chairman Tom Dorman, city council members, *Orlando Sentinel* publisher Tip Lifvendahl, and others, seeking to build support for a team. He retained sports attorney Robert Fraley to guide him through the maze of legal requirements. He talked to business leaders and began assembling an ownership group.

Things kept moving forward through the fall. By December, I was sitting in snowbound Philadelphia imagining what life would be like in all that endless Orlando sunshine. I had another speaking engagement in central Florida, so I boarded a plane and winged my way back to that magical city I was beginning to think of as my new hometown. While in Orlando, I met with John and Jimmy and others who were interested in this dream of ours. I asked a lot of questions about Orlando. They asked a lot of questions about running a pro basketball team. It was clear by the time I left Orlando that this idea was picking up steam.

Arriving back home in Philadelphia, I picked up my phone messages and found one from Bill Gaither. Bill is an old friend and a gospel music mogul, the songwriter behind songs like "Something Beautiful" and "The King is Coming." He is the Babe Ruth of gospel music—and he's a colossal hoops fan. I called him and we got to talking, and right out of the blue Bill said, "Pat, when I give up this music business, what I really want to do is get into your business—the basketball business. I'd really like to own a piece of a team someday—preferably an expansion team."

"If you could pick any place in the country, where would you put your expansion team?"

"Oh, that's easy," he said. "Orlando, Florida."

I was stunned, speechless. I hadn't given Bill one hint of the talks I had been having about starting a team in Orlando. I hadn't even mentioned to him that I had just flown in from Orlando. I stammered and sputtered and finally said, "Bill, that's unbelievable! Why did you say Orlando?"

"Well," he said, "of all the places we travel on our concert tours, there is just one place that really stands out above the rest, and that's Orlando, Florida. There's just something about that whole area—the spirit of the community, the attitude of the people. I keep thinking it would be a nice place to retire to, and if I could be a part-owner of an NBA team in Orlando, that would just complete the dream."

As things turned out, Bill Gaither never did buy a piece of the team. But he tossed his dream out there where I could see it, and it gave a little added impetus to my own dream. The timing of his comment was so astounding that it seemed to go beyond mere coincidence. I had to see where this dream was leading us.

During the winter, as Jimmy Hewitt was assembling an ownership group and getting the wheels in motion for construction of an arena, I was on the phone with him almost daily. Then, on January 22, 1986, Jimmy flew to New York and met with NBA commissioner David Stern. Jimmy took with him John Tolson and Don Dizney, CEO of United Medical and an owner of the Orlando Renegades of the United States Football League. Stern was impressed with the delegation, and he gave a conditional green light to proceed. He also encouraged the organizers to go to Dallas and meet with Norm Sonju, which they did.

In April, Jimmy Hewitt called me and said, "Bubba, this thing is rolling down the tracks and gathering speed. We've got the ownership group. We've got the arena on the way. I've gone as far with it as I can. You'd better jump on quick if this thing is gonna happen. Either get down here and head it up, or we've got to let it drop."

Those were heady days in the NBA. There were expansion plans in other cities, including Miami, Tampa–St. Petersburg, Minnesota, and Charlotte. If Orlando was going to be a contender, I was going to have to jump in with both feet. "Jimmy," I said, "Count me in. I'm committed to Orlando."

Jill was ready to go, too. "I'm ready for some sunshine and balmy breezes," she told me.

Meanwhile, I still had a team to manage in Philadelphia. The Sixers had another good regular season run and got into the playoffs. The first round was against the Washington Bullets, and Moses, our big man, was sidelined with an eye injury. Our lineup was held together with ankle tape and Band-Aids, but we scraped by, beating the Bullets and advancing to the next round against the Bucks. We battled the Bucks to a standoff, three games to three, with the seventh and deciding game to be held on the same Sunday as the NBA lottery draw.

While the team journeyed west to Milwaukee, I went to New York's Grand Hyatt for the lottery. As important as the lottery was, I had more on my mind than draft picks. The NBA was closely guarding its intentions about expansion, and there was a good chance that if I jumped from the Sixers and cast my lot with Orlando, I would end up without any team at all. When you have a family of seven to feed, you think about such matters as staying employed. Going to Orlando without a commitment from the league would be a risky move, and I wanted to make sure it was a well-calculated risk.

After lunch on the day of the lottery, I went into the men's room—and there, just a few porcelain fixtures away, was David Stern, the NBA commish. Coming out of the rest room, we stepped into a corner of the hallway and chatted. "David," I said, "there's a lot of momentum building for a team in Orlando, and they want me to jump on board. Can you tell me anything at all about the league's intentions?"

"Sorry, I can't," he said. "There's just no way to predict what the league's going to decide. The only thing I can tell you is that if you're willing to take your shot, a warm-weather site like Florida isn't the worst thing in the world. I wish I could tell you which way to bet, but I don't know myself. But look at it this way, if you really think you've finished your run in Philly, what do you have to lose?"

Even though David was careful not to encourage or discourage me, what he said helped to clarify my choices: I could stay in chilly Philly and keep doing my same old stuff—or I could make a leap of faith and hope there was a safety net waiting in Orlando. Whether I landed on my feet or in a big splat, one thing was for sure: It would not be dull. It would be an adventure. After my talk with David, I was leaning toward taking the plunge.

After talking to David, I quickly shifted mental gears and focused on the lottery. The Sixers' draft pick was one we had gotten in 1979 when we sent Joe Bryant to the Clippers in exchange for their 1986 number one pick. The draw was to be televised during halftime at the Sixers-Bucks game. It was a simple open lottery, not based on the teams' win-loss records, as it is today. The league simply placed seven cards in a metal drum, the drum was turned, and the cards were drawn by hand and placed on an easel. The cards, marked with team logos, were revealed in reverse order, from lowest to highest, to build suspense toward the number one pick. So I watched in mounting suspense as the cards were turned over, one by one. Finally, only two cards remained. Either the 76ers or the Boston Celtics were going to win the lottery.

So there I was, wreathed in a cloud of blue smoke from the Celtics' Red Auerbach as David Stern pulled the second-pick card from the barrel.

It was Boston's, which meant the Sixers would choose first!

My next thought was, *What am I all excited about? I'm not staying in Philly—I'm going to Orlando! But should I? Maybe I should stay in Philly. After all, now we've got this terrific new kid, Barkley, and we've got the first pick of the draft—things could get very interesting around here.* So that draft pick really put me in a quandary.

With head spinning, I spent the next hour giving exuberant quotes to the press, then I rushed to the hotel room, snapped on the snowy TV screen, and watched the last ten seconds of the big seventh playoff game against Milwaukee. My heart leaped into my throat. The Sixers were down by one. Dr. J had the ball and was working it down the floor as the last few seconds drained out of the clock. Sixteen feet from the hole, he took a majestic leap and seemed to float in midair as he released the ball.

The ball bounded off the iron. The horn sounded, like the last trump before Judgment Day.

Our season was over.

But at the same time, that loss at the buzzer tilted me toward a decision. This season in Philly had ended as so many others— in disappointment and frustration. I was ready for a change. Something new was happening—something big. And it was happening in Orlando.

## Grapefruit War

A month after the lottery came the NBA draft. The night before the draft, trades were flying every which way. The Sixers ended up trading Moses Malone and Terry Catledge to Washington in exchange for Jeff Ruland and Cliff Robinson. Then we traded the number one pick we had gotten in the lottery to Cleveland for Roy Hinson and cash. How much cash? Therein hangs a tale—and another lesson in Katzonomics.

This is at the very tag-end of my tenure with the Sixers, just before my move to Orlando. So the 76ers front office decides to trade our number one pick to Cleveland in exchange for Roy Hinson—just a straight-across trade, no money changing hands. I call my counterpart in Cleveland and say, "Listen, we'll do the deal, our pick for Hinson." Then, on an absolute whim, just to be outlandish, I improvised and threw in an additional condition: "But you're going to have to kick in a million dollars." I knew they'd never go for it, but I thought, *What the heck? You don't get it if you don't ask.*

The guy in Cleveland said, "I've gotta check with the owners." Half an hour later, he called back and said, "I couldn't get a million, only eight hundred thousand." I almost dropped the phone. They actually went for it! I closed the deal, then went to Harold Katz and said, "I made the trade as you wanted—

plus I got Cleveland to kick in eight hundred thousand dollars." His response: "Why didn't you get a million?"

See what I mean? Katzonomics.

Understand, that's not a complaint; that's awe talking. Harold was full of surprises and contradictions. That's his charm. I loved working for Harold, because you never knew what he would do or say from moment to moment. He was an endlessly fascinating owner. Best of all, he never skimped when it came to winning.

Harold and I had a great relationship. He loved it when I would put on my Don Rickles face and rip him and roast him in front of the media. So at my final press conference in Philly, which was called to announce my move to Orlando, Harold was there to wish me well. I gave him this parting shot. "I'd like to give Harold something as a remembrance of my years here in Philly," I told the reporters as Harold looked on, "but I couldn't figure out a way to get an ulcer framed." Harold broke out laughing. He loved it.

Well, we had traded away Moses Malone and a number one draft pick, and at the time, it seemed like the right thing to do. Even the Philly sportswriters thought we had made the right move. The fans, however, thought we had lost our minds. As the following season unfolded, the fans were proved right. With the pick we traded, Cleveland drafted North Carolina's Brad Daugherty, who quickly became an all-star. Moses Malone performed quite well in Washington. Roy Hinson didn't pan out in Philly, and Ruland and Robinson suffered career-ending injuries.

After all that, it was a good thing I was getting out of town, because it just wasn't safe for me in the City of Brotherly Love anymore. I officially separated from the 76ers organization in June 1986 and prepared to move to Florida.

On June 18, the evening after the NBA draft, I was scheduled to introduce Dr. J at a charity event in Philly. The next morning, I was scheduled to be in Orlando for a press conference to begin the drive to sell season tickets for our team-to-be. On the morning of the 18th, Jill went to a T-shirt shop at a mall near Philly and had a special shirt made.

When I was introduced in Orlando the next day, I said, "Folks, we've got some good news and some bad news. The good news is that we're in the running to bring an NBA team to Orlando. The bad news is that we're competing with some other cities—and we've got some catching up to do."

As I talked, I started removing my coat, my tie, and my shirt, to reveal my T-shirt, the front of which read:

Orlando
On the Way to the NBA!

On the back were these words:

Together We Can Do It!

I went on to lay out what we needed to do to make the dream a reality. We had to demonstrate the team's viability to the NBA, and that meant selling a lot of reservations for season tickets. Immediately after that press conference, orders for tickets began pouring in, beginning with *Sentinel* publisher Tip Lifvendahl's order for one hundred season tickets and a skybox. I even sold some tickets while waiting to check out at a health food store. A man in line recognized me and said he'd been meaning to buy some tickets, so I went to my car, grabbed an order form, and took his check for four hundred dollars on the spot.

One of my comments in the June 19 press conference set off a firestorm of controversy that led to the rivalry between the Miami Heat and the Orlando Magic that continues to this day. Orlando sportscaster Rod Luck asked why I thought the league would choose Orlando over Miami as a site for an expansion team (the league eventually would choose both cities—but we didn't know that then). I replied by listing all the factors in Orlando's favor, then concluded, "And we all know the problems Miami has." I didn't mean any offense to Miami, honest. I just figured it was commonly understood that Miami had a few drawbacks—such as heat, humidity, drugs, and crime—that weren't characteristic of life in Orlando.

But the comment was picked up and magnified by the media, resulting in howls of outrage in Miami. By this time, I wasn't the only person who had left the Sixers to head for sunnier weather. Billy Cunningham had gone to Miami to be the point man for launching that city's NBA franchise. So when I got back to Philadelphia, my phone was jangling off the wall. It was Billy, and he was in high holy dudgeon over my remark. It seems the *Miami Herald* had run a headline that read something like:

Orlando Enters Chase
Williams Blasts Miami

I hadn't blasted anybody. I didn't think I had even said anything remotely controversial—but I couldn't convince Billy of that. All he knew was what he read in the papers. So the Miami-Orlando "grapefruit war" was launched before either city had an NBA team—and the Heat and the Magic have been gunning for each other ever since.

## Orlando Believes in Magic

In late June 1986, Jimmy Hewitt, Bobby Hewitt, and I went to the NBA offices in New York to present our hundred-thousand-dollar application check and enter the expansion sweepstakes. The media were invited, and as Jimmy handed the enlarged cardboard check to David Stern, I slyly popped a set of Mickey Mouse ears onto the commissioner's head. I was amazed at how quickly he removed the ears—lest the world think he was partial to Orlando! But I had come prepared. I had a second set of mouse ears behind my back, and he no sooner had removed the first set when I slapped the others onto his head. A dozen flashbulbs went off, recording the moment. The commish handled it well. Jimmy, Bobby, and I were ecstatic—and I knew that somewhere Disney's Michael Eisner was smiling.

The next hurdle was the league owners' meeting in Phoenix. We had four months to prepare ourselves for that meeting—

and that meant we had to sell a lot of tickets, begin construction of the arena, select a team name, and create a logo. I figured the name and logo would be the easy part. I was wrong.

The *Sentinel* launched a contest to name the team, and we were buried in suggestions—more than four thousand of them. Some were awful beyond belief. Some were terrific. Our selection committee narrowed this list down to four finalists: Heat, Tropics, Juice, and Magic. We canned Heat because it was not one of the city's more marketable assets, according to the Chamber of Commerce. We scratched Tropics because we were not technically in the tropical latitudes. We sluiced Juice because it didn't sound tough enough, compared with Bulls, Bullets, Pistons, Warriors, Rockets, and Hawks.

We were leaning toward Magic—but I still wasn't 100 percent sold. The Sunday before the meeting at which the name would be finalized, I flew my seven-year-old daughter Karyn down to Orlando for a big birthday weekend (we were still living in New Jersey and preparing for the move). Karyn went through the whole Orlando experience—Disney's Magic Kingdom, Sea World, dinner at Morrison's Cafeteria, plus swimming and boating at a lake. When it was over, she didn't want to go home. "Daddy, it's so wonderful here!" she said. "This place is magic!"

I was sold. Magic it was. Magic it would be. Not black magic, not sorcery, not sleight of hand. The Magic basketball team would represent the real magic of central Florida—the abundant sunshine, the endless entertainment opportunities, the juice-laden orange groves, the golfing and boating and skiing, the good life.

We assembled a staff to midwife the birth of the Magic. Some were hired, some were investors, and some simply volunteered their time because they wanted to see NBA basketball in central Florida. Our staff included Stewart Crane, a minority investor with an accounting background who became our volunteer controller-bookkeeper-ticket manager; Jacob Stuart, energetic director of the Greater Orlando Chamber of Commerce, who advised me on political strategy and put me in touch with all the right people (including Cari Haught and Marlin Ferrell of his staff); Jane Hames, a PR whiz who plotted our marketing strategy; and a zany, pop-eyed, brillo-headed ex-wrestler and certified nut-case named Doug Minear, head of The Advertising Works and creative genius behind the design of the Magic logo, floor design, mascot, and uniforms. Cari is now Cari Coats, and Marlin, my trusty assistant, is now Marlin Busher. They were two of our first full-time employees when the Magic became a reality in 1987.

Norm Sonju had told me that the most time-consuming aspect of getting the Dallas Mavericks launched had been designing a logo. I laughed, but he hadn't been kidding. A logo is far from a trivial matter. It is the identifying brand of your team and must be intensively marketed to the public so that it becomes as familiar and distinguishable as McDonald's golden arches or the distinctive script that spells Coca-Cola. We sorted through—and rejected—dozens of designs before we settled on the star-spangled image of a meteorlike basketball and casual lettering that is now synonymous with the Orlando Magic.

For team and logo colors, we began working with my favorites, yellow, gold, and black. What can I say? I'm a Wake Forest man, through and through. But I soon found myself in the minority. Our principal investor, Bill du Pont, was not a big fan of yellow. And John Christison, who was in charge of the Orlando Arena project, said yellow did not show up well on a basketball court. Besides, there was a conflict with the University of Central Florida, whose colors were black and gold. Finally, Doug Minear showed us a design in a hue that can only be described as Magic blue, trimmed in quicksilver and midnight black—an instant hit.

In October, we went to Phoenix for the presentation in the NBA owners meeting. By that time, six cities were vying for four expansion franchises. League officials were afraid that things could get out of hand, with representatives from the cities putting on multimedia extravaganzas replete with fireworks, laser light shows, dancing girls, and wrestling bears—or worse, wrestling girls and dancing bears. So they set some ground rules: thirty-minute oral presentations were to be accompanied by printed materials bound in standard three-ring notebooks.

We brought in white binders emblazoned with the words "Orlando Believes in Magic." Inside were marketing data, financial projections, letters from local big-wigs, newspaper clippings, architectural renderings of the Orlando Arena, and a detailed audit of our 14,046 paid season-ticket reservations. With Jimmy Hewitt, his brother Bobby, and Stew Crane at my side, I gave my pitch.

Norm Sonju later told me that one of the owners remarked, "Did you notice that Williams did that whole talk without notes? Wasn't that incredible?" Not so incredible. Who needs notes to give the same speech for the umpteen-hundredth time, the pitch I had already presented to clubs, corporations, and civic organizations all over central Florida?

The NBA owners made the decision to expand, and formed a committee to scout the aspiring cities and make recommendations to the league in April.

## Flirting with Mickey Mouse

The road to an NBA franchise had a lot more twists and turns before we reached our destination. For example, before we could begin construction on the arena, we needed a thumbs-up from the city council—which we only narrowly received in a 3-2 vote. That decision hinged on an amazing coincidence. Shortly after Thanksgiving 1986, I was in Houston to speak at a dinner honoring Bill Fitch, coach of the Houston Rockets. At the dinner, I was introduced to a man named Vince Barresi, general manager of a Houston television station, whom I had known from my days in Philadelphia. "You know," he said, "my mother-in-law is on the city council in Orlando. Her name is Pat Schwartz."

"Oh, yes, I know her," I said. "Vince, if you've got any influence with her, I sure would appreciate you putting a good word in for the arena."

So Vince called his mother-in-law, told her how important pro basketball was to the city of Houston, and urged her to support the effort in Orlando. She had been undecided up to that point—but her son-in-law convinced her to vote yes. Hers was the crucial swing vote. If not for her, the NBA expansion committee would have arrived in Orlando three months later and found a vacant lot instead of the beginnings of the O-rena. And if the committee hadn't seen a building taking shape, we would have been dead in the water.

On December 8, Jimmy and Bobby Hewitt and I were summoned to New York to hear the decision of the NBA. I didn't know if Orlando had been selected or eliminated—but I was hoping David Stern hadn't called us all the way to New York just to turn us down. He got right to the point. "Two cities have been eliminated: Toronto and Anaheim." My heart did a backflip inside my chest. "That leaves four cities that are qualified for expansion franchises—Charlotte, Miami, Minneapolis, and Orlando."

*Yes!* But there was more. It was one of those good news, bad news deals—and he had given us the good news first. We had been told it would cost the owners group around twenty million dollars in up-front franchise fees, which could be paid to the league over five years. "The price has gone up," Stern continued. "The number is now $32.5 million." My heart turned to lead. And the news got worse. "The entire amount has to be paid in cash up front—no five-year payout."

It was a stunner for all of us. We left the commissioner's office in shock. "What have they done to us, Bubba?" Jimmy asked. "Why did they jack up the price on us? Where are we going to come up with that kind of money?"

Our next task was to find a heavy hitter who could pump in the cash we needed to buy our way into the NBA. I talked to Bruce Starling of Orlando-based Harcourt Brace Jovanovich publishers. Starling considered the possibility, but turned us down.

I talked to Bob Allen, the vice president of Disney World, and he was interested enough to send an accountant over to examine our books. Later, Jill and I were invited to Disney's fifteenth anniversary celebration of EPCOT Center at Walt Disney World. There I bumped into Buell Duncan, chairman of SunBank, and he said, "Pat, the guy you ought to talk to is Michael Eisner."

I blinked. "You mean *the* Michael Eisner, the chairman of Disney?"

"Sure," said Duncan. "He's over at the American Pavilion, giving a speech. Come with me."

So I accompanied Duncan to the American Pavilion, and Eisner was there all right—along with Chief Justice Warren Burger of the U.S. Supreme Court, Sen. Ted Kennedy of Massachusetts, and a swarm of other dignitaries. "Gee," I said, "he looks kind of busy."

"Go ahead and say hi," said Duncan. "He'll be glad to meet you."

So as soon as Eisner's speech was over, I pushed my way through the crowd, thrust my hand out, and said, "Mr. Eisner, I'm—"

"Pat Williams!" Eisner said, astonishing me. I had no idea he knew who I was. "You're just the man I want to talk to! Tell you what—let's meet in France at nine. We can talk there."

France? Oh, right! The French pavilion at EPCOT.

So I went to France and staked out a street corner. Around nine o'clock, Eisner came strolling up and we found a table at a little bistro and chatted like long-lost cousins. It turned out Michael Eisner is a big-time hoops fan. His kids went to the same southern California school as the children of the Lakers' Michael Cooper and Kareem Abdul-Jabbar. What's more, the famous "I'm going to Disneyland" commercials were his wife's idea.

"I've been following your odyssey," he told me, "and I'd love to see the Magic succeed. David Stern is a friend of mine, and I want to help if I can."

That meeting kicked off an exploration by Eisner and company into the possibility of teaming up with the Magic ownership to get the franchise off the ground. Disney came up with a plan that would have linked "Sport Goofy" and other Disney characters to our basketball games, provided Disney designs for our logos, uniforms, and merchandise, used Disney as our advertising agency, linked the Magic to Disney's media and promotional power (such as promotion of the team over the Disney Channel), and more.

In the end, the NBA and Disney were unable to come to terms on financial and other arrangements, but the mere possibility opened our eyes to creative ways to bring in the infusion of big money we needed. Though Disney did not become a partner in the Magic venture, the two organizations have continued to enjoy a warm and mutually supportive relationship.

On January 6, 1987, Jimmy Hewitt introduced me to William du Pont III. Bill du Pont was already a limited partner, but Jimmy thought Bill could give us the financial clout we needed, and he encouraged Bill to increase his investment and become a general partner. In the end, Jimmy—who had been the driving force for this dream from the beginning—would graciously step aside as a general partner to make room for Bill du Pont. Everyone hated to see Jimmy pull out, but the NBA left little choice.

The league was concerned that our syndicate-style ownership group was too large and diffuse, and we needed to reduce the ownership to one or two general partners who had the principal financial stake and decision-making power. If ownership wasn't consolidated to the league's liking, there would be no franchise. The du Pont name conveyed a certain substantiality that the NBA trusted—and the process moved forward with Bill at the helm.

Bill du Pont and I got along well from the moment we first shook hands in the boardroom of the law office of Swann and Haddock. I had grown up around the du Pont family, having been raised in Wilmington, Delaware, headquarters of the DuPont Company. There had been du Pont children in every grade at Tower Hill prep. The grandmother of my best friend, Ruly Carpenter, was a du Pont. A soft-spoken man wearing wire-rim glasses, blue jeans, and an open-necked sport shirt, Bill reminded me a lot of Ruly. He was part of Pillar-Bryton Partners, a commercial real estate and development company in Orlando. When asked to become a lead owner, he acted decisively—and affirmatively.

We were rapidly moving toward the creation of a team. The money was coming together. The arena was coming together. The ownership group was coming together.

Magic was in the air.

# 11

# Shaq and Penny

As long as the NBA was expanding, the Williams family decided it was only fitting that we expand, too. We already had six kids scuffing up our carpets and knocking over lamps—how much damage could a couple more do? So we applied for another pair of children from Korea—boys this time. Photos of two five-year-old boys came in the mail from the agency. Their names were Sang Wan and Sang Hyung, and in the pictures they looked lonely and sad beneath unruly mops of black hair.

"Why aren't they smiling?" asked one of our children.

"They need a family to love them," I replied. "When they have a home to belong to, with brothers and sisters, then you'll see them smile."

We submitted the paperwork in January 1987. Then we waited. And we jumped through hoops of paperwork. Then we waited some more. We waited while the U.S. Immigration and Naturalization Service wrapped a few miles of red tape around our application. We agonized through the month of February, when the Korean government announced a new policy prohibiting the adoption of Korean children by families with more than four children. During this time of suspense, I read a book by Dr.

Richard Strauss, who wrote, "God already knows the future. It's a finished event for Him." That was an encouragement.

We breathed a sigh of relief when the government of Korea relented (after a strong pitch by Susan Cox of Holt International) and made an exception in our case on the grounds that we had applied prior to the new policy. Finally, on May 1, 1987, our family gathered at the Orlando airport to welcome Sang Wan and Sang Hyung to their new home—only now, their names were Stephen and Thomas Williams. Arriving home from the airport, we all piled out of the van and walked to the front door. There Stephen and Thomas stopped, carefully removed their shoes, and lined them up neatly beside the door.

Surprised and delighted by this Korean ritual, Jill had an idea. "Hold it!" she called. "Everybody take off your shoes and line them up like Thomas and Stephen did." The children all complied.

And that was the beginning of a Williams family tradition. From then on, before children entered the house, they had to take off their shoes and line them up by the front door. It was not just a matter of homage to Thomas and Stephen's culture—it also saved a lot of wear and tear on the carpets in the family domicile. Eventually, it reached the point where on any given day you could find eighteen pairs of shoes outside our door!

## In the Basketball Business

As the league owners and commissioner concluded their deliberations on expansion, the final issue they had to settle was the alignment of divisions. The Atlantic Division was short-handed at the time but wasn't eager to absorb the lion's share of the expansion. If it took in two new teams, Atlantic Division teams would have to play seven or eight of forty-one home games against expansion teams. Games against expansion teams do not draw large crowds. If some plan could be worked out that would equitably realign the divisions, the owners would consent to a four-team expansion—the Orlando Magic, the

Miami Heat, the Charlotte Hornets, and the Minnesota Timberwolves.

The solution came from league attorney Gary Bettman (who is now commissioner of the National Hockey League). In a meeting with David Stern and NBA executive vice president Russ Granik, Bettman took out a legal pad and began scribbling various permutations. Then an inspiration struck: Why not rotate the three Eastern teams—Orlando, Miami, and Charlotte—to different conferences and divisions during the first three years, just to keep it fair? It didn't make sense from a travel point of view, of course, to have Orlando in the Western Conference or the T-wolves in the Eastern Conference—but we could make it work for a few years, then settle the teams into permanent divisions. It was a plan that would get everybody to agree on expansion.

On April 22, 1987, Bill du Pont was at Winged Foot Golf Club in Westchester County, New York, playing a round of golf with his wife, Pam. After playing the front nine, he went to a pay phone and called the NBA office to check in. A league staffer told him, "We've been trying to reach you. You need to be at the Helmsley Palace Hotel in an hour."

"What's up?" asked Bill.

"All I know is you need to be there."

So Bill dashed home, showered, and threw on a suit and tie in record time, then jumped into the car. Pam drove as they sped down the FDR Expressway, took an offramp for midtown, and promptly got stuck in Manhattan traffic. Inching along, Bill saw he was not going to make it by car, so he kissed Pam good-bye, leaped from the car, and raced down the sidewalk. Arriving at the Helmsley precisely on time, he took a deep breath, smoothed the creases in his suit, and strolled in, calm and collected.

At a meeting with the league brass, Bill was told how the franchise deal would work: The Orlando franchise would begin in the Central Division the first year, go to the Midwest Division for a year, then settle in for good in the Atlantic Division. Was that okay?

Better than okay, it was beautiful. Who cared what division we were in? All that mattered was that we were in the basketball business.

After the meeting, Bill called the Orlando office. His first words were: "The bad news is we don't play our first game until '89. Now you know what the good news is."

Bill du Pont's news flash from New York set off a wave of celebration across Orlando. Crowds celebrated around Church Street Station and the Cheyenne Saloon. Men in conservative business suits whooped and hollered and traded high fives. Jimmy Hewitt, Stew Crane, and I pulled on our "We Believe in Magic" T-shirts and gushed to any reporter who would stick a microphone in our faces.

I was disappointed in the bad news part of Bill's message—that we would not launch our first season until '89. Charlotte and Miami would be fielding teams a year earlier. I was eager to hear the sound of dribbling balls and crashing boards in Orlando. But the bad news turned out to be good news after all, because we needed that extra year to get our proverbial ducks in a row.

Soon after the franchise approval, I had a long talk with Billy Cunningham and his partner Lewis Schaffel in Miami. Billy and I had worked together for eight years in Philly, and I wanted to patch up the relationship that had been strained by misunderstandings that arose in the competition for a franchise. Our conversation went well, and Billy was very open-hearted.

"But you know," I added, "Bill Veeck always told me, 'Rivalries are good for business, and if you're going to have a rivalry, don't keep it a secret. If you're going to hate the other city, hate everything about them, even their park benches.' We have the makings of a great rivalry here. The press loves it, the fans love it, I think you and I ought to have some fun with it."

Billy dubiously and tentatively agreed.

So I went back to Orlando and began sharpening my verbal harpoons for the grapefruit war between Orlando and Miami. When a story hit the papers about a shortage of rest rooms at the Miami Arena, I called for an NBA investigation into the "Pottygate" scandal. When news broke of sagging ticket sales in Miami, I announced that the only difference between the *Titanic* and the Miami Heat is that the *Titanic* had a band. I casually mentioned hearing that a family moved into a Miami neighborhood the other day and was fired on by the Welcome Wagon. I said that the mayor of Miami had given me the key to the city—and Billy Cunningham had all the locks changed.

A *Miami Herald* humor writer by the name of Dave Barry got into the act. Yes, *that* Dave Barry. Though he is now one of the top nationally syndicated columnists in the country, I had never heard of him at the time. He coined a new term for all of us who live in Orlando: "Orlandoids." He described us as a race of low-foreheaded, knuckle-dragging yahoos whose greatest joy in life is standing in line at a theme park, and whose idea of haute cuisine is the fare at the corner wafflehouse. Every column he unleashed in our direction had me doubled up in laughter. I like to think that our grapefruit war launched Dave's career, and I've pointed out to him that if not for us knuckle-dragging Orlandoids, nobody ever would have heard of him.

## Assembling the Organization

In 1988, we hired Matt Guokas to be the first head coach of the Orlando Magic. He had just been fired by Harold Katz as the Sixers' head coach when, midway through the season, the team had a losing record of 20-23. I understood why Harold was disappointed in the team's falling below .500, but I also thought Matty was doing a good job, considering the raw mate- rial he had to work with. The Philadelphia 76ers were not the same team that had made it deep into the playoffs every year. I knew Matty coached the kind of game we wanted our team to play: full-court, fast, and furious—a crowd-pleasing game. I also knew that he was fiercely competitive—few coaches hated losing and loved winning as much as Matt Guokas—and had the patient disposition needed to deal with the difficulties of getting an expansion team off the ground.

Landing Matty was a big step toward putting together the athletic side of our basketball show. We also spent that first year of preparation working on the entertainment side. It took that entire year just to assemble our dance team, the Magic Girls. We held tryouts all over the region, recruiting dancers from around the state. We wanted to emulate the excitement and energy of the Laker Girls out on the left coast—but without the blatant sexuality. This is Orlando, the world capital of family entertainment, and we needed upbeat yet wholesome girl-next-door types—we weren't looking to have one of our home games raided by the vice squad. We held the selection of the final sixteen Magic Girls at J. J. Whispers nightclub, and drew a crowd of fifteen hundred.

A pair of magicians, Giovanni and Tim, approached us to say they wanted to entertain during Orlando Magic halftime shows. We had them work a few promotional events for the organization, and they did a good job. We kept them on as entertainment for the games, and it soon became evident that we had invented something the world had never seen before: sports magic! The magicians worked the crowd with all kinds of gimmicks, contests, games, and stunts. They came up with giant slingshots (now in use around the league) to send T-shirts and other items hurtling all over the arena, even to the fans in the upper decks.

We spent a full year working on a costume and a concept for our mascot, Stuff. We hired several different designers to produce ideas and sketches, including character designers Bonnie Erickson and Wade Harrison, who had worked with Disney and Jim Henson's Muppets. We considered dozens of ideas—a top-hatted rabbit, several varieties of magicians and sorcerers, a number of weird Muppet-like creatures, a touristy character with stars for eyes, and even a big bean with eyes and legs. ("A bean?" we all wondered, scratching our heads and puzzling over the artist's state of mind.) Finally we settled on Stuff—a play on "stuffing" the basket and a certain magic dragon made famous by Peter, Paul, and Mary.

Many sports teams figure you can put anybody in a mascot suit and who's going to know or care? But we knew better. We had seen one mascot—Big Shot—fall flat during my days with the Philadelphia 76ers. We had replaced the lumbering Big Shot with a smaller, more mobile Sesame Street–style character named Hoops—but Hoops wasn't much more successful than Big Shot, because we couldn't find the right person to fill the suit. To prove how important it is to have the right guy in the costume, we hired Dave Raymond, who filled the Philly Phanatic suit for the Phillies baseball club, to play Hoops for a night during a Celtics-Sixers game. I tell you, Dave took over that arena, and the crowd loved him.

Unfortunately, Dave couldn't play Hoops on a regular basis because of his commitment to the Phillies. But I had caught the mascot bug. I had to see for myself what was so hard about jumping around in a mascot suit and making people cheer. So for a game against the Seattle Supersonics in January 1982, I put on the suit. I did things I never would have dared do in my suit and tie. I led cheers, high-fived the kids, swiped shoes off the feet of unwary women, and mocked the refs.

During a time-out, I flopped onto my carpeted belly and sneaked right up to the Sonics huddle. Sonics coach Lenny Wilkens spotted me—not knowing it was me—and came after me with homicide in his eyes. To the amusement of the Sixers fans, Lenny chased me away from his huddle and right off the floor. Well, that was an exhilarating experience, but not wanting to risk life and limb anymore, I retired after my one and only appearance as a mascot.

The experience taught me that you've got to have the right talent in that suit, or all the time and money you spent designing the character is wasted. With time running short before Stuff's official unveiling, we tried out at least a dozen people, but weren't happy with any of them. So for Stuff's unveiling on October 31, 1987, we flew David Raymond in from Philly to perform the role.

The show was held downtown at Church Street Station. Curly Neal, our goodwill ambassador, and our magicians, Giovanni and Tim, revved up the crowd. The climactic moment came as the magicians crammed Curly into a huge box and raised it up a tall pole. When the box opened, Curly had disappeared—and there was Stuff, sliding down the pole to the oohs and aahs of the crowd. The rock anthem "Shout!" began thumping from the loudspeakers, and Stuff rocked out. He was all over the place, waving at the crowd, mussing the heads of kids, tossing balls and presents all over the mall. The introduction of Stuff was a resounding success.

The next day, I walked into the office feeling on top of the world—and was quickly brought down to earth. David had called and left a message of apology. It took me a while to piece the whole story together, but this is what happened. Arriving at his room at the Radisson Hotel after the triumphant debut, David took the Stuff suit off and hung it on a hook by the closet. The suit was too heavy for the hook, and it fell down, catching the handle of a fire alarm. The alarm sounded, and the sprinkler system came on, drenching David, the hotel room, and the suit.

David grabbed a robe and raced out of the room—and it wasn't until he heard the snick of the door behind him that he realized he didn't have the room key. He was locked out. The hallway filled with people and the alarm continued to jangle. David tried to calm everyone down—"It's not a fire!" he called. No use. People were racing all over the place.

David narrowly escaped being arrested for raising a false alarm. And then there was the water damage to the room. And of course, Stuff was pretty well ruined. And David missed his flight back to Philly. And . . . well, you get the picture. It was a disaster—and it was howlingly funny. I doubt that David Raymond has dared set foot in Orlando again.

We had the costume repaired and located a local performer to be the stuffing in Stuff—and the mascot has continued to thrill and delight O-town crowds ever since. The identity of Stuff is a closely guarded secret, but I can assure you there is no truth to the rumor that Stuff and Pat Williams are never seen together.

## Return of the Master of Disaster

As we approached the task of building our team, up popped Darryl Dawkins, the Double D from the planet Lovetron, Sir

Slam, Chocolate Thunder, the Master of Disaster—the same hulking center I had first seen when I was on a Sixers scouting trip to Orlando in 1975. He was a hometown hero, and he had charisma, but he had been cut by the Detroit Pistons partway through his fourteenth season. Now he wanted to make his comeback with the Orlando Magic. Mugging for the news cameras, he declared, "Pat Williams, get my contract ready! And make it *big!*"

Well, we had already dealt Dawkins off to the Nets once, when I was with the Sixers. If I was going to hire him again in Orlando, I wanted to make sure he could still do his stuff. Frankly, I had my doubts.

We invited Double D to our first free-agent camp in May 1988 to see what he could do. His "financial reverend," the Reverend Mr. Judge, assured us that Darryl would be there. But a few days before camp, Darryl told the *Sentinel* he would not participate in camp without a guaranteed contract. Alarmed, I called Judge, and he again assured me that Darryl would be at camp. The day before camp, Darryl showed up, along with Judge. I gave them a tour of the Magic facilities—then Darryl cornered me and began laying down a list of complaints. He was not happy about having to pay for his own airline upgrade. He also wasn't about to try out like the rest of those unknowns in camp—after all, he was a bona fide star. Besides, what if he got injured?

So Darryl didn't suit up and Darryl didn't try out. Judge seemed embarrassed by Darryl's behavior.

Still, we were interested enough to invite him back for the preseason camp in the fall at the University of Central Florida. He showed up in uniform, but refused to play. He had another list of gripes.

"Darryl," I told him, "this is your shot. If you want to get back into basketball, you're going to have to play ball right here, right now. You don't get a contract until we see your stuff."

Well, we didn't see his stuff, and he didn't see our contract.

But that wasn't the end of it. A few months later, as Darryl read news accounts of how the Magic was filling its roster with expansion and draft players, he realized his phone wasn't ringing. He began to get the message that maybe the Magic wasn't so desperate for his services after all. Soon we got another visit from the Reverend Mr. Judge, appealing for us to give the Dawk one more chance. Against our better judgment, we agreed to take one last look.

Shortly before a series of workouts and summer-league scrimmages involving players from Miami, Charlotte, and Atlanta, a full-page ad appeared in the *Orlando Times*, a neighborhood paper. It showed Double D in a Sixers uniform going up for a slam dunk, along with the words, "Have Shoes—Will Travel." Judge paid $1,140 out of his own pocket for the ad. He assured us one more time that Darryl would be there for the workouts.

The day of the workouts came. No Darryl. He had decided to sit it out at his home in New Jersey. Judge was mortified. "Judge," I said, "what are you going to tell the media?"

"I don't know," he glumly replied.

"And Judge," I asked, "what do I tell the media?"

"You tell them, 'I don't know, either.'"

I chuckled ruefully. It was funny. And it was so sad. The Reverend Mr. Judge had tried so hard to save Darryl from himself, but some people refuse to be saved. Darryl was the master of his own disaster.

## We Have a Team

The scouting of player prospects was handled by John Gabriel, our scouting director; Jack Swope, assistant general manager and marketing director; and me. I brought Jack and John down from the 76ers, where we had worked together for years. Gabe watched hours and hours of videotape of college games. I had a satellite dish and VCR installed in my home so I could catch all the games myself. We narrowed the field of likely college picks down from hundreds to dozens to four: Georgia Tech forward Tom Hammonds, Florida State bomber George

McCloud, Todd Lichti from Stanford, and shooting guard Nick Anderson from the University of Illinois.

On June 7, 1988, we received our expansion lists from the other NBA teams by overnight carrier. The media came in and photographed me as I opened the packages that had streamed in from around the country, listing players we could grab from the other teams to build our roster. Our office manager, Marlin Ferrell, and our bookkeeper, Danny Durso, helped me open the packages and compile the list of exposed players. The next day, I flew to Chicago to join Matty, assistant coach Bobby Weiss, and John Gabriel at the NBA scouting camp. We had a very short time to research the players and make our selection. We made our picks and crossed our fingers.

A few days later, at a halftime ceremony during the Lakers-Pistons finals, a flip of a coin would decide our fate in the college draft. On one side of the coin was the logo of the Magic, on the other side the logo of the Minnesota Timberwolves. The toss determined which of the two teams would go first in the expansion draft. I had never had much luck with coin tosses, so we sent Matty out to L.A. to call the toss.

Usually, things like big-stakes coin tosses make a nervous wreck out of me—but on that day, I was surprisingly calm. That morning, I had gotten a call from my friend, Watson Spoelstra, a retired Detroit sportswriter living in St. Pete. "I know this is a big day for you, with that coin toss and all," said Waddy. "But I want you to take a moment to look up Proverbs 16:33 in *The Living Bible*. I think it will help you survive the suspense of the day."

I looked up the verse, written long ago by a wise man named Solomon: "Man rolls the dice, but God determines the outcome." Just what I needed to hear.

We had a telephone hookup between L.A. and a conference room at the O-rena. Our conference room was filled with people from the press and the Magic organization, all anxiously awaiting the news.

Out in L.A., Commissioner David Stern flipped the coin.

The future of our team glittered in the air.

The coin landed on the carpet, bounced once . . .

And came up Magic.

The draft was on June 15—a week earlier than originally scheduled, due to the Pistons' four-game sweep of the Lakers in the finals. Along with Jimmy and Bobby Hewitt, John Tolson, Bill du Pont, and a lot of other people, I had spent the last three years working toward that day, hammering a misty dream into a solid, money-making, crowd-pleasing reality—and it was about to come true. We were about to experience our first expansion draft.

We went into the Magic conference room at 1:50 P.M., and the NBA posted a security rep to make sure no one entered or left the room—not even to go to the rest room. The league wanted to leave no opportunity for word to get out about the draft choices. Around the conference table were coaches Matty and Bobby, Bill du Pont, our accountant Danny Durso, Jack Swope, attorney Robert Fraley, his assistant Rick Neal, our publicist Alex Martins, and me. At 2:02, we got the conference call from New York. League attorney Gary Bettman came on the line, we introduced ourselves, the league officials in New York and the Timberwolves officials in Minnesota did the same, and the draft began.

We made our first pick: Sidney Green, a big forward from the Knicks. Next we took Reggie Theus, a scoring guard from the Atlanta Hawks. Then Bullets power forward Terry Catledge (we had drafted him in '85 for the Sixers). Then point guard Sam Vincent of the Bulls and guard Otis Smith of the Warriors. Smith was from nearby Jacksonville, and local heroes who can play are good for the gate.

Next we took point guard Scott Skiles, a kamikaze player if there ever was one—a physical player who's not afraid to leave blood on the floor, whether his or someone else's. Some of us at the table were tempted to use a later pick on Skiles, but Matty said, "Let's take him now. I want that madman on my team— let's not gamble." So Matty got his kamikaze.

In the seventh round, we took swingman Jerry Reynolds of Seattle. By the eighth round, we had a problem: no center. So we settled on Mark Acres from Boston. In the ninth round, we took rookie guard Morlon Wiley from the Mavs—a guy Bobby

Weiss was high on. By the tenth round, Danny Durso warned that we were coming up to the salary cap. We closed the final three rounds by staying away from contract players, settling on restricted free agents Jim Farmer of Utah, Keith Lee of New Jersey, and Floridian Frank Johnson of the Rockets. By the time we were through, we were amazed at the depth of this draft—we had gotten all the players we wanted through the ninth round, and Minnesota had only taken players we were not interested in.

Both teams had done their homework and knew exactly what they wanted in a team. Though the league had allotted four hours for the draft process, we finished in only fifty minutes.

In the college draft, we took Nick Anderson, an outstanding guard from Illinois, and Michael Ansley from Alabama. (As I write, almost ten years have passed since the Magic's inception, and Nick Anderson is the only player still on the team who was there from the beginning—a solid, productive player who recently emerged as a genuine star.) By the time we had filled our first roster, we were satisfied that we had harvested a good crop of talent. And we were ecstatic that it was actually happening. After three years of work, sweat, sacrifice, and suspense, the dream had finally come true.

We had a team.

## Highlights and Lowlights

The city of Orlando pulled off a major promotional coup in landing Bill Cosby to perform at the opening night of the arena on January 31, 1989. He did his act in a blue warm-up suit with the Orlando Magic logo prominently displayed across the front.

The tip-off for our first season came in November of '89. In our first exhibition game, we hosted the Detroit Pistons—the defending world champions. Our new building, the Orlando Arena, was sold out clear to the ceiling. It seemed as if the whole town turned out. The crowd was pumped. What a night!

Came time for the introductions, and in came Chuck Daly's Detroit Pistons, starring Isiah Thomas, Joe Dumars, Mark Aguirre, Vinnie Johnson, James Edwards, and Bill Laimbeer. And incredibly this little expansion team, playing its first-ever game, beat the NBA champs! Instantly everyone in town was talking about the Magic taking the championship its first year out. Inside the organization, we knew better. The Magic had enjoyed a good night, and had caught the Pistons off their game. We had a nice team, a strong physical team—but we knew we were an expansion team, not a championship team.

We muddled through the preseason, then went into the regular season. We lost our first regular home game against the New Jersey Nets. It was a close game, we were in it, and we had a chance to win—but the Magic fell apart in the closing minutes. We just couldn't get it done. All of us were very disappointed.

But then we came back the next Monday, played Patrick Ewing and the Knicks at the O-rena, and won. It was one of the most memorable nights of my life, watching our expansion team beating the mighty Knicks. Our franchise was launched and we had a decent season. We beat the Bulls twice in Orlando. In a road game against the Lakers just before Christmas, we battled back from a deep deficit to win in the fourth quarter—an unforgettable game.

Those were the highlights, but there were plenty of lows. The fact is that an expansion team is going to do more losing than winning in its first year, and that's what the Orlando Magic did in the 1989–90 season. We limped to a first-year record of 18-64.

We went into the lottery and came up with the fourth pick in the draft. With that pick, we selected Dennis Scott from Georgia Tech, who became known as 3-D because of his beautifully accurate three-point shot. With the addition of Dennis (who made the All-Rookie Team that year), we were set for the '90–91 season.

Even before this time, in the midst of our first year in the NBA, Major League Baseball began making noises about expansion. So I went to our principal owner, Bill du Pont and said, "Bill, now that we've got pro basketball, pro baseball is next.

There's going to be a run on expansions, and somebody is going to want to get involved in bringing major league baseball to Orlando. It seems to me that we ought to be the ones to do it."

"I agree," said Bill. He was quick to buy into the idea.

But by mid-1990, Bill du Pont's real estate development business was running into problems because several major investments had not really panned out as planned. Bill's bean counters told him he needed to unload—not take on new projects. He was not going to be in a position to pursue pro baseball, and he was probably going to have to sell some of his interest in the Magic. The basketball franchise was doing extremely well, and he could maximize it by converting some of his equity in the Magic into cash. In July, we had a brief meeting in which he told me I should try to find another principal owner for the team because he could no longer serve in that role.

At that point, our baseball plans hit the wall. Our application to the league had to list an owner, and we couldn't find anyone who could come up with the requisite amount of scratch—which was a very steep ninety-five million dollars.

## The Amway King

One day that summer I was talking to Bobby Richardson, former Yankee second baseman, who is a good friend of mine. I explained the financial mountain we had to climb to bring major league baseball to Orlando. "Bobby," I asked, "what do you suggest?"

"You need to get hold of our friend Billy Zeoli," said Bobby. "He knows Rich DeVos real well, and he can introduce the two of you." I knew the reputation of Rich DeVos—the cofounder of Amway, a strong Christian, and one of the wealthiest men on the planet. I've known Billy Zeoli for years—he's president of Gospel Films, and Rich DeVos is that company's chairman of the board.

So I called Billy Zeoli and told him what was going on. I said, "Z, I'd be forever grateful if you would check with Rich DeVos and see if he would have any interest in becoming a team owner."

"Sure," he said, "I'll check it out."

Zeoli called me back the following week and said, "Rich is interested. Let me set up a meeting." So he arranged a meeting in Atlanta, but DeVos had to cancel a few days later. Now we're getting on into August, so I called Zeoli again and said, "Z, we're running out of time. We must have an owner in place and get our application in by Labor Day."

"I'm still working on it," he replied. "I'll get back to you." He called back later and said, "I've got it set for August 30. You'll stay at the Amway Grand Plaza in downtown Grand Rapids."

"Well, okay," I said, "but we're really cutting it close."

So I flew to Grand Rapids, Michigan, and Billy Zeoli picked me up at the airport and took me to the hotel. First thing the next morning, we drove out to the Amway headquarters in the nearby town of Ada. There I met with Bill Nicholson, a top exec at Amway and a very sports-minded guy. I laid out the whole picture with Bill about baseball. He listened to my pitch, but what he really wanted to talk about was basketball. He was an ex-player and avidly followed all our games on his satellite dish. He was very knowledgeable about the first season we had just completed in Orlando.

As Nicholson and I were wrapping up, Z came in, looking ashen-faced. "There's a problem," he said. "Rich is at his summer home in Holland."

"He has a place in the Netherlands?"

"Holland, Michigan."

"Ah."

"He really doesn't want to come in to the office. I told him you've come all the way up here from Florida, so he said he'd come in this afternoon."

Z and I went to lunch and returned to Amway headquarters at around one. He said, "Wait here in the lobby. I'll see if Rich is in yet."

"Okay."

"If you see Rich DeVos walking across the lobby, do not approach him. Just sit, and don't let him see you."

"Huh?"

"Well, he's liable to get into conversation right here in the lobby, and I don't want that to happen. I want you to have a nice, quiet setting for your meeting—up in his office, not here in the lobby."

"Okay."

Z took off, and I sat down and waited. A few minutes later, there was a loud, rumbling noise and a lot of commotion from people talking at once. Then I saw about a dozen Japanese tourists with cameras race out of the lobby to the grassy area in front of the building. I went out to see what was up and saw a helicopter landing there. I instantly recognized Rich DeVos from his picture as he stepped out of the helicopter. He obligingly posed for the Japanese shutterbugs, who apparently were Amway people on a pilgrimage to Multilevel Marketing Mecca. I went back inside and, as Z had instructed, made myself invisible behind a potted palm as DeVos strode across the lobby and disappeared inside his headquarters.

A few minutes later, Billy Zeoli returned and ushered me up to DeVos's office. Z introduced us. I said, "Mr. DeVos, it's a pleasure to meet you, sir."

He shook my hand and said, "Skip that 'Mr. DeVos' stuff. I'm Rich."

I thought, *I know you're rich. That's why I'm here.*

So we sat down and talked, and I told him what we were trying to accomplish in Orlando with major league baseball, and the problems that had developed with ownership. Would DeVos consider becoming the principal owner? I didn't know it then, but that was the beginning of what would become a warm friendship between Rich DeVos and me. I found him to be not only astute and decisive, as most great businessmen are, but also warm and open. After about forty-five minutes, he said, "Tell you what—would you step out into the hall for a few minutes? I'll get right back to you." So I strolled the halls and looked at the pictures that lined the walls, a photo-journal of the history of Amway. About ten minutes later, Z came out and beckoned me back into the office.

I walked back in, and Rich said, "Tell the league I'll go forward with baseball in Orlando. I don't know all the details, I don't know where it's all leading, but submit my name and tell them I'll go forward."

I was stunned. Billy Zeoli ushered me out of the office and said, "We've got to get to the airport."

"Sure," I said, "as soon as I understand something."

"What's not to understand?"

"Z, I'm a little confused here. Tell me what just happened in there."

"Well," Zeoli replied, "Rich just told you to go ahead and put his name on the application as principal owner. He said he's going forward with you."

"You mean," I asked in an awed voice, "Mr. DeVos made a ninety-five-million-dollar decision—just like that?"

"Exactly," said Z. "He said he would go forward, and that's what he means. He's with you one-hundred percent."

"Wow!"

I was so energized and ecstatic that I almost beat the plane back to Orlando. But the expansion plans for baseball in Orlando never materialized. The National League bypassed Orlando in favor of Denver and Miami. Still, something good came out of those efforts. Rich DeVos and other members of the DeVos family became entranced with the magic of Orlando, Florida. In the spring and summer of '91, the DeVos family negotiated to purchase the Magic, and the sale was consummated in August of that year.

Rich and Helen DeVos have four grown children—Dick, Dan, Cheri, and Doug. Dick became the first president of the Orlando Magic, representing the DeVos family. After Dick moved up to take the reins of the Amway empire, Cheri and her husband, Bob Vander Weide, made Orlando their home. Bob took over the operation of the DeVos sports organization, RDV Sports. Bob is a bright young businessman with extraordinary people skills, and he has overseen the enormous growth of the Orlando Magic and related sports businesses. Rich DeVos is one of the best owners I've ever worked with, and a true friend. He has certainly made his mark in professional sports.

# The Old Baseball Bug

In February of 1990, just before my fiftieth birthday, I saw an article in the *Orlando Sentinel* about Hank Henry, who bench-pressed 350 pounds on his sixty-fifth birthday. The photo of Hank was awesome—and I was inspired. Right then I decided I wanted to look like Hank on my sixty-fifth birthday. So I started pumping iron, and I've been pumping ever since. I installed a weight room in our porch area and joined a couple of clubs. Nobody has mistaken me for Charles Atlas, but I've never felt better, and I love the idea of improving with age. I intend to outrun, outlift, and outdo my grandkids when I'm into my eighties and beyond.

If there is one disappointment in my career, it is that I never got to operate a major league baseball team. From the time I left the Phillies organization in 1968, I always thought that one day I'd get back into baseball. Over the years, I was contacted by a number of teams, and I interviewed for positions with the Cubs, Rangers, Pirates, Braves, Orioles, and Cardinals. Each time, either I decided to stay put or the team went with another candidate. When I left the 76ers in '69 to go to Chicago, I told my friend Ruly Carpenter about my decision, and he replied, "I'm sorry to hear that—I always thought you and I would run the Phillies together." That meant a lot to me.

When Major League Baseball shifted into the expansion mode in the late '80s, just as I landed in the fertile growth area of central Florida, my imagination was fired, my enthusiasm was fueled. MLB and Orlando seemed like a marriage made in baseball heaven.

In 1990, the du Pont sports ownership group purchased the Minnesota Twins double-A farm club in Orlando. This would give the du Pont group territorial rights if Major League Baseball ever came to central Florida. I became president of the team (a part-time occupation)—and that was a real thrill. It was Spartanburg all over again—back to my minor league baseball roots after a twenty-five-year absence. It was also a great experience for my thirteen-year-old son, Bobby, who got to go on the road with the team that summer as a bat boy. I'll always remember the team we had, including Chuck Knoblauch, Scott Erickson, Denny Neagle, and Lenny Webster, all of whom went on to outstanding major league careers.

The old baseball promotion bug still had a grip on me. One night in 1990 still stacks up as one of my favorites. Jerry Greene, a sports columnist for the *Sentinel,* wrote a piece blistering our O-town sports fans. The gist of it was, "You Orlando fans think you're ready for major league baseball? Come on! You aren't even supporting double-A! You people couldn't fill up the ballpark if they let you in free!" He closed with the challenge, "If you fill up the ballpark, I'll eat my words."

Well, that was just what we needed. We jumped all over Greene's challenge. We worked with the *Sentinel* and put on a big promotion called "Jerry Greene Eat My Words Night." The *Sentinel* offered scads of free tickets, and we ended up putting six thousand people in a ballpark that was supposed to seat five thousand. That night, we set up a dining table in the middle of the field with a beautiful candelabra. I was on hand, along with a waiter in tie and tails who ladled red marinara sauce onto a bowl of shredded newsprint. And there sat Jerry, a guy who, from the look of him, hasn't missed many meals in his life. He dove into that plate of newsprint "pasta," twirled some of it on his fork, and proceeded to choke down every bit of it. As a photographer stepped up to capture the look on Jerry's face as he ate his own words, I leaned over and pointed derisively at Jerry's plate. The picture is on the wall of my office, a memento of one of my favorite promotions.

The old baseball bug has also led me, every winter since I moved to Florida, to participate in several Dream Week old timers' games held annually in the state. Though I never realized my dream of playing in the big leagues, a couple of times a year I get to strap on the tools of ignorance and play with and against some of the most legendary names of major league baseball history. I play on the same field with such greats as Bob Feller, Bob Gibson, Brooks Robinson, Al Oliver, Pete Rose, and Harmon Killebrew. Thirty years after I caught for him as an eighteen-year-old rookie with the minor league Miami Marlins,

I got to catch again for Hall of Famer Ferguson Jenkins. I even got to catch in two exhibition games against the Silver Bullets, the women's professional team.

In January 1997, I was catching in a Phillies-Cardinals Dream Week game at Al Lang Field in St. Petersburg. It was a dark, rainy day when ex-Phillies relief pitcher Larry Andersen came in during the seventh. Larry wasn't interested in throwing easy lobs. He was firing hard. He threw a nasty slider that literally ripped off my glove. I looked down and saw the top joint of my left thumb pointing off to the side. It was dislocated.

I ran over to the dugout, and the trainer pulled on the thumb and popped it back into place. As I looked over his shoulder, I saw seventy-seven-year-old Andy Seminick—who had been my manager in the minors in Miami—sitting on the dugout bench. And I remembered something he had told the Miami team back in '62: "You've gotta be tough! You've gotta play hurt!" So I put my glove back on, ran back onto the field, and finished catching the game.

Each winter, I also participate in ceremonies at the Ted Williams Museum and Hitters Hall of Fame in Citrus Hills near Ocala. There, I again rub shoulders with all my boyhood heroes. Florida is baseball heaven, and life is good.

## From Carpooling to Buspooling

A parallel storyline during those years is the growth of our rapidly expanding family. Our concern for children in the poverty-ridden Third World intensified after Jill and our son Bobby accompanied Lorraine Boisselle of the Adoption Centre in Orlando on a trip through some poor towns and encampments in Guatemala. They were profoundly moved by the sight of entire families living in shacks with cardboard roofs and dirt floors, of grimy children with matted hair playing on train tracks. Jill and Lorraine tried to work out a process that would enable abandoned Guatemalan children to be adopted by families in the States, but their plan was thwarted by a dishonest

Guatemalan attorney and an indifferent Guatemalan government.

That same year, however, we learned of four Filipino brothers who had been turned over to the courts of the Philippines when their mother could no longer care for them. Their names were Leifvan, age nine, Marty, eight, Windell, seven, and Artem, four. Coming soon after our adoption of Thomas and Stephen from Korea, this development meant we faced a tough decision over the possibility of expanding our tribe from eight to twelve. We considered what it was going to cost—remodeling and enlarging the house, getting more bunk beds, buying another van, and of course down the road, paying all that college tuition. Jill, who understood the practical issues better than I did, really struggled with the big change this would bring to our family—but it was something I wanted to do, and I pushed hard for the adoption. To be candid, I think I simply wore Jill down until she finally said yes.

At the family conference we held to discuss the matter, our oldest boy, Jimmy, was initially opposed to the idea. He had taken a lot of ribbing from his friends about living in an "orphanage." And he was worried about what he might have to sacrifice to accommodate four new brothers. Most of the kids, however, gave the plan thumbs up—though the girls, worried about being outnumbered, lobbied for more sisters instead of brothers.

But when everyone saw the photo of those boys standing in front of the Christian orphanage in the Philippines with smiles on their faces despite the hardship they had endured—well, we all just knew that God was calling us to make more room in our house and our hearts. Even Jimmy came around—not with great enthusiasm, but he's a team player, and he genuinely supported the family decision.

The biggest obstacles to adopting the four boys, however, turned out to be the U.S. government and a typhoon. The boys were tested for tuberculosis, and the U.S. embassy claimed that the boys tested positive. We obtained the test results and X-rays and had them evaluated by two medical experts, who determined that the boys did not have TB. The embassy, however, insisted that the boys be retested, so they went back to the clinic for more tests. The next day, a typhoon blew through Manila, bringing floods as deep as seven feet. The boys' tests were washed away in the flood. Jill and I turned to Sen. Bob Graham of Florida for help, and the embassy finally relented.

Our four Filipino sons—whom we renamed David, Peter, Brian, and Samuel—joined our family in November 1988.

At the end of 1989, the communist government of Romania fell. That's when the Western world learned that the country's deposed communist leader, Nicolae Ceausescu, wanting to build a mighty army, had ordered families to have large numbers of children. Of course, those poor families were unable to care for so many children, and the children ended up in state orphanages to be raised by the government. There were thousands of homeless children in Romanian orphanages. When Jill and her friend, Lorraine Boisselle, heard of this in early 1990, they flew off to Romania to see the situation for themselves, and to take medicine and clothing into the country.

Jill did not go into Romania with the idea of adopting more children. But as she toured the orphanages and looked at the faces of those boys and girls, her heart was broken. She was visiting an orphanage in a Carpathian mountain village when she spotted a four-year-old girl who completely captivated her. This little elf's name was Gabriela—and Jill came home bonded with this child. Jill showed me pictures of Gabriela and another little girl from Bucharest—Katarina (we named her after skater Katarina Witt).

No adoption agency was set up to find homes for Romanian children, so Jill had to go to Romania to dicker, argue, and wheedle her way through the chaotic national welfare system. She made four trips to Romania, and the process took over a year. But in the end, she was able to bring back our two little girls, who by that time were five years old. Gabriela became part of our family in May 1991, and Katarina joined us in September.

At that point, we had fourteen children—and we were far beyond carpooling. We were a buspooling family.

# The Big Guy

The Magic finished the '90–91 season with a record of 31 wins, 51 losses. It was the last season for owner Bill du Pont, who had overseen the birth and infancy of the organization.

The 1991–92 season began the DeVos era. I made it clear to Rich and his family that we were in for a long, exasperating year. "Prepare yourselves for a lot of suffering," I said. As an expansion team in our third year, we were not ready to compete on an equal footing with the rest of the NBA. The '91 draft brought us two rookies: Brian Williams from Arizona and Stanley Roberts from LSU. They worked their way into the Magic system, and we still had Nick Anderson and Dennis Scott, who were starting to come along as young players.

But as the year unfolded, everything that could go wrong went wrong. Apparently, that famous lawmaker named Murphy had bought a season ticket for our games. Williams was late signing. Roberts showed up terribly out of shape. Scott injured his knee, and that injury cost him almost the whole year. Anderson had an eye injury unrelated to basketball and was sidelined for months. And so it went—a disastrous 21-61 record, the second worst in the league.

It was an emotionally tough season to get through, but in the spring of '92, there was a silver lining. Our season was so miserable that we entered the lottery with ten of the sixty-six Ping-Pong balls in the lottery machine. And it turned out to be one of the most significant lotteries in the annals of the NBA, because that was the year a once-in-a-lifetime player—a 7′1″, 300 pound center from Louisiana State University—announced he was leaving after his junior year to enter the draft. His name was Shaquille O'Neal.

Shaq was going to be the easiest draft choice anybody ever had—whoever won the lottery won Shaq. (The next most obvious pick that year was Alonzo Mourning.) The lottery was held at the NBA Films headquarters in north Jersey, not far from where we used to live when I was with the Sixers. I flew up the night before the draft and stayed in Philadelphia—my first visit to Philly since I had left six years earlier. I rented a car and drove through the old neighborhood just to look around.

The lottery was conducted late on a Sunday during a play-off game. I arrived in the afternoon, and everything ran late because the game was long. The lottery is always a scene of high anxiety, but this one was especially intense because of Shaquille O'Neal. You could feel the edge of emotion in the air, because many people in that room knew that their lives and careers were going to be affected for years because of the random action of some Ping-Pong balls in a lottery machine.

All eleven clubs that did not make the playoffs took part in the lottery. Each had a Shaq jersey made up and waiting in case it won the lottery for the right to make the first draft pick. Only one club would be able to pull out that jersey and show it to the TV cameras. The other ten would trash their Shaq jerseys and slink out of town in the dark of night.

I remember walking through the back of the auditorium that evening. NBC had a video crew set up and the network's Bob Costas, who was emceeing the event, was on the podium getting ready for the telecast. I knew he would be interviewing the representative of whichever team won the lottery, so as I walked by him, I said, "Bob, keep my seat warm up there. I'll be up to talk to you right after the lottery."

So the ceremony commenced. Our representative, Jack Swope, counted to make sure all ten of our Ping-Pong balls were in the machine. The other clubs did the same. David Stern officiated and a representative from a major accounting firm was on hand to certify the results. The room was locked—no one would go in or out until the ceremony was completed. The results were indicated by an arrangement of cards printed with team logos. The cards were turned face-down; then, as the network cameras rolled, David Stern turned over the logos in order, from eleventh to first. As each logo was turned, I watched and prayed. The suspense was murder.

Sitting to my right was Don Carter, owner of the Dallas Mavericks, a team that really struggled that season. They had experienced nothing but frustration, and he would have loved to hang a Mavericks jersey on Shaquille O'Neal. He sat there in his cowboy hat with a lucky coyote tooth on the front. His team's logo came up at number four. His disgust was palpable.

Sitting to my left was former NFL linebacker Bob Stein, president of the Minnesota Timberwolves. The T-wolves' logo surfaced at number three. Bob growled his frustration.

Who was left? Charlotte and Orlando. Charlotte was number one in the lottery last year and used its pick to grab Larry Johnson of the University of Nevada at Las Vegas. I said to myself, "Not Charlotte again. It cannot be! Life would not be so cruel and unfair that Charlotte could get *both* Larry Johnson *and* Shaq!"

David Stern moved to the second logo, turned it face up—

A Hornet. A Charlotte Hornet!

The Orlando Magic had won the lottery.

They tell me the TV shot of my face is something people will never forget. I was stunned and ecstatic all at once. I wanted to leap out of my chair and hug somebody. But I could see that coyote-tooth on my right was not in a hugging mood, nor was the grizzled old linebacker on my left. Before the proceedings, Stern had warned us all, "Don't anybody come up and hug me. Two years ago, the Nets won the lottery and Willis Reed—all 6'10", 280 pounds of him—came up and hugged me, and my ribs are still sore. So no hugging."

I numbly moved to the podium to be congratulated by David Stern, and I held up our Shaq jersey—but I was so stunned that I just stood there, looking silly. *I can't believe it,* I thought. *I just can't believe it. Rich DeVos must be our lucky charm. There are teams in this league that have gone decades without a break— and the DeVos family hits the jackpot its first year in the basketball business!*

Next, I went over to be interviewed by Bob Costas, and he said, "Pat Williams, you told me before the lottery to keep your chair warm, because you were going to be back here to talk about winning the first pick—and here you are."

And there I was. Unbelievable.

## The Pick That Almost Didn't Happen

We had won Shaq in the lottery. But getting him to Orlando was another story.

Shaq was represented by Leonard Armato, a sports attorney with the territorial tenacity of a junkyard dog. Under Armato's canny guidance, one of the shrewdest games of cat and mouse in sports history began. Though it was obvious that Orlando would pick Shaquille O'Neal, all Shaq would say was that he was honored to be considered the likely first pick. He avoided any mention of the Magic. He played his hand beautifully. A story began to circulate that he wanted to go to Los Angeles, and the fans in Orlando began to despair of ever landing him. Sure, he didn't have many options for 1992—but he could have sat out that year and gone back into the draft in '93.

The five weeks between the lottery and the draft were weeks of misery and suspense for the Magic organization and its fans. We talked with Armato but had to be very careful in what we said because NBA rules would not allow us to open negotiations until we had drafted O'Neal. So we could not talk money.

As the draft approached, we were adamant about bringing Shaq to Orlando, which is standard operating procedure with draft prospects—you fly them down, show them around, interview them. Armato kept putting us off, saying, "Why do you want to bring Shaq down? You know who you're going to pick." We kept saying, "We just want to be thorough and check him out." At the last minute, Armato agreed to let Shaq come down and meet us. We arranged a flight by private plane the Friday before the draft, which would be on Tuesday. We brought Shaq; his father, Sergeant Harrison; and his younger brother, twelve-year-old Jamal Harrison, into Orlando. When they landed at the downtown airport, a lot of people were gathered to greet him. Shaq, his father, and brother were very quiet as they got into my car. Sergeant Harrison had a cellular phone with him, and as we drove into the city, I heard him calling Shaq's mother, Lucille, to tell her what was going on.

We started at the Magic Team Store and gave Shaq and his family a shopping spree—they loved it, filling several bags with Magic paraphernalia. Then I took them over to our house to meet our big family. I could see that Sergeant Harrison was a family-oriented man who loved kids—and we had plenty of kids to show him. Our kids, of course, were thrilled and awed to meet Shaq. They had never seen anyone the size of this guy. He just blots out the sun—yet he was a very gentle giant with our kids, and he enjoyed them. We had a very nice visit.

I said, "Shaq, would Jamal like to stay here and play while we go look over the arena?" Shaq and the sergeant called Lucille, then said, "Yeah, he can stay here." So Jamal stayed at our place and whooped it up all day with my kids. They went out in the boat and hung out and had all kinds of fun with the Williams clan. I wanted Shaq to see the genuineness of our family and to know that the Magic organization is a family and that Orlando, Florida, is a family-oriented town. We wanted to get him excited about Orlando.

Shaq, the sergeant, and our staff spent the rest of the day in interviews and meetings and tours. Rich DeVos flew in that afternoon. Rich is the ultimate salesman, and if you can get him together with people, they're going to come away impressed. We had dinner in a private room at the Omni Hotel, across the plaza from the arena. It was a big deal, with Shaq, his father, Jamal, Rich, Bob Vander Weide, Matt Guokas, John Gabriel, and some other Magic bigwigs—about a dozen people.

I'll always remember the playfulness and childlike quality of Shaquille O'Neal that night. Here he was, getting ready to do a multimillion-dollar deal, and he and his brother were at one end of the table by Matty, goofing around like brothers do—grinning, bumping each other, poking each other, taking food off each other's plate. Nothing wild or rude—just having fun. I thought it was great that Shaq wasn't overwhelmed by the bigness of everything. Perhaps it is fitting that the name Shaquille is Arabic for "Little Warrior." Shaq truly is a warrior-child, a kid who has fun playing his game—a kid who happens to stand over seven feet tall and weigh 300 pounds.

That evening, we took Shaq and his family to the airport and they flew off into the warm Florida evening. We felt we had scored. They liked us, and they liked Orlando.

The draft—which is normally held in New York every year—was in Portland that year because of the World Games. All the players in the draft had to go to Oregon to be introduced on national television. It was a major media event, and Shaq and his family were on hand for all of it. We carried it live on our giant Magic Vision screens at the Orlando Arena, and about ten thousand people filled the stands.

We had it set up so that the fans would be a part of Magic history in the making. I would stand on a podium in the middle of the Orlando Arena, and the fans could see me make the draft pick in person while watching the rest of the draft on the big scoreboard screen. All I had to do was speak through the long-distance phone hookup and say, "The Orlando Magic selects Shaquille O'Neal of LSU." Moments later, NBA commish David Stern would echo our selection to the world from Portland.

Everything had been tested and double-checked in advance. It was one of those high-tech, computerized, satellite linkups which guaranteed that nothing could go wrong . . . go wrong . . . go wrong . . . At exactly the right moment, I picked up the phone, punched the buttons as I had been instructed, smiled to the crowd, and heard—

Nothing.

No dial tone, no nothing. The line was dead.

I looked around for help. The technical people just shrugged and looked at each other. "Try it again," they whispered.

I tried it again. No dial tone. I'm getting nothing but a rising sense of panic, edging toward terror. Sweating artillery shells, I think about the fact that the commissioner has given us five minutes to make up our selection. Everyone in the world knows we don't even need five *seconds*. Yet here we are, issuing a thunderous silence from Orlando—and I realize we have no contingency plan. We hadn't allowed for a technology breakdown. We had never told our representatives in Portland, "If anything goes wrong, just take Shaq."

As I had my nervous breakdown right in the middle of our arena, the fans began to suspect something was wrong. A murmur rippled through the crowd—something along the lines of, "The idiot! What's he standing there for? Why doesn't he take Shaq and get on with it?"

I was frantically telling my assistants on the floor, "If we don't get through right now, we forfeit our pick!"

Then I saw our ace publicity director, Alex Martins, cooly dialing his cellular phone. In seconds, Alex was in touch with our representative at the Magic table in Portland. "Tell the commissioner," he said calmly, "we're taking Shaquille O'Neal of LSU." Minutes later, the commissioner announced our pick on national television.

To this day, there are times I wake up in a cold sweat, thinking how our night of triumph nearly became a night of horror—the night of the pick that almost didn't happen. The press later commented on the strange lag in our announcement, though I don't think the full reason for it was ever reported.

So we drafted Shaquille O'Neal—but the big man himself was still silent. He had still not declared himself for Orlando.

The next day, Shaq flew to Orlando for a press conference. We wanted to honor the selection and get Shaq off to a good start. A band and the Magic Girls and hundreds of fans greeted him at the airport. The town was in a tizzy. The celebration culminated in a luncheon at the Expo Center downtown with more than three hundred of Orlando's leading citizens attending. Near the conclusion of the luncheon, Shaq stepped to the podium to make his speech—without question, one of the briefest speeches I've ever heard and one of the most powerful. The crowd strained to hear his words.

"I'm very excited about starting my NBA career . . ." He paused for an eternity—maybe an eternity and a half. Then he concluded, "Right here in Orlando."

The crowd jumped to its feet and applauded uproariously.

We still had a difficult summer ahead of us. The toughest job belonged to our "capologists," the financial wizards whose job it was to figure out how to pay Shaq's asking price and still stay under the salary cap. The leaders of our capology division were our president, Bob Vander Weide, who has an extremely acute financial mind, player personnel director John Gabriel, and director of finance Scott Herring. We also had a couple of sharp lawyers out of Cleveland, Irv Leonard and Dan Hagen, who were indispensable in our effort to bring Shaq aboard.

We had a lot of maneuvering to do, including convincing five players to rewrite their contracts downward to make room for O'Neal—something that was unheard of at that point. We had to structure the deal in such a way that the players would take less at first, then get it back later—and they were willing to do that, if it meant getting the Magic positioned for a real run at the championship. We also traded Sam Vincent to Milwaukee to get his salary off our books.

Shaq wasn't difficult to negotiate with—he wanted to get the deal done as much as we did. But he clearly had a high market value, and we had to find creative ways to afford his obvious value.

In the middle of it all, Dallas threw out an offer sheet on center Stanley Roberts, who became a free agent in '92. That created turmoil and additional financial pressure. It was a cagey move by the Mavs, because they knew if they could drive up the price for signing Roberts while we were struggling to get under the cap, we would not be able to match their offer. Roberts would simply slip away and we would get nothing. We had to get Shaq signed before we could deal with Roberts. So it was a summer of incredible pressure and intensity, and we were all involved in it twenty-four hours a day. I mean that literally—we got phone calls and attended meetings at the strangest of hours.

We finally got everything resolved and squeezed Shaq's multiple-year, forty-plus-million-dollar contract under our cap with a little room to spare. We called a press conference in August and announced that we had signed Shaquille O'Neal and we were matching the Mavs' offer on Stanley Roberts. As soon as Roberts was matched, we began to pursue trades. John Gabriel negotiated a trade that sent Roberts to the Clippers for two future first-round picks. That may seem crazy, fighting so hard to keep Roberts, then trading him away. But because he was a free agent, he could have ended up in Dallas and we would have gotten no cash, trade, or draft picks in return. Once we matched the Mavs' offer, we had contractual control of Roberts and could protect our investment.

Shaq had an outstanding year in 1992–93 and took Rookie of the Year honors. Were there rough edges to his game? Absolutely. He never had a hook shot, and—more important— he was a poor free throw shooter. Most of the big men in the game have had trouble connecting from the stripe. Wilt Chamberlain, Bill Russell, and Bill Walton all struggled. One exception to the rule was Kareem Abdul-Jabbar, who could really hit free throws.

But the fact is that Shaq struggled at the line, no doubt about it, and many teams learned to exploit this weakness with a tactic that came to be called "Hack-a-Shaq." He was fouled so often that, had he been only a 70 percent free throw shooter, we never would have lost a game. We tried everything imaginable to elevate Shaq's free throw stats—seminars, extra practice, and one-on-one tutoring with shot doctor Buzz Braman. All our efforts produced only marginal improvement.

All of that, of course, is mere quibbling next to the rim-bending, glass-rattling power he provided down low. Offensively, he dominated any player in the league in the low post. Defensively, he was a shot-blocking monster. He was deservedly included on the 1996 Olympic Dream Team in Atlanta. Clearly, Shaq was the pivotal reason for the upswing in our fortunes, lifting us from a 21-win record in '91–92 to a respectable 41-41 mark in the '92–93 season.

## Eighteen Is Enough

The process of stuffing Shaq into a Magic jersey by July 1992 pretty much wiped out the Williams family vacation. At the end of August, I told Jill, "We've got to go somewhere—even if it's just for a few days." Jill had met Vini Jaquery, a missionary in Brazil, at a luncheon when he visited Orlando. We had heard about the plight of masses of children in Brazil, and we decided to head down there for a few days to see for ourselves.

Our week in Brazil was the most incredible experience imaginable. Hosted by Vini and social worker Andrew Saunders, Jill and I saw Brazil in the raw—the slums, prisons, and orphanages of Sao Paulo and Rio, scenes you don't find in the travel brochures. Although Jill had been to Guatemala, Romania, and other troubled lands, this was my first trip to the Third World, and it was a real eye-opener. As we visited several orphanages, I found myself falling in love with kids by the dozens. It was a scary experience, because I soon found myself "kid-shopping." Everywhere we went, I said, "Let's get that kid; and that one," even though I knew we couldn't afford to take in every lost child we saw. That I was so strongly and emotionally pulled by the sight of these children genuinely frightened me.

Andrew took us to a courthouse during our next to last day in the enormous city of Sao Paulo. "I want you to meet a girl named Rita Gomez," he said. He showed us into a room where we spent about ten minutes with a charming eleven-year-old. When our meeting was over, Jill said, "Can you picture her in the halls at Lee Middle School back home?" Well, I sure could. Little Rita stole our hearts.

I couldn't stop thinking about her during the rest of the trip, and neither could Jill. Later, as Andrew was driving us to the airport, I told him, "We would like to adopt Rita, but I also want a Brazilian boy."

So Andrew reached back into his briefcase, pulled out a pair of color snapshots of a handsome eleven-year-old boy, and said, "I've been trying to find a home for this one. His name is Anderson D'Oliviera."

Jill took one look at those photos and said, "We'll take him." So we started the adoption process for these two children in September 1992 and returned to Brazil February 1, 1993, to finalize the process. The two children were put in our care immediately, though Jill had to stay in Brazil another three weeks before she could bring them home. We renamed the boy Richie, after my friend Rich DeVos. And Rita chose her own new name—Daniela. We welcomed Richie and Dani into the

Williams family on February 22, 1993, bringing the number of children in our home to sixteen.

During that return trip to Brazil in February, Andrew Saunders had taken us to visit a holding center where many orphaned children were temporarily housed. Jill and I had walked into a room where about ten children were having lunch. A couple of kids who appeared to be brother and sister were eating from bowls of rice and beans. "Andrew," I said, "tell me about those two."

"Their father is dead," he replied. "Their mother is in jail."

"Well, what's going to become of them?" I asked.

"Statistically," said Andrew, "the boy probably won't live to see his eighteenth birthday. The little girl will probably grow up to become a teenage prostitute."

"No, she won't," I said. "We're going to take those two."

The process of adopting those children—Kelly, age ten, and Denis, eight—lasted until December 1993. We went down and brought them back to the States on Christmas night. They arrived in Orlando to a great media fanfare. Deborah Norville reported on the event for CBS and Olympic swimmer Diana Nyad hosted a syndicated show on the kids' arrival. An NBC story aired at halftime during an NBA game Christmas night. Kelly and Denis gave themselves new names: Caroline and Alan. Our family now numbered eighteen children—and we decided eighteen was enough.

One summer afternoon, about six months after Caroline had come into our home, I was sitting with her and several of our other kids, watching a rented video of the movie *Annie*, the story of the comic strip character Little Orphan Annie. After the movie, most of the kids ran out to go swimming, but Caroline stayed behind. I noticed she was crying. I said, "Why are you crying, honey?"

She ran to me, threw her arms around me, and kept sobbing for a while. Then she lifted her head and said, "I'm so glad I've got a daddy!"

Wow! That's what it's all about.

I keep hoping and praying that more people will begin to share this dream in which all of God's children, whether they come from Latin America, Eastern Europe, Africa, Asia, or right here in America—would have mommies and daddies and the love to which every child has a God-given right. We could only take in so many, but we've encouraged many more families to look around the world, see the need, and make room for a child or two.

## Shiny Penny

The Orlando Magic's .500 record for 1992–93 was a twenty-game improvement over the previous season. We were in a dead heat with Indiana for the last playoff spot, and we went through a set of tie-breaker guidelines, with the advantage going to Indiana based on some insignificant statistic. After the great year we had, missing the playoffs by a gnat's eyelash was a tough disappointment.

The good news, however, was that our record was just poor enough to get us into the draft sweepstakes again. That was a big consolation, even though we knew that, with only one Ping-Pong ball in the lottery this year instead of ten, our odds of getting the number one pick were considerably steeper: a mere one in sixty-six.

The draft lottery was conducted at the Sheraton Hotel in midtown Manhattan. I made the trek, even though I wasn't up for it. Why travel all that way just to sit there and be disappointed? It was a wasted weekend, as far as I was concerned.

I arrived in New York in the morning and went into the men's room of the hotel to put my contact lenses in. Both eyes rejected them. My eyes just said no. I took it as a bad sign. I left the men's room and called Dial-A-Prayer. The line was busy. I called the people at the suicide hotline. They hung up on me. I just knew this was not going to be my day.

In the big ballroom where the draft would take place, I took my seat in the eleventh chair. That year, it was pretty much a sure thing that Chris Webber would be Da Man, the inevitable first pick. The next three players, in the minds of most handicappers, were Anfernee "Penny" Hardaway, Jamal Mashburn, and big Shawn Bradley (7′7″), who had been away from basketball for two years while on a Mormon mission in Australia.

The lottery began and David Stern flipped over the eleventh card. I expected to see the Magic logo. Without my glasses or my contacts, I couldn't see well, but I could tell by the color scheme that the Detroit Pistons had drawn number eleven. *Hmm*, I thought, *so Motown has even worse luck than O-town.*

The draft continued and the excitement and disbelief kept building in that room as we got down to the last few cards with Orlando still in the running. At number three, the Golden State Warriors's card turned up. That left Philly and Orlando.

Understand, there was a big difference in the atmosphere in that room in '93. The previous year, Orlando was the underdog, with a lousy 21-win season. Everybody figured, "Heck, Orlando deserves a break. Let 'em have Shaq." People were happy for us. But once we had Shaq, once we had improved our record by twenty games, people thought one break was enough. If we scored two number one picks back to back, that would be too much. That would be unfair. The other people in that room wouldn't congratulate us—they'd lynch us!

So David Stern turned the card over for the number two pick—

And it was the Philadelphia 76ers' card.

A miracle—again! I couldn't believe our good fortune—and neither could anyone else. If looks could kill, I'd have been dead ten times over.

Our second straight lottery win set off an immediate round of controversy over the lottery. The most common comment was, "This is not good for basketball. We need to keep teams from winning two years in a row." Stern came under a lot of pressure to change the lottery system again. It had been changed ten years earlier to keep teams from dumping games to get advantageous draft picks. Every year, the lottery is altered or tweaked to make it more fair. But a lottery is a game of chance, and by the luck of the draw, we had beaten odds of one in sixty-six to win the '93 lottery. It wasn't as if anyone had given us a free pass; the scales were deliberately weighted against us. God simply smiled on us.

No one in that room was more stunned than I was. As I walked on rubbery legs up to the podium, David Stern glared at me as if to say, *What are you doing here again?* I shook his hand and tried like crazy to keep from smiling. I didn't dare let the faintest trace of gloating or even satisfaction cross my face—not if I wanted to get out of that room alive.

Afterward, I did the Bob Costas interview. Then I floated back to Orlando. The story in the press was that it was going to be Shaq and Chris Webber side-by-side. Even Shaq thought so. He came out the next day and exulted, "Hey, man, we got to get Webber! That's the pick!"

Between the lottery and the draft, Matt Guokas, tired of the rigors of coaching, decided to resign his coaching post and pursue opportunities in the front office or the broadcast booth. Rather than hire a new head coach from the outside, we decided to elevate his assistant, Brian Hill, to the top spot. Brian had paid his dues, the players respected him, and he had made a good impression with the front office, so we stuck with him.

We brought Chris Webber in for interviews and a two-day workout. This was unheard of; top picks usually will not do that. But the workout was revealing. We saw Webber's talent, and we liked his size and his moves—but we had a few nagging questions about him. Webber was not a great free throw shooter, and that was a concern. What if we have Shaq and Webber on the floor in a tight game, and they're getting fouled and can't make free throws down the stretch? That will certainly cost us games.

We were also concerned because Webber had not completed all his NBA medical exams—he had pulled out early without an explanation. But the most troubling thing of all was an indefinable factor called *attitude*. Webber was in a foul temper when he arrived in Orlando for a second visit—possibly because he didn't feel he should have to go through a physical. Attitude is always a consideration in a prospective player. Is he coachable? Is he a team player? Or does he have an ego problem or a chip on his shoulder? After meeting Webber, John Gabriel was alarmed about what he saw as a potential problem in that department.

We also brought in Jamal Mashburn—a wonderful offensive player who has become a very good scorer. We brought in Shawn Bradley—not that it made much sense to have two seven-plus-footers in our lineup, but just to check him out and study him.

Near the end of the process, we brought in Anfernee "Penny" Hardaway, a highly rated guard from Memphis University. (He's been Penny, by the way, ever since he was a baby and his grandmother said he was as pretty as a shiny new penny.) We interviewed him, worked him out, studied him—but as we got closer to the draft, it was apparent to us that Webber was the safe pick. We had a gaping hole at power forward. So at the June board meeting with Rich DeVos and the rest of the family, we informed ownership that Webber was our man. Being from Michigan, they were very pleased that we had settled on a University of Michigan star. So we were comfortable with our choice and that was that.

Well, not quite. On the Sunday before Wednesday's draft, John Gabriel, our basketball operations director, called me at home and said, "Pat, I want to bring Hardaway back in for another workout."

"What do you want to do that for, Gabe?" I asked. "What's your thinking?"

"Well," he said, "Penny and Shaq are out in Hollywood. They're making this movie, *Blue Chips*. They're out on the set, they're playing a lot of basketball in their free time, and Shaq keeps calling and saying, 'Man, this guy is the real thing. He's a player, man. We gotta think about taking him.' And I'm also hearing from Hardaway. He doesn't think he got a good look in the first workout. He's willing to come back in if we'll look him over again. He really wants to be in Orlando."

"Okay, Gabe," I said, "whatever you have to do to satisfy yourself. We might as well be thorough. Bring him back in."

So Hardaway flew back to Orlando on Monday. This, too, was practically unheard of—that close to the draft, NBA draft prospects don't do workouts. They don't want to see anybody.

They hide out and wait for their name to be called. John Gabriel told him, "Penny, just tell me what you need for this tryout, and I'll do it."

And Penny said, "All I want is one hour of pickup ball."

The game started at one o'clock in the afternoon in a church gym, no referees. It was an old-fashioned shirts-and-skins game, up and down the floor, with some of our Magic players—Jeff Turner, Dennis Scott, Anthony Bowie, Greg Kite—plus some college guys. In the course of this workout, some truly astonishing things happened. Hardaway made unbelievable passes and hit incredible shots. He was finding people, guarding people, stealing the ball, leading the fast break, hitting shots from everywhere on the court—layups to way downtown. Penny did everything but change the light bulbs and sweep the floor. I kept glancing at the faces of the front office guys who were sitting with me in the stands. There was consternation and amazement all around.

Finally, the workout was nearly finished with the game tied. Hardaway had the ball out past the arc and pulled the trigger—and it must have been a thirty-five footer. It hit nothing but net, as sweet a three-point shot as you'll ever want to see. Then he nonchalantly walked off the floor, looking up at us as if to say, "Seen enough?"

Well, we had seen enough. We had witnessed the Michael Jordan-like versatility of a 6'7" swing man who was equally strong inside and outside. Not only was he a brilliant shooter and a dazzling ball-handler, but he unselfishly distributed the ball and set up opportunities for other players. Shaq was right: Anfernee Hardaway was the real thing.

After Penny left that church gym to catch a plane for Detroit, the site of the draft ceremony, I turned to John Gabriel and shook my head. "John," I said facetiously, "you have really messed things up. We have a very tough decision to make."

The biggest headache we faced was the enormous media and fan expectation surrounding Chris Webber. Everyone assumed Webber was Orlando-bound. He was the number one college player in the country, a household name among NCAA fans—

and we sorely needed to fill the position he played. It would be insanity not to take the guy.

Penny, on the other hand, was not a marquee player, even though he had been named Great Midwest Conference Player of the Year twice and been selected for the All-America first team in 1993. The public and the press had not seen that shirts-and-skins game in the church gym. They didn't know about the interaction between Shaq and Penny out in California, and the wonderful chemistry that emerged between takes on the set of *Blue Chips*. We knew that if we took Penny instead of Chris Webber, it would be Pearl Harbor all over again.

Two hours before the draft, we were all still in agony about what to do. I sat down with John Gabriel, looked him in the eye, and said, "Gabe, forget the public, forget the media, forget your coaches, forget everybody. This one decision will determine the next ten or fifteen years of the Magic's destiny, and we're never going to have a shot like this again. So we can't just do the safe thing—we have to do the right thing. What does your gut tell you?"

"I am absolutely convinced," he said, "that we have a better chance of winning championships with Shaq and Hardaway than with Shaq and Webber."

I sighed, knowing that we were about to walk right into the spinning propeller. "Okay, you know best. Let's go with Hardaway."

We pulled the whole group together from the front office, including president Bob Vander Weide. Gabriel told the group what he'd told me, and we all agreed: Penny was our man. Don Nelson, the general manager of the Warriors, had been after us to deal Webber to him, so we worked out a deal in which we would take Webber first, the Warriors would take Penny, then we would trade Webber for Penny plus three future first picks.

And that's the way the draft unfolded. When we took Webber, the fans went wild—all ten thousand of them who were present at our draft party in the arena. You'd have thought we had just won an NBA championship. Twenty minutes later, we traded Chris Webber and it was my job to walk out on the platform in the middle of the court and explain our decision. Bob

Vander Weide agreed to go with me. On our way out, I saw a life-size cardboard cut-out of Penny that he had sent us as a promotional gimmick—I think the city of Memphis had made up a bunch of these things as part of a local antidrug campaign. So I grabbed the cutout and carried it out with me as a cheerleading prop.

One problem: There were no cheers to lead.

Instead, Bob and I faced a sea of hostile faces, all demanding to know which idiot was responsible for trading away Chris Webber. Talk about a tough room—that crowd was ugly. The fans booed us. They insulted our lineage. They threatened our lives. I lifted the Penny Hardaway cutout over my head and shouted into the microphone, "You're booing tonight, folks, but Penny Hardaway will turn your jeers into cheers." Then Bob and I hurried off the platform.

My words were prophetic. Some of the early reviews from fans and press were unkind to the Magic organization and to Penny. But as soon as jersey number 1, Anfernee Hardaway, started showing his stuff on the court—his speed, his agility, his slammin' and jammin' and no-look wraparound passes—it became hard to find a single person in Orlando who would admit to ever having doubted us. Penny averaged 16 points and 5.4 rebounds per game his rookie year and made a huge impact on our team and on the NBA. Webber and Penny finished a tight first and second for Rookie of the Year honors—so close in the voting that it easily could have gone the other way.

Once our decision was made to go with Penny, we never doubted it. We had put our money on Penny, and we knew we had made the right bet. We were poised to take a run at the championship.

# 12

# New Beginnings
# and Happy Endings

Great sports teams don't just happen. A championship team isn't just a bunch of guys who can run, shoot, and hang from the hoop better than any other bunch of guys. Championships are the result of talent, planning, sacrifice, attitude, work, chemistry, and much more. A championship team is an ever-changing puzzle composed of moving parts that interact with each other in complex and often unpredictable ways. A level of strategy and thinking goes into the building of a team that makes a game of chess look like tiddledywinks.

In the 1993–94 season, it became clear that we had achieved a rare and magical alchemy with the O'Neal-Hardaway combination. Shaq reigned supreme in the middle, while Penny scored from everywhere on the court. Nick Anderson and Dennis Scott prowled the outer edges of the arc, adding fire to the game by lobbing missiles with radar-guided accuracy. That season, the Magic racked up fifty wins, clinching a second-place finish in the Atlantic division—and our first trip to the playoffs.

Though we were knocked out in the first round by the Indiana Pacers, our young team had tasted a real winning season and had set one foot in the promised land of the playoffs. The players were hungry to do it again, and do it better, the following year.

Each year, our organization sets goals and objectives which enable us to focus all our efforts on the tasks that will make us successful on the court and at the gate. Those goals and objectives are focused on quality, profitability, customer satisfaction, employee satisfaction, and community leadership. And every year we renew our commitment to winning an NBA championship. We had gotten where we were with the help of some magical good fortune in back-to-back draft lotteries—but we couldn't count on that again. For one thing, we didn't want to end up in the lottery again, since your ticket to a lottery is a losing season. One more lottery, and we'd all be out of a job.

In 1994, we knew we had to make our own breaks. We took a hard look at our team and realized that one thing had to happen for us even to have a chance to win the championship: we had to fill a hole at the power forward slot.

As it happened, a brilliant power forward became a free agent in the summer of '94: Horace Grant of the Chicago Bulls. Grant had been a huge rebounder for the Bulls in their NBA championship years of 1991, '92, and '93. A lot of teams were clamoring for Grant's attention, including the Bulls, who didn't want to lose him. We needed and wanted him in Orlando, so we brought him down to visit our operation and meet the people. We squired him around Orlando, put him up in a Disney hotel, and gave him a real taste of the central Florida community. We also took him up to Holland, Michigan, to spend some time with Rich DeVos, and the two of them hit it off right from the start.

Obviously, Grant was lured by the chance to play alongside Shaquille O'Neal and Anfernee Hardaway, two of the hottest tickets in the NBA. But I truly believe it was the community and family atmosphere of the Magic that sold him. Grant donned his Magic jersey in August 1994. From the moment of his arrival, he merged with our system, providing not only strong rebounding but seasoned leadership for our young team. With three NBA championship rings in his possession, this battle-hardened veteran could show our young players how to win some rings of their own.

With Grant at power forward, the Magic ratcheted up another notch during the 1994–95 season, improving to fifty-seven wins and twenty-five losses. We captured our first division title and battled our way through Boston in the first round. Then we took on Chicago in the Eastern semifinals. That was the year Michael Jordan returned from retirement and minor league baseball, and he was not quite the M. J. of old. We beat Chicago in six games, winning the last game in Chicago.

We went on to the conference finals against the Indiana Pacers. It was an intense series, and the Magic needed all seven games to subdue the Pacers—though our final victory before our home crowd was a thirty-point blowout. Not a bad showing for an expansion team that had started as a pipe dream in Jimmy Hewitt's car back in '85.

Now it was on to the finals. All that lay between us and an NBA title was Houston.

## Rocked by the Rockets

We begin the finals with the home-court advantage over the defending champions, the Houston Rockets. Rich DeVos has come up with the slogan: "Why not us? Why not now?"—a bold statement that, while we are a young team without a depth of playoff experience, we are brimming with talent, energy, and competitive attitude.

As we approach the first game, the much-anticipated matchup between the two towering centers—Shaquille O'Neal and the Rockets' Hakeem "Dream" Olajuwon—lives up to its billing. In scoring and rebounding, they are evenly matched. In game one, we jump all over Houston, opening a 15-point lead in the first quarter, and extending that lead to 20 points by halftime. Horace Grant grabs nine rebounds in the first quarter, versus eight for the entire Houston team.

Orlando is heavily favored to win the series. The Rockets are seeded sixth in the Western Conference, having won only 47 regular-season games, compared with our 57. So we're confident that the Magic will win the title. But there is a weakness to our game: Penny and Shaq are carrying our entire offense. Though our team has had the hot hand throughout the play-offs, our hand turns cold. Dennis Scott's jumper is not hitting the mark. And Nick Anderson's confidence seems to have deserted him.

The Rockets, meanwhile, are getting outstanding contributions from every player, especially 6'3" point guards Kenny Smith and Sam Cassell, who combine to neutralize Penny's 6'7" height advantage in the second half. In the final moments of regulation play, with the Magic ahead 110-107, Anderson is fouled and goes to the line for two shots, either of which would put the game out of reach of even the luckiest desperation three-pointer by Houston.

Nick shoots the first free throw—and misses. He shoots the second—and misses that one. I'm astonished. Nick never misses two in a row. Luckily, he gets his own rebound—and is deliberately fouled again. So Nick goes back to the line and he has two more chances to put the game away. Incredibly, he misses them both.

I can't believe it. Nick can't believe it. No one who is watching the game in the arena or on TV can believe it.

With 1.6 seconds left in regulation, Houston's Kenny Smith launches a shot from beyond the arc—and hits it, tying the score and sending the game into overtime. A game we had seemingly won begins to slip away from us. It nearly goes into double over-time, but it ends with an Olajuwon tip-in with only three-tenths of a second on the clock. Olajuwon finishes the night with 31 points and 7 assists. Final score: Houston 120, Orlando 118.

Most of the team tries to boost Nick after the loss. Obviously, he blames himself for the loss. Though he feels deeply wounded because of those four missed free throws, he goes before the national media and handles it like an absolute pro.

But at the same time, it is clear that there has been a major shift in our mindset as a team, as an organization, as a fan base.

In a matter of seconds, we had seen a sure, in-the-bag win turn to complete disaster and disarray. In all my years in the NBA, I don't remember ever witnessing such an incredible emotional turnaround, such an enormous letdown in an arena and a community. I walk out of the building thinking, *It doesn't get any lower than this.*

Comes game two, and we are dead. Emotionally, we're just shot. We have no resources, nothing. There's no question that the first loss has left the team and the fans utterly dispirited.

In the first game, we had double- and triple-teamed Olajuwon, which left Cassell and Smith open to hit the jumpers— the Rockets had hit 14 three-point shots in game one. This time, Shaq and Dream go one-on-one, and Olajuwon collects 34 points—and Cassell still scores 31. Equally dangerous is Robert Horry, who shocks the Magic with a flurry of outside shots, rebounds, and seven steals.

It is no surprise that we get whipped at home again. The final score: 117-106. Now we have to go to The Summit in Houston—and we are in deep trouble.

In game three, Orlando shoots only 46.9 percent from the field—and a dismal 8 for 31 (25.8 percent) from behind the arc. The star of game three is Houston's Clyde Drexler—a thirty-two-year-old veteran who has never won a championship. Brought aboard at midseason from the Portland Trail Blazers, Drexler brings an added something to the Houston team: intense hunger. He wants that ring so bad he can taste it—and that's how he plays in game three, scoring 25 points, grabbing 13 rebounds, making 7 assists. Houston wins 106-103.

All hope for the Magic disappears in a puff of smoke. No team in NBA history has ever come back from being down three games to zip in any playoff series, much less the finals. Orlando is on the verge of being the first team since the '89 Lakers to be swept in the finals.

Game four begins well for us. Our outside shooters hit 9 of 14 from the three-point line in the first half (by the end of the game, we will hit 14 three-pointers, tying a finals record). Dennis Scott scores 7 points in the first quarter. By halftime, the Magic has 51 to Houston's 47. But Houston comes on strong in the third quarter, scoring inside and outside, and the lead changes hands again and again. Down the fourth-quarter stretch, however, the Magic's shooting goes cold. The team's inexperience shows in a series of frustrating turnovers, which Houston converts into fast-break scoring opportunities. The Rockets streak away from the Magic. Olajuwon has a series-high 35 points and 15 rebounds—capped by an astonishing feat for a center: a three-point shot just 11.5 seconds before the buzzer.

The Houston Rockets have won back-to-back NBA titles, sending the Magic home not merely empty, but hollowed out with despair. Final score: Rockets 113, Magic 101.

Did we underestimate the Rockets? Probably. So did Utah, Phoenix, and San Antonio, all with at least 59 regular season wins, all with the home-court advantage. Houston accomplished the impossible that year. Not only was it the lowest seeded team ever to win an NBA title, they also won a league-record nine times on the road, including seven straight. Twice in the playoffs the Rockets came from behind, being down two to one against Utah and three to one against Phoenix. Give coach Rudy Tomjanovich and his players their due—it was an incredible accomplishment.

For us, it was a tough way to end the series. It was the thrill of getting to the finals mingled with the agony of defeat—but that's what this crazy suffering business is all about. We moved into the off-season disappointed but with tremendous optimism and positive feelings about the future. Experiences such as this bring about the seasoning and maturity that lead to playoffs and championships.

## The Darkest Period of My Life

Jill's mother passed away from cancer in February 1994, and Jill began to pull away from me after that. Jill's personal loss wasn't the cause of her separation from me—she had been dissatisfied with our relationship for years. But it was, apparently, the catalyst. When her mother died, a piece of Jill seemed to die. Soon after that, I came home and found that Jill had moved out of the main house and into the guest house.

The curtain of finality had fallen. She would not discuss the possibility of salvaging our marriage. As a practical matter, our marriage was over. All that remained were the legal details.

I prayed. I tried to maintain a positive attitude. I tried to keep our family focused, motivated, and moving forward. Jill, meanwhile, bought a house and moved away.

So I entered the darkest period of my life.

My biggest struggle was with an overwhelming sense of shame and embarrassment. I had a deep sense of failure coupled with the fear that everything I had ever worked for would fall apart. For months, I didn't want anyone to know that Jill and I had separated and seemed to be headed for divorce. I didn't think anyone knew, but I was probably naive and in denial.

Three things happened during the summer of 1995 that gave me encouragement and hope of surviving the experience. The first came when I was in North Carolina for a speaking engagement in July. I drove down to Sumter, South Carolina, to have dinner with Bobby and Betsy Richardson and a mutual friend, Tara McClary, who was visiting them. After dinner, I just felt God urging me to open up and tell my friends what was happening in my life.

At first, I resisted, but then I felt God's Spirit saying to me, *It's okay. Trust them. Trust me.* So I took a deep breath and told them that Jill had left me and that I felt completely shattered. I was amazed by their response. Rather than a sense of rejection or failure, I felt their acceptance and love. They embraced me, encouraged me, and prayed with me. I came away with an uplifting sense of comfort and reassurance.

The second event happened a month later at a staff retreat on Mackinac Island. There are no automobiles on this Victorian-style resort island in northern Michigan—only horse-drawn carriages and bicycles. So everyone was out bicycling during a break. Bob Vander Weide took me aside and said, "Pat, let's grab a couple of bikes and get some fresh air." So we went riding.

Out on the bike path, Bob said, "Tell me what's happening at home." Bob's a very compassionate person, and I felt free to open up. He obviously knew something was not right in my life, even if he didn't know the details. So I accepted his invitation and unburdened myself. He listened—and of course, authentic caring and attention are two of the greatest gifts you can give to someone who is hurting. Then Bob said, "I want you to know that everyone in the organization stands behind you. I stand behind you. If there's anything we can do to help you and your family, anything at all, just let me know." That meant the world to me.

The third encouraging event took place at the end of our stay on Mackinac. John Gabriel, a good friend from my Philly days whom I had brought to Orlando, handed me a note as we were leaving the island. The note read:

> Pat,
>
> I feel for you and I can relate to your situation. Always know that I'm here to support you, or to just talk. Always remember what you have! You have a fascinating combo of good looks (ta-dah!), brains, and wit, making you the envy of thousands of men and women alike.
>
> Gabe

You can't even measure what that meant to me at that moment, because I just couldn't imagine I was the envy of anybody. Gabe's note was an extraordinarily powerful encouragement at a time I really needed it.

## A Fascinating Woman

Each year, our company, RDV Sports, holds a two-day retreat called Magic University. On the second day of our September 1995 retreat on the theme of time management, I sat waiting for the afternoon seminar on organizational skills to begin. It was to be led by a representative from Franklin Quest (now Franklin-Covey Co.), maker of the Franklin Planner.

I was thinking, *Oh, boy! I've got to fight this drowsiness—I've got another four hours to go. I don't know how I'm going to get through one more of these sessions.* But then this pert, five-foot-three blond came out, dressed in a beige business suit, and launched right into her presentation. This woman was unique. She whipped out her marking pens and started working with the overhead projector as she talked. She moved animatedly around the stage, told stories, made us laugh, inspired us, and thoroughly riveted our attention. I was captivated. Her name was Ruth Hanchey.

After the seminar, I chatted with her for a few minutes, then walked her out to the parking lot. Central Florida in September can be pretty hot and humid, and this day was sweltering— yet we stood in that parking lot and talked for more than an hour.

I learned that Ruth lived in Tampa. With a degree in English from LSU and a master's in psychology from Rollins College in Winter Park, Florida, she was working on a doctorate in human behavior. I also learned that she was a dedicated Christian, an avid runner, had a daughter in her twenties, had been divorced for five years, and loved children.

Even though I had not told many people what I'd been going through for the past year, I felt comfortable telling Ruth about my personal life—the struggle to keep moving forward as my marriage to Jill was deteriorating, the wrestling and wrangling with lawyers, the stress and emotional pain. She understood it. She had been through it.

We exchanged business cards and said our good-byes, and as she drove away, I said to myself, "Wow! There goes a fascinating woman."

At the end of 1995, Jill filed for divorce and I became caught up in the mechanics of divorce—dealing with papers and attorneys and accountants. Divorce is a fate worse than death. My occasional conversations with Ruth helped make the process a little more tolerable. She became a good friend during the toughest year of my life.

## A Hole at Center

The year 1996 was tough professionally, too. The Magic had its best ever regular season with a record of 60 wins and 22 losses. There was, however, one miscalculation on our part: Michael Jordan was back in full form. After being so soundly defeated by the Magic in the previous year's playoffs, the Bulls were really snorting fire. We got to the Eastern Conference finals—a much-anticipated series—and were waffled by the Bulls in four straight games.

Shortly after that, we were all profoundly disappointed by the defection of Shaquille O'Neal, who opted for free agency and a record-high contract with the L.A. Lakers. I was particularly displeased with the way Shaq parted company, taking completely unnecessary shots at his teammates and at Orlando (a city that had loved him, and which he dismissed as a "dried-up pond"). Our front office was stunned by the fact that Shaq's agent, Leonard Armato, never gave us the opportunity to make a final offer. After weeks of Shaq's public wobbling and repeated attempts by John Gabriel and Bob Vander Weide to negotiate in good faith, there was an abrupt announcement that Shaq was signing with the Lakers. Shaq knew that we had come up with a better compensation package than that of the Lakers, and he knew he had a better shot at a championship in Orlando than in L.A. I suspect he simply wanted to "go Hollywood" and grab the fast-lane celebrity lifestyle of southern California.

But the departure of Shaquille O'Neal was only the beginning of our woes. A few weeks after he left, Shaq's replacement, Jon Koncak, suffered a career-ending injury during practice. We had just taken two big hits at center—and we were reeling. No franchise in NBA history had faced such dramatic changes in its lineup as we did in the fall of 1996. We had to completely change direction and overhaul our strategy. We had to rebuild our team around the speed and skill of Penny Hardaway.

## God Is Not Locked In

When the divorce was being finalized at the end of 1996, I felt emptiness and sadness mingled with relief. The ordeal was over. My life was beginning again.

For more than a year, Ruth and I had maintained a discreet friendship, even though we both knew that we had the basis of a romantic relationship. It was clear that we were both interested in exploring the possibilities—but I was also aware that it is important not to rush into a new relationship right after a previous one ends.

"Ruth," I said, "I'm not sure where we go from here. But all the textbooks say that after a divorce, you need time to get stabilized—time to let the emotional dust settle. I think I really need to do that. But I really want to stay in touch with you and maintain our friendship."

"Well, how long does this dust-settling thing usually take?" she asked.

"One of the books I read says you should wait two years—"

"Okay," she said, "if that's the way you want it." I detected coolness in her response, and I immediately wished we could have talked in person instead of over the phone.

After that conversation, our relationship was not the same as it had been. I would call Ruth and she would not seem as cordial and warm as before. I took the kids to a Solar Bears hockey game at the Orlando Arena and during the game, I slipped away to my office to call Ruth in Tampa. She seemed particularly aloof.

"Is anything wrong?" I asked.

"I just can't talk right now," she said. "I'm going out to dinner with a friend tonight, and I'm going to the Buccaneers' game tomorrow. Why don't you call me after the game?"

"Okay."

I called the next night and got her answering machine. I called a few more times, got the machine each time, and thought, *What's this all about?*

I tracked Ruth down the following week and said, "I know you couldn't talk the other night—can you talk now? I don't understand what's going on."

"I recently met a very interesting man," she said.

A chill went through me—a tingle of terror mingled with jealousy. At that moment, it hit me like a sledgehammer how I really felt about Ruth. I wanted her to be more than just a friend. And now she was slipping away from me.

"This man," she continued, "was introduced to me by some mutual friends. He was the one who took me to the Bucs' game the other day."

Now, when I'm in pursuit of something I want, I charge hard. I realized I wanted Ruth. I was charging after her like a bull rhino—and getting nowhere. I was beside myself.

While I was going through the divorce process with Jill, I had introduced Ruth to my good friend and advisor Jay Strack, who lives in Orlando. Jay and his wife, Diane, had gotten to know Ruth and had built a friendship with her, independent of me. So I confided my problem to the Stracks. "I thought the right thing for me to do would be to wait an appropriate interval before pursuing any romantic relationship with Ruth," I explained. "At least, that's what the books say."

"Pat, you're not going to find another Ruth," Diane said bluntly.

"I know all that," I said. "It's just that the book says—"

"Would you forget about that stupid book!" Jay interjected. "See here, Pat, God is not locked into any one pattern, any one formula. I think that two-year theory is probably good advice for most people. But sometimes, God chooses to short-circuit the process a little. When he does, you need to be flexible. You need to listen to what he's telling you. When he brought Ruth into your life, Pat, that was no accident."

"Around the Strack house," Diane added gently, "when something happens we can't explain any other way, we just say, 'It's a God thing.'"

I sighed. My friends were right. "But I messed everything up! She's dating another guy!"

"Well," said Jay, "we'll just have to pray about it and ask God to untangle this mess you've made of things."

I left Jay and Diane's house feeling I had received a blessing from God—and a big eye-opening epiphany. The only problem was that Ruth didn't get epiphanied at the same time. Over the next few weeks, I kept calling her, asking to talk to her or meet with her, and she kept saying, "Please don't pressure me. I'd rather you just left me alone. I just can't deal with this right now."

My kids had gotten to know Ruth when she had baby-sat in our home while I was traveling. They loved her, and they could see that I loved her and that I was struggling and hurting. So Karyn, who was a senior in high school, took me out to Wendy's for lunch. She said, "Dad, Ruth is awesome! You'd better not let her get away! I'd really like to have her as a stepmother."

Well, my tears just flowed over my grilled chicken sandwich. I was sure that I had already let Ruth get away and that there wasn't anything I could do about it.

In addition to confiding in the Stracks, I sought out four pastors in the country who were longtime friends and whose counsel I respected greatly. I talked through the situation with them, and they gave me the same advice Jay had. I also called Ruth's father in Mississippi, a man in his mid-eighties whom I had never met, just to get his slant on the situation. "Well," he said diplomatically after hearing me out, "we've always taught Ruth to be very independent and to make her own decisions."

And, of course, I had a lot of long talks with the only one who could really do anything about the situation. If Ruth and I were going to come together, God himself was going to have to work out the details.

## Professional and Personal Transition

Around this time I was elevated to a new position, senior executive vice president of RDV Sports and the Magic. It sounds lofty, but I found it troubling at first, because I was relieved of the day-to-day responsibilities of running a basketball team, which had been my life for twenty-five years. John Gabriel moved into the role of general manager—and it was absolutely the logical move. He was truly ready to take on all the daily activities, something I was far better off without.

So it was an adjustment, but I quickly became accustomed to the freedom of concentrating on the bigger issues related to RDV Sports. More significantly, my corporate speaking career had been exploding, and I had an intense desire to produce the books that were in my mind. I have specific ideas for a book a year for the next sixteen years.

Also, the Women's NBA was beginning to take off, thanks to the big boost women's basketball received during the '96 Olympics in Atlanta. I really wanted to help Orlando acquire a WNBA franchise and take part in the birthing of another team. So I was reaching an interesting transition point in my professional life—and in my personal life, too.

## A New Beginning

Just before Christmas 1996, I learned that Ruth was flying into Orlando for a speaking engagement. I called her and said I'd like to meet the plane, which was arriving at quarter to ten at night.

"Pat, please don't come," she said. "I'm just not prepared to talk right now."

Well, that was pretty unambiguous. So I had a major decision to make: Should I abide by her wishes—or disregard them? I disregarded them.

Arriving at the airport, I learned that her plane would be four hours late due to bad weather. Finally, at ten till two, a group of beleaguered passengers filed off the Delta flight from Atlanta. Soon I saw Ruth, pulling her suitcase on a little cart, looking as if she had survived a long, miserable day. As she walked along the concourse, I stepped up behind her and followed her, my heart thudding like a jackhammer.

Soon I was alongside her, with Ruth completely unaware of my presence. What would she think when she saw me? What would she say? Suddenly, she knew I was there—I don't know if she saw me out of the corner of her eye or if she just sensed I was there. She stopped and looked at me with an expression of shock.

This was it. She was either going to be glad to see me or light into me for showing up when she told me not to.

For a seemingly eternal moment, she didn't speak.

Then her expression turned to joy, enthusiasm, animation. She hugged me and said, "I'm so glad you came! I was going to leave a message for you, but this is even better. You'll never guess who I sat beside on the plane from Mobile to Atlanta."

"Who?"

"Hank Aaron."

"You're kidding! Really?"

"Yep! Look, I have to rent a car—"

"Ruth, where are you staying?"

"The Marriott International Drive."

"You don't want to wait in line to rent a car at two in the morning. Why don't you just let me drive you to your hotel?"

"Well—okay."

During the drive, we talked and talked like long-lost friends—which, in a way, we were. We pulled into the parking lot at about 2:30, but we didn't get out. We just kept talking. We were still talking as the sun came up at six in the morning.

"Well, I'd better let you go inside and get some rest—before I let you go, I want you to know that my two-year plan is out the window. When you know something is the right thing to do, why should you wait two years to do it?"

"What do you mean?"

"Ruth, before I leave here, I have to tell you three things. First, I love you. Second, I want to give you a ring. Third, I want to marry you."

Then I held my breath and waited for her reaction. I didn't have to wait long.

Ruth put her arms around me and said, "Yes, I'd love to marry you. That's what I've wanted to do since I met you!"

A few hours earlier, I had been debating whether to approach her, thinking she didn't want to even see me. Now we were engaged!

"Well," she said, "you're about to have a house full of ecstatic kids."

"You bet we are! Tell you what, let's look at your speaking schedule and mine, and let's find a time when we can get married."

So we pulled out our Franklin Planners, compared schedules, and settled on April 5, 1997. The next question was who should perform the service. We looked at each other and in unison said, "Jay Strack!"

So I went home and called Jay Strack. It was Jay, of course, who had told me that I needed to pray, and that God would be able to untangle this mess I had made of things. I couldn't wait to tell Jay that God had answered that prayer.

So for the next three and a half months, we planned the wedding. Ruth also oversaw the remodeling of the house while she continued working full-time and prepared to become a stepmother to eighteen children.

April 5 arrived—a gorgeous day in central Florida. We gathered at the Stracks—my kids, my mother, Ruth's family, and about a hundred friends. The ceremony was conducted out on the dock. Karyn sang a moving song called "Household of Faith." In the middle of it, my eyes met Karyn's, and both of us completely broke, tears streaming down our faces. Somehow, Karyn got through the song. It was a powerful moment, and soon there was not a dry eye anyplace in the Stracks' big backyard.

## Life after Divorce

After my divorce, I had felt my life, career, and public platform as a speaker and writer were destroyed. I was wrong. Those areas of my life have flourished in ways I never imagined. God has transformed the pain of separation and divorce into the fulfillment of a new ministry to divorced people. I get at least a dozen calls and letters every week from people saying, "My marriage has fallen apart. My life is shattered. What do I do? Where do I turn?"

My response: There *is* life after divorce. The God I know is a God of second chances.

I never knew how terrific marriage could be until Ruth came along. Ruth and I started as friends. Today we are soulmates. She loves all the things I love—she loves the Lord, she's as passionate and ambitious about life as I am, she enjoys sports, particularly running and weight-training. Forget the "opposites attract" stuff. She and I are alike in every way except gender (viva *that* difference!). She's smart, patient, gentle, strong, family-oriented, positive, and a great listener. Ruth's best friend, Peggy Bohart, told me shortly before our wedding, "Ruth is one of the most stable, even-keeled people you'll ever know." Diane Strack told me, "Ruth doesn't react, she responds." And she's one of the best public speakers I know.

Best of all, the kids love her. She has given the gift of her love, her counsel, and a wonderful Christian example. A sweet country song by Tracy Byrd was sung at our wedding. It contains these lines, which perfectly express the way I feel today:

I tip my hat to the Keeper of the Stars;
He sure knew what he was doin' when he joined these two
   hearts.

The Keeper of the Stars worked a miracle in my life. He has led me through some tough times—and he has given me a gift beyond my imagination. Ruth is awesome. Life is awesome. God is awesome.

# Epilogue

## A Passion for Distinction

When I think back over my career, and this passion for sports and for distinction that has swept me along through life, I think of beautiful Duncan Park, set down in the Carolina woods, packed with happy people who had gathered to take life easy and to fill those woods with cheers and laughter. Those minor league baseball memories are still fresh within me, and they bring joy to my heart.

I think of a cold night in Chicago, the Bulls versus the Bucks, Kareem battling head to head with Tom Boerwinkle and Jerry Sloan battling toe to toe with Oscar Robinson while twenty thousand screaming fans filled that old barn with an ear-splitting din. I think of a packed Spectrum in Philly, as Julius Erving levitated and did impossible things with a basketball while thousands of fans erupted with wonder and joy.

I think of Penny Hardaway flipping a pass the length of the court to Shaq, who finished the play with a booming thunder-dunk as wildly enthusiastic Orlando fans raised the arena's roof. That has been the music of my life; that is what I have lived for. To me, there is no sweeter sound than that.

I told you at the beginning of this book that I've had a wonderful life. It continues to be filled with wonders.

Most wonder-full of all, I've had the privilege of walking with God. I've found him to be a powerful, caring, loving friend—a God of second chances, a God of infinite grace and mercy.

After the separation and divorce, I became the day-to-day parent—with the help and support of a number of terrific people, including several nannies; our cook, Dan Littlefield; our handyman, Angel Garcia; and many caring friends. When I remarried, Ruth stepped in and became an integral part of our family. She has been a wonderful stepmother to the children, and has enlarged our family with a daughter, Stephanie, who is grown, educated, and out in the workforce.

Jill and I continue to coparent, while all the kids live permanently with me. Eight children are at home, and the rest are grown or have gone off to boarding school or college. People ask if I plan to adopt any more kids. The answer is a reluctant but firm no. While my heartstrings continue to be tugged from time to time, God has truly sealed off the desire to enlarge our family again.

## A Fascinating Psych Job

The Williams clan is unusual, to say the least. We are not the Cleavers, and we are not Ozzie and Harriet. There are up days and down days, times we feel we are succeeding, and times we feel we are failing miserably. No one ever wrote a manual on how to raise a family like this.

When we got into this, I didn't sit down with our accountant or financial planner and count the cost. I just jumped in with both feet. Amazingly, Ruth has jumped right in beside me, adding her 100 percent commitment to mine. Not long ago, it hit me that when the last kid is out of college, I'll be seventy years old—so I'm working as hard as I can just to pay the bills.

In the aftermath of my first marriage, I've been doing a fascinating psych job on myself. I've tried to understand where this fire in my soul came from—taking Jill's desire to adopt a few kids and turning it into a personal crusade. All I know is that I'd see those needy kids and seem to hear God saying, "These are my children—help them, receive them, make them yours." I've discovered that I no longer can travel to foreign countries and go to the barrios and orphanages. I'm like the gambling addict who never again can go to Vegas, the recovering alcoholic who never again can go to a bar. I'll become too emotionally involved; I can't trust myself with that temptation.

All I can do now is spread the word. If I were to receive just one letter from a couple who read this and felt moved to take in one child, I'd find all the work of writing this book justified.

I don't want to leave a false and rosy impression about international adoption. There are plenty of warm fuzzies when you bring that child into your home for the first time—but the warm fuzzies fade and the reality of life sets in. These are kids with troubled backgrounds. Some are kids of the streets who have been knocked around by life. It's not easy for them to mesh into a new family with a new language in a new culture. The transition is tough for the adopted child, the adoptive parents, and the children already in the family.

It pays to look ahead—something I failed to do while busily taking all of these children into my home. One situation I didn't adequately anticipate is that I'm now dealing daily with sixteen teenagers. One or two teenagers at a time is enough for most parents—but *sixteen!*

And what about the next generation? Here's a staggering thought: How many grandchildren can we expect to have? The average family in America has 2.3 children (don't you feel sorry for that three-tenths of a kid?). Playing the averages, we can expect to have 41.4 grandkids. And what if each of our children has three or four or five kids? What if they catch the adoption bug like I did? I could have seventy, a hundred, two hundred grandkids. Can you imagine Thanksgiving at our house a few years from now? We'd need to start our own turkey farm and buy our own cranberry bog.

## Nothing Exceeds Like Excess

For the first ten years of our marriage, Jill had expressed a strong desire to adopt children from overseas, but I hadn't wanted to hear about it. After our first two Korean kids arrived, however, I became smitten with it. I realize now that, near the end of the process, Jill was trying to put the brakes on what had become this adoption mania of mine. And so were other members of my family. At one point, our son Jimmy laughingly asked, "Don't you think you could get some other families to adopt some kids, too?" I realized there was a serious point to that question. Over the years, I've worked to make Jimmy's suggestion a reality.

For that reason, we allowed our family to be spotlighted in books and magazines and on various television shows, such as *The Maury Povich Show.* What few people realize, however, is that we tried to adopt many other children, from Ecuador to Russia, over a ten-year period. For one reason or another, we couldn't get them. If we had adopted them all, we'd be looking at a house filled with almost three dozen children—absolutely impossible!

I was so obsessed with international adoptions that during the summer of 1993—when the Magic signed Penny Hardaway—Jill and I went to Colombia to view the orphan situation in that country. I was absolutely charmed by two sisters and an unrelated boy, and I returned to the States on fire about helping kids in that country. So I began an attempt to adopt these three Colombian children, unaware that while a lawyer friend, Mel Martinez, was helping me get adoption papers translated from Spanish to English, Jill was working on divorce papers.

During the summer and fall of '93, I became acquainted with a general in the Peruvian army and I asked him to dinner to talk about opening Peru for international adoptions. I had no idea that while I was interviewing this general, Jill was interviewing divorce attorneys. In fact, Jill moved out of the house in early spring of 1994—only three months after Caroline and Alan arrived from Brazil.

If I have one great strength in life it is this: When I am on a mission, I am unstoppable. But my great strength is also, at times, my great weakness. I took the same intense passion, drive, and focus that has made me successful in my career, and I let it power my obsession for international adoptions. To paraphrase the old saying, nothing exceeds like excess.

I offer this word of caution. Find your passion and pursue it, but make sure you rule your passion. Don't let it rule you.

Do I regret taking fourteen adoptive children into my home? Not for a moment! My kids are the joy of my life. If I had to do it all again, I would take in every one of those kids. I might try to plan things better, but I wouldn't trade any one of my eighteen children for anything you could offer. Why do I feel that way? Let me give you just one reason out of many—a handwritten letter I received from our Brazilian daughter, Caroline, who was eleven at the time and had only been a part of our family for six months:

Dear Dad,
    I'm doing very good at school, and I'm almost doing good at swiming. I'm realy geting good at school. I remember when I got here and I didn't know a single word in inglesh. Because of you and mom I already know now to speak inglesh. Thank you for puting me in Killarney Elementry and for puting me in E.S.O.I. class.
    I do remember when you went to Brazil and pick me and Alan to U.S.A. Because of you dad, I have now a knew life and knew family and my brothers & sisters. Now me and alan is not thos peoples from street that begs from door to door for food.
    Dad I want to say thank you for all the things you did for me. God bless you and keep you for ever. In whatever you do.
Thanks again for everything dad.

Love you daddie
Caroline

That one letter makes everything worthwhile—and I get that kind of feedback from my kids all the time, every day. On Father's Day 1998, my twenty-one-year-old son, Bobby, wrote me, "I can't begin to tell you how much I appreciate everything you have done for me. You are the best thing that ever happened to me. I love you." So I heartily agree with Psalm 127:3, which tells us that children are a reward or gift from the Lord. One translation calls them a heritage. So, children are also a treasure to be invested in, because they are our future.

My prayer for all our nineteen kids is that, as they begin to carve out their own lives, they will all want to walk with God and serve him. I pray that we will end up as good friends, that we will enjoy each other. I pray that we will someday look back on the days when they were growing up—including the tough times—with a sense of awe and wonder and gratitude.

I hope our children will truly take hold of life and shake it, so that all the blessings life can bring will rain down on them. I've tried to instill in each of them the passion I've always had for living, for growing, for learning, for distinction. I try daily to foster within them a passion for doing their best, for trying their hardest, for never saying, "That's good enough." I have never been content to live in the gray areas of life, and I don't want our children to be, either. My wish for all of them is that their lives will stand for something, be significant, make a difference, and really count.

And that is also my wish for you.

## Ten Rules for a Wonderful Life

Life today is just as exciting as it ever was. We've learned that Orlando has been awarded a WNBA franchise for 1999, so I'm going to be part of building another new expansion team from the ground up—and best of all, we get to do it in the magical city of Orlando again.

That's my great passion—to help bring dying teams back to life and produce new teams out of magical dreams. That has been my entire career—and here I am in my late fifties, getting to do it all over again, promoting and selling tickets and drumming up more hoopla than a carny-barker. I live for that.

In my job, you can get away with just about anything! At a luncheon with more than three hundred women, all leaders and businesswomen in the central Florida community, my job was to get them motivated and excited about the new WNBA franchise. Because this was a women-only luncheon, the only way they'd allow me in was in disguise. So I put on a platinum-blonde wig with one of Ruth's sunhats and got up in front of that group of women to promote and sell. Darned if we didn't walk out of there with deposits for two hundred season tickets! It made the TV news and all the sports pages—Pat Williams in a wig, up to his usual nonsense, doing whatever it takes to make a dream come true!

I am excited about every speech I'm about to give, every book I'm about to write, every marathon I'm about to run, every new experience that comes my way. I can't wait to charge into every new experience with the RDV Sports family. Most of all, I look forward to every new day I get to enjoy with Ruth and the children. I truly believe that the rest of my life is the best of my life.

It's been a profound experience, as I've been going back over this story, to reflect on all the lessons I've learned along the way, and I've distilled them into a set of simple principles. Here are Pat Williams' Ten Rules for a Wonderful Life:

*1. Pursue your passion.* Find out what you truly love, that one passion that thrills and energizes you—then *invest your life* in it. Pursue it with a vengeance, every day of your life. When you live that way, every day is filled with wonder, fascination, and excitement.

*2. Develop key friendships every day.* As a young man, I went out of my way to meet people in my chosen field of endeavor. I hung around the Phillies locker room and met my heroes in baseball. I reached out to people who could mentor me in the sports world—Bill Durney, Bill Veeck, R. E. Littlejohn, and countless others. I also built friendships with people who were clearly success-oriented and ambitious, even though they hadn't arrived yet—people like Sparky Anderson, Larry King, Ferguson Jenkins, Billy Packer, and many more. They have contributed much to my success, and I hope that I have been able to repay or at least thank and acknowledge them in some way.

*3. Sell yourself.* Be confident, exude competence, show yourself to be dependable and trustworthy. Make sure people are impressed with you when they meet you and that they remain impressed with their memory of you.

*4. Focus on building character and integrity.* Character seems increasingly rare, and that means character is more important than ever. There is a great need for people who prize truthfulness and honor above momentary gain. Some people will say character and integrity aren't important anymore. Don't you believe it. If you want to be a person of distinction, be a person of character.

*5. Be teachable and coachable—then teach others.* A successful person wants other people to influence his or her life. Instead of trying to impress others with what you know, be humble and willing to learn. Accept coaching with a patient, hungry-to-learn attitude—then be a mentor and teacher to others. Adam Lippard is a bright young exec in the RDV Sports organization who has a wonderful future. Though in his twenties, Adam has had an opportunity to be involved with virtually every aspect of our organization. I once asked if he had any idea how fortunate he was.

"I sure do," he said, "and I'm really grateful. But I'm also frustrated."

"Frustrated? Why?"

"Because I don't have anyone to share it with! I've learned so much, and I'd like to be able to pass it on to others—but I don't have anyone to teach it to."

I thought, *Wow! What an attitude!*

"Adam," I said, "Why don't you gather all the interns together every two weeks. Just have a coffee klatch, and share everything you are learning?" And Adam has begun doing just that.

*6. Take risks.* Don't hold back. The saddest thing in the world would be to come to the end of life and say, "If only I'd attempted this; if only I'd tried that." The only experiences you'll regret in life are the ones you didn't have. I made a decision early that I didn't want to have any regrets. I figured life is a smorgasbord, and I was going to have a taste of every positive thing before I was done.

As I was trying to decide whether to meet Ruth at the airport, I thought of the words of business leader Holbrook Jackson: "When in doubt, risk it!" I did—and I have no regrets. Don't shrink back from opportunities—live bold, live large, take risks.

7. *Work hard.* Be willing to sacrifice some ease and pleasure to win what really counts. Mister R. E. used to say, "The man who rows the boat generally doesn't have time to rock it." So put in the hours and pay your dues. But don't work *too* hard. When it's time to relax, relax. Mister R. E. often quoted Vance Havner: "If you don't come apart, you'll come apart." Life is a marathon, not a sprint, and you have to pace yourself to go the distance.

8. *Set goals.* While writing this book, I spoke at an Amway convention in Orlando. I asked my host how many of these rallies he had attended. "About eighty," he said.

"Who were the most memorable speakers you've heard?"

Without hesitation, he replied, "Norman Schwarzkopf and Norman Vincent Peale. I'll never forget when Dr. Peale came to speak. He was ninety-two years old at the time, and he gave an absolutely rousing, inspiring talk. I was to take him to the airport the next day for a 10 A.M. flight, so I asked, 'What time should I pick you up?' He said, 'Six A.M.' 'Dr. Peale,' I said, 'You don't have to leave that early—the airport's not that far away.' He said, 'Oh, I like to get there early. I use the time to catch up on my reading and writing. At the moment, I'm working on my goals for the next ten years.'"

9. *Read books.* The power of books is amazing. When you open a book, you open the life and heart of another human being—and you are forever changed by the encounter. My life was changed at the age of seven by *Pop Warner's Book for Boys.* The lessons of that book continue to reverberate in my life.

Another book that made a profound impact on me was Bill Veeck's 1962 autobiography, *Veeck as in Wreck.* I made life-altering decisions about my future as I was reading it, and I reread it once a year as a refresher.

After becoming a Christian, I decided to dig everything I could out of the Bible, which I am convinced is the inspired Word of God. The Bible has transformed my life.

*10. Seek friendship with God.* This is the biggie. There is no true success, no true satisfaction, no true meaning and distinction apart from a relationship with the Lord. I was twenty-seven when I made this discovery, and I only wish I had been seven. Jesus put it this way: "What good will it be for a man if he gains the whole world, yet forfeits his soul? Or what can a man give in exchange for his soul?"[6] So don't put it off—start living for the Lord today.

I've opened my life to you for one reason: I hope that, in some way, my story will encourage you to commit to a life of distinction. I hope you will never settle for living in the gray areas but that instead you will reach for some magnificent goal. And I believe you *can* achieve that goal.

If you fail, make sure you fail brilliantly, valiantly, so that all the world will marvel at your courage in making the attempt. Failure is never final unless you allow it to be. I guarantee this: You are capable of achieving far more than you can possibly imagine, and if you persist, one day you will triumph.

So pursue your passion. Be bold. Live large. And above all—have yourself a wonderful life!

# Notes

1. New American Standard version.
2. Adapted from *The Four Spiritual Laws* by Dr. Bill Bright, copyright © 1965, 1995 by Campus Crusade for Christ. All rights reserved. Internet version copyright © 1995 by Campus Crusade for Christ International, electronically retrieved from http://www.ccci.org/laws/.
3. Psalm 37:4.
4. 1 Thessalonians 5:18.
5. Romans 8:28.
6. Matthew 16:26.

Pat Williams travels the country speaking to conventions, corporations, churches, retreats, and civic groups. Please contact Pat's office in Orlando, Florida, at 407-916-2404 or fax him at 407-916-2810.